Asia and the Road Ahead

ASIA and the Road Ahead

Issues for the Major Powers

by Robert A. Scalapino

UNIVERSITY OF CALIFORNIA PRESS
Berkeley, Los Angeles, London

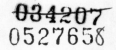

University of California Press
Berkeley and Los Angeles, California
University of California Press, Ltd.
London, England
Copyright © 1975, by
The Regents of the University of California
ISBN 0-520-03066-4
Library of Congress Catalog Card Number: 75-15219
Printed in the United States of America

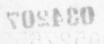

To Jaull, Deeya, Iian, and Analisa

Contents

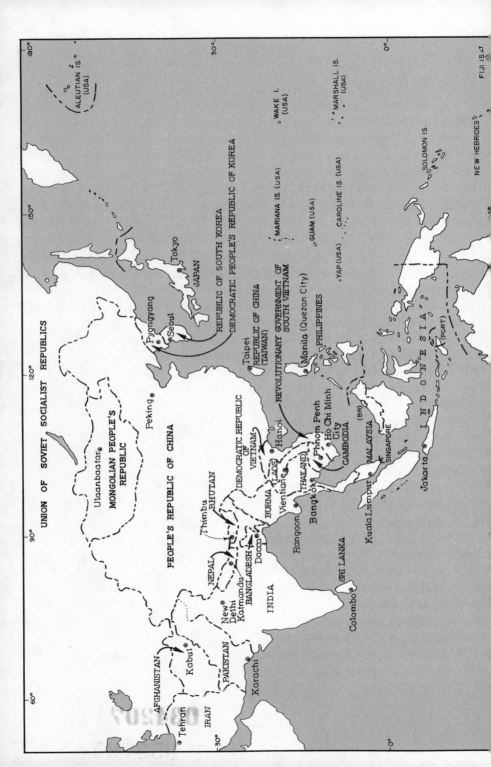

Preface

It scarcely needs to be said that the hazards of undertaking a study of trends and alternatives in the foreign policies of the major Asian-Pacific societies are formidable, given the fluid, uncertain nature of our times. Yet perhaps it is precisely at this point that one should ask basic questions and bring to bear such data as are available in an effort to survey alternatives and likely prospects.

Six societies are the focus of my inquiry: Japan, the People's Republic of China, India, Indonesia, the Union of Soviet Socialist Republics, and the United States. I have also found it essential to divide the vast area with which this work is concerned into five regions: the Pacific Ocean, Northeast Asia, the Continental Center, Southeast Asia, and South Asia. In dealing with these regions, I have often explored the roles and positions of states other than those toward which the study is primarily directed and, in addition, have sought to highlight the domestic factors that influence foreign policy.

Although I have attempted to set forth those contrary arguments and positions that seem most persuasive, I have not hesitated to make my own predilections clear, together with the reasons for them. It is my firm belief, for example, that the United States must continue to be involved seriously in the Asian-Pacific World, and must accept the fact that critical linkages within that world do not permit an enclave policy. As will be seen, this is not to argue for a continuance of all old policies, nor to make a brief for undifferentiated internationalism. Priorities must be established. The mix among economic, political, and military instruments of foreign policy must be periodically reexamined and adjusted. But if the trauma of America's first major political-military defeat, that in Indochina, leads to a triumph of isolationism, new or old, we shall, in my opinion, face grave problems in the not distant future.

Because this study is an attempt to sum up my reflections and experiences of many years, I have appended a brief bibliographic essay rather than pursuing the footnote route. Portions of the chapter on China have been adapted from my article in the January 1974 issue of *Foreign Affairs,* "China and the Balance of Power." And, I am deeply conscious of my debt to literally hundreds of authors and informants—Asian, American, Russian, and others. My three-months' trip to the Soviet Union and Asia in the summer of 1974 was my twenty-sixth trip since the end of World War II, and I could not begin to express my appreciation adequately to all those who have sought to instruct me during those years. I must, however, mention the colleagues who read and commented on all or part of this specific work or aided in the bibliography: George Breslauer, Allan Goodman, Donald Hellmann, Karl Jackson, Chalmers Johnson, Ram Joshi, Gail Lapidus, William Lockwood, Guy Pauker, Nelson Polsby, Leo Rose, Allan Samson, Paul Seabury, Lawrence Shrader, and W.R. Smyser. These individuals should not be burdened with responsibility for my interpretations and views, but they were generous with their time and suggestions, for which I am most appreciative.

To Louise Lindquist and Darlene Goulding, my secretaries, I am deeply indebted for services far beyond the call of duty.

And to my wife, Dee, for whom this has been a time of difficulty, I can only express my profound admiration. She has brought new meaning to the word *courage*.

ROBERT A. SCALAPINO

May 1, 1975
Berkeley, California

Chapter 1

The Setting

The end of the twentieth century approaches amid predictions of catastrophe. Even observers properly leery of perennial doomsayers incline toward deepening concern. In a time of unprecedented problems, we have thus far not merely failed to find "solutions"; more seriously, we have been unable to create a viable international order conducive to the search for solutions.

Challenge, it is said, evokes suitable response, but that has not yet proved true in this instance. This is an era marked by a series of extraordinary paradoxes. In the face of great challenge, political leadership with few exceptions is itself in crisis—uninspired and uninspiring. Despite the commitment to economic development, at least among "emerging" states, only a few political elites are prepared to fashion priorities and policies realistically to that end, and seldom are the masses stimulated to move decisively away from those old values and life styles that constitute massive roadblocks to true emergence. Even within so-called revolutionary states, sloganeering frequently serves as a substitute for reality. Moreover, the economic gains achieved often flow in substantial measure to new elites, or to augment state power, resulting in relatively modest advances for the average citizen, accompanied by a retrogression with respect to his individual rights.

Few would doubt that at a time when near-universal homage is paid it, democracy is in deep trouble, even in the nations of its origin. In essence, the issue is what admixture of

1

freedom and authority, of rights and responsibility, is required in these times, and whether democratic institutions are conducive to workable compromises in a period when the tendency is toward extremes—on the one hand, highly authoritarian systems where self-selected elites proclaim themselves capable of reflecting mass desires, hence democratic; on the other hand, societies standing on the frontiers of total freedom, with various private interests, powerfully organized and strongly articulated, vying with the state itself in power and authority.

Paradoxes are not confined to the arena of the nation-state. Note the international scene: at a time when the need for an effective internationalism is steadily becoming more apparent, the signs of a sharp nationalist resurgence abound. Moreover, this resurgence is present in "emerging" and "advanced" states alike. The pursuit of "self-interest" to the exclusion of the interests of others in the end will prove chimerical, especially for major societies. But who is to say at present that it will not be tried again?

To acknowledge the strong element of crisis in contemporary political and economic affairs is not to assert that all is darkness. The ledger contains assets, real or potential, some of them substantial. Perhaps the processes of negotiation and conference, underway in a wide variety of settings and covering a significant number of issues, will prove more decisive in establishing a new viable world order than is now apparent. In any case, one central objective of the policy-maker today must be to find the means to uncover and exploit the assets available. Nevertheless, it would be foolish to ignore the accumulating signs of trouble. Indeed, these signs must serve as an important part of the broader context in which Pacific-Asian relations today are placed.

The focus of this study is on the attitudes and policies of the major Pacific-Asian powers, present and future. Hence, it is necessary at the outset to define the term *major powers* as it is used here. A major power, for our purposes, is a state having the capacity to influence the attitudes and actions of other societies on either a regional or global basis as a result of its particular mix of military, political, and economic capabilities. Three Pacific-Asian states may be considered to have global impact, albeit in different respects: the United States, the Soviet Union, and Japan. A fourth state, the People's Republic of China, is essentially a regional power today, but one having some global influence. Two other states, India and Indonesia, are regional powers of significance, although neither has truly global reach at present. It is with these six states that we shall be primarily concerned.

Our concern with individual states requires scant justification. Despite our growing interdependence and the impressive range of problems not susceptible to solutions at its level, the nation-state remains the most critical link in the international decision-making process of our times. To understand a given national position, moreover, demands an intimate knowledge of that nation's internal circumstances. Only then do policies that may appear needlessly irrational at the international level assume a certain rationality or, at least, explicability. Political culture, socioeconomic structure, and leadership are only some of the factors bearing heavily on attitudes and priorities.

Nevertheless, each nation, through its leadership, now acquires a growing part of its sense of problem—and promise—from the larger region of which it is an immediate part. The regional component in such elemental issues as security and economic growth often rivals the national one. Some analysts, indeed, believe that the greatest economic and political advances of the next several decades will come through the further development of regional institutions. In any case, no one would doubt that regional relations, positive and negative, constitute a substantial portion of the foreign policies of the major societies.

For the Pacific-Asian area, the identification of appropriate regional subunits is of special importance. We are dealing here with nearly one-half of the world, whether measured in size or population. It is an area, moreover, containing the widest possible diversity of cultures, political institutions, and stages of economic development. We must not be oblivious to certain overarching problems that cut across regions and areas, assuming a truly global character. We have touched on some of these here, and we shall return to them. It may well be that our ability or inability to deal creatively with these problems will determine the basic health of the international order. But it may also be—and the time has come to face up squarely to this possibility—that internationalism in its broader dimensions will fail, in part if not in whole, temporarily if not permanently. Many, including myself, would describe this as a probability, not merely a possibility. Failure, in whatever form, will clearly have more adverse effects on some states and regions than on others. Mankind will survive, however, and both bilateral and regional relations will remain vitally important.

The Pacific-Asian Regions

Fortunately, to establish suitable regional divisions for the Pacific-Asian area is not difficult, providing we do not seek to treat these regions as completely exclusive, being prepared to accept a certain duplication of constituency. We can then divide the Pacific-Asian area as a whole into five regions.

The Pacific Ocean Region is currently dominated strategically by the United States, but with the interests of the USSR and the People's Republic of China (PRC) both increasing. This is a region, moreover, of great importance to the key nations of the Western Hemisphere fronting on the Pacific, notably Canada, Mexico, and several Latin American states. It is also vital to the island nations of the eastern Pacific from Japan in the north to Australia, New Zealand, and Indonesia among others in the south.

Northeast Asia centers on Japan, but this is a region in which Russia, China, and the United States each has very strong commitments, and it includes also such smaller states as the two Koreas and Taiwan.

The Continental Center focuses on those two major protagonists of recent years, the USSR and China. Scarcely a buffer state comes between them except for the People's Republic of Mongolia, although the Korean peninsula, and particularly North Korea, are so placed geographically as to be inextricably involved in Sino-Soviet relations, as are portions of southern Asia.

Southeast Asia has been defined conventionally to include the Asian mainland states comprising the old Indochina, Malaysia, Thailand, and Burma; it also includes the island states of the Philippines, Singapore, and Indonesia—and by extension, Papua-New Guinea and Australia.

Finally, South Asia involves the great subcontinent now dominated by India, with the Himalayan states of Nepal and Bhutan on its northern tier, Bangladesh and Pakistan on its flanks, and Sri Lanka to the south.

Before turning directly to the policy alternatives confronting the major powers, let us seek out those conditions and issues that give to each region its special character and contribute most markedly to relations among the major powers.

The Pacific Ocean Region

The Pacific Ocean Region can be treated either in terms of its center or in a much broader sense, taking into account the various states on its peripheries. Both treatments are warranted. The Pacific center now poses two major issues: security and resource management. It consists of many island clusters spread unevenly over a vast expanse of water. The approximately 115,000 people of Micronesia (excluding the residents of Guam), for example, live in an area encompassing some three million square miles. The population is not only sparse, but lacking in homogeneity. A wide range of cultures, colonial antecedents, and economic resources are to be found.

Since World War II, the Pacific center has been under the strategic control of the United States. That control rests on two conditions: acquisition of most of the Pacific islands previously held by Japan, and the absence of any other major power in the region. In recent years, however, the Pacific Ocean Region has been affected by the same issues of local autonomy or independence that have swept the rest of the world. Thus, in the south, New Guinea-Papua has achieved independence, as have certain smaller territories. Naturally, pressures have gradually mounted, both internal and external, with respect to Micronesia, largely an American trusteeship.

From the 1960s onward, autonomy or self-government became a cause among some Micronesians, with this issue being juxtaposed against the continuous requirements advanced in the name of the security of the United States, and its treaty obligations to Asian-Pacific allies. American authorities have always defined security with respect to this region in two senses. Positively, it has meant the availability of military facilities sufficient to serve both as fall-back positions to underwrite treaty commitments as the United States reduces its military bases in the populous areas of Asia, and as adequate outer defenses for the United States itself. Negatively, security has been based on the concept of denying central Pacific bases to any other major power.

In recent years, military technology has undergone revolutionary changes. Are U.S. strategic concepts relating to the Pacific-Asian region abreast of these developments? Some would argue that mid-Pacific bases, at least on any expanded scale, are unnecessary from a strategic standpoint and unwise from the standpoint of their political reverberations. They also question whether the objective of denying Pacific bases to others is feasible, given the independent status of certain Pacific territories. Others strongly defend the need for expanded U.S.

bases here, but doubt that such bases alone will suffice, particularly with respect to naval facilities, to fulfill American commitments in Asia. Thus, they insist that certain bases in Asia proper will continue to be essential if present American commitments are maintained. We must explore these questions further at a later point, but it should be clear that the case for a thorough reexamination of American strategic planning is overwhelming. Such a reexamination, moreover, must weigh economic and political realities together with strategic considerations.

Meanwhile, the political destinies of the Pacific island peoples are in the course of being determined, at least for the near future. It seems likely that differing courses are to be pursued. For some, it will be full independence, as in the case of New Guinea-Papua. In other cases, it will be extensive autonomy, with certain reserved areas for the former governing authority, such as defense and foreign affairs. In still other situations, it will be an arrangement representing commonwealth status, but short of full incorporation into an existing national framework. Will such political arrangements be conducive to stability and the progress of the peoples concerned? Will they be acceptable also to the major powers interested in the area?

These questions become more germane if it is presumed that the near-monopoly of power held by the United States in the Pacific region since 1945 may be coming to an end. Clearly, Japanese economic interest in the region, once considerable, is again rising rapidly. It is quite possible, indeed, that Japan will have become the dominant economic force throughout the Pacific at some point in the 1980s. Meanwhile, both the Soviet Union and, to a lesser extent, the People's Republic of China have shown an increased strategic interest in this region. In the latter case, this interest is connected at least partly with the Taiwan issue. In the former case, a major expansion of Pacific military facilities is underway, at this point with the China problem in mind, but available for other purposes. Is there not good reason, therefore, to assume that within a decade, both Soviet and Chinese military power will be of greater significance in the Pacific?

Beyond the Pacific center lie major and diverse societies, both in Asia and in the Western Hemisphere. There also exist states like Australia and New Zealand that fall precisely into neither category. These latter states, especially Australia, are in the process once again of seeking a shift in basic orientation. Having gravitated out of the British political orbit at the close of World War II when the empire was being dismantled, and having looked to the United States for support, Australia now appears to be in the process of disengaging from its special ties with Washington and seeking to establish itself as a state primarily committed to and involved in Asia. Increasingly, its concerns are with such diverse states as Japan, where extensive and vital economic relations have been developed; Indonesia, its close, rich, and populous neighbor; and the People's Republic of China, a nation affording some political and economic counterbalance. In lesser degree, New Zealand is following suit.

These efforts contain a substantial degree of logic, but they do not negate the fact that for Asians, Australia and New Zealand will always be Western states, with certain Asian attitudes and policies affected accordingly. These two states, moreover, cannot influence the Asian-Pacific strategic balance in any significant sense. On the political and economic fronts, their impact is meaningful, but not in itself critical.

Thus, a broader issue is raised. Should an effort be made at this point to develop a more vital Pacific Basin Community? Is it time to move toward a more ambitious regional program, with additional organizational facilities, in this sector of the world? Could such a community resolve or mitigate some of the thorny problems existent or lying ahead with respect to maritime jurisdiction, resource management, trade, investment, multinational corporations, and the growing economic gap within the region between poor and rich? Could it revitalize the interest of peoples, including Americans, in mutual cooperation across national lines? Or is this idea unfeasible in the present climate, and possibly unnecessary, given the plethora of supranational organizations already in existence?

If the concept has merit, a host of more practical issues must be resolved. What should be its structure and membership? How should it relate to bilateral efforts which it most certainly would not replace, or to other regional and international groups and organizations seeking to perform somewhat similar functions?

In these questions, many of the Pacific nations have a stake, but none is more vitally affected than the United States and Japan. For these two major states, the Pacific is destined to be an arena of close interaction, both cooperative and competitive. Indeed, it is probably no exaggeration to say that the entire tenor of American-Japanese relations will be strongly influenced by the manner in which the issues of the Pacific region itself are handled.

Northeast Asia

Among the regions of the Pacific-Asian area, Northeast Asia is in many respects the most critical with respect to determining the basic international trends of our times. Japan, central to the region, is itself a major power, albeit one largely confined at present to the economic realm. Its relations with the United States, the Soviet Union, and the People's Republic of China are of vital importance to international relations on a global scale. Each of the other major powers, moreover, has extensive interests and commitments in Northeast Asia. Indeed, in few if any other parts of the world are the triangular relations of the United States, the USSR, and China of such import as here.

Thus, Northeast Asia is one important testing ground for the principles of peaceful coexistence, a region where war/peace issues take on special significance. This fact is underlined by the existence of two so-called divided states within the region, namely, South and North Korea and China and Taiwan. Can the issues pertaining to these states be resolved peacefully, or does violence lie in the future, and if so, will it be restricted to the parties most immediately involved?

In economic terms also, Northeast Asia assumes a unique importance. To what extent is economic cooperation between non-Communist and Communist states possible in this era of tentative détente, and what are its likely consequences, political and strategic as well as economic? Specifically, can and should the extraordinary skills and technology of Japan and the United States be put to the service of modernizing the Soviet Union and China? Or will the political and strategic issues posed from both sides provide barriers that limit the feasibility of such a relationship?

The future of Japan's relations with the advanced Western world are of no less consequence. Is it to be new breakthroughs in international economic institutions and policies conducive to a fruitful, increasingly harmonious interaction? Or will we witness a sharp turn toward the type of highly nationalistic, competitive policies productive of escalating friction? Or will some combination of these courses ensue?

The natural resources now being discovered or commencing to be exploited in Northeast Asia add both to opportunities and to potential difficulties. Some of them lie in disputed ocean beds, raising the complex problem of maritime jurisdiction. Others relate to Siberia and mainland China, thereby involving strategic and political as well as economic questions. Thus, cooperation and competition over resources has a very special meaning for this region.

Finally, the vital connection between domestic and international politics is also displayed in Northeast Asia in a most telling fashion. Japan, one of the truly open societies of Asia, is currently undergoing travails similar to other societies of its type. Thus, the questions are posed: how stable will Japanese society be in the decade ahead, and how capable of playing a constructive role in the international scene? Perhaps the issue should be put in broader, more dramatic form: can parliamentary democracy survive in our times, and can open societies, subject as they are to numerous and visible strains and tensions, compete effectively with closed societies in the international arena?

The Continental Center

When a definitive history of the twentieth century is finally written, the Sino-Soviet cleavage may well be recorded as one of the most significant events of this highly eventful era. An alliance potentially capable of dominating the vast Eurasian continent dissolved into bitter hostility no more than a decade after its consummation. In recent years, moreover, this hostility has shaped in major degree the foreign policies of both major Communist powers, and affected their domestic policies as well. Today, the Churchillian image of an iron curtain has more applicability to the Asian continental center than to the lines demarking Western and Eastern Europe. Massive military forces face each other along the 4,800-mile Sino-Soviet frontier, and on occasion the outbreak of large-scale warfare has seemed perilously close.

The basic causes of the Sino-Soviet split were complex, but at root the division stemmed from three broad issues. First, the problems of adjusting to authority relationships within the Communist world were implicit in the emergence of many Communist states after 1945. No longer was the Kremlin the sole repository of Communist power. Nationalism, moreover, vied with Marxism-Leninism as a foremost expression of the new Communist states. Thus, Soviet dominance—itself long an expression of Russian nationalism—was certain to be challenged, and one logical source of such a challenge was Peking.

Second, the imbalance in economic and technical relations inevitably caused problems. Was Soviet aid sufficiently generous? Did the Russians use such aid to apply political leverage? Over time, Soviet paternalism, sometimes heavy-handed, rubbed against Chinese xenophobia. But the apogee came with the Chinese decision that the Soviet developmental model had less applicability to China than was initially assumed, and that consequently China had to create its own developmental pattern. This fundamental decision produced both Soviet resentment and further division.

The issues of most immediate import, however, lay in the military-strategic realm, and centered on the question of how to deal with the United States. The Soviet acquisition of nuclear weapons and its movement toward military parity with the United States produced divergent responses from the two major Communist states: on the part of the Russians, some growth in self-confidence and security, combined with an increasing disinterest in taking the risks of nuclear war—the beginnings of sentiments conducive to limited détente; on the Chinese side, a call for boldness, product of China's profound dissatisfaction with the status quo and the strong ideological flavor of a first-generation revolutionary elite.

These differing responses culminated in the events of 1957–1958, when in the course of the Taiwan Straits crisis China was caused to realize the limits of Soviet support in any episode threatening confrontation with the United States, and the Russians were caused to fear that Mao's "recklessness" had as its ultimate aim a Soviet-American nuclear conflict from which China would emerge the real victor. Under these circumstances, it was natural that Russian leaders would retrench from earlier pledges of support for Chinese nuclearization, and that an atmosphere of distrust would quickly replace that of cooperation in the international arena. The manifestations of this shift were seen shortly with respect to such diverse issues as

Sino-Indian relations, Soviet-Eastern European problems, and the explosive Cuban missile crisis.

Over time, these highly practical issues were presented to the world via ideological disputation, as benefited rival Communist elites. Religion thus became centrally involved. It was not merely who was wrong, but who was a heretic, and conversely who deserved to inherit the mantle of Marx and Lenin. In addition to adding to the bitterness of the dispute, the ideological component had important implications for the international order. Each party sought to read the other out of the socialist world. By the end of the 1960s, that world had ceased to exist as a unified force, both in practice and in theory, particularly as far as China was concerned.

By that time also, earlier issues had blended into a single, overriding concern—security. Along the Sino-Soviet frontier, vast armies had been deployed, with the most modern weaponry available to each side. Limited military conflict sporadically broke out, and intense efforts at subversion were launched. The issue of borders now occupied the center of the stage, and tensions culminated in a Soviet threat—widely disseminated—that if Chinese recalcitrance provoked war the Russians would not limit themselves to conventional weapons. This threat brought the Chinese to the negotiating table, but it also produced a major shift in Chinese foreign policy. In a dramatic volte-face, Mao and his followers abandoned the isolationist policies of the Cultural Revolution and, in moves reminiscent of the united front policies against Japan pursued by the Chinese Communists after 1935, sought to build a united front against the Soviet menace. Because the United States was correctly perceived to be the key to such a policy, a new chapter in Sino-American relations commenced.

To appreciate this background is essential if we are to understand current trends and future possibilities with respect to Sino-Soviet relations, as well as their respective policies toward the other major powers. Is there a strong likelihood of war between the two Communist states, and what would be the consequences of such a war, both on the immediate region and in the global scene? Or in the opposite direction, is there a reasonable possiblity of détente, or even a renewed alliance between Russia and China, and what impact would either of these developments have on Asia and the world?

While the Asian continental center is dominated by Sino-Soviet relations, it serves to illustrate the problems and options of small states living in the shadows of rival, massive powers. Unlike Central Europe, Central Asia provides no natural buffer-state system at present. There are no Finlands, Austrias, and Yugoslavias to support a disengagement process. On the contrary, the Russians and Chinese must live cheek-by-jowl with each other. Only the People's Republic of Mongolia, with scarcely one million people, lies directly between the two giants. Long ago, Mongolia was drawn into the Soviet orbit, opting voluntarily or involuntarily for a distinctly subordinate relation to one major power in order to avoid domination by the other.

Certain other small states of the region seek another option, that of playing off China and Russia. In essence, that has been the thrust of North Korean politics in recent years, albeit with a pronounced tilt toward China at most points. It is also a factor in the politics of the other small Communist state to the south, North Vietnam. Nor is it an unwelcome concept for such non-Communist states as South Korea, and many of the states of Southern Asia.

Can balance-of-power politics or "neutralization" efforts work for such states? And what are the risks and gains, both for them and for others?

Like Northeast Asia, the Continental Center illustrates in its own way the intimate relation between domestic and international politics. If Central Asia lacks a buffer-state system, it has long represented a region heavily populated by ethnic minorities on both the Russian and Chinese sides of the borders. Hence, viewed from the perspective of Moscow or Pe-king, it is a region of uncertain loyalties. In each case, the Soviet Union and the People's Republic of China have inherited great empires, albeit empires contiguous to their own heartlands. These empires are composed of diverse peoples not yet fully in-corporated into either the social or political systems dominated by Slavs and Han.

Consequently, the borderlands of Central Asia represent tempting fishing grounds for both sides. Faced with definite security threats, the dominant response has been to people the border areas with increasing numbers of Russians and Chinese, while at the same time putting an equal premium on economic and military development. Generally, this is the course of action followed by each government. But one result of such policies is to increase fear on both sides and bring two hostile governments into closer proximity with each other, eliminating such sense of buffer as a sparsely populated, wholly underdeveloped Central Asia could bring. Can a modus vivendi under the new conditions be found?

In yet another respect, domestic politics in this region casts its shadow across the international horizon. The likelihood of recurrent political instability in China during the immediate post-Mao era is high. To what extent will foreign policy be used as a weapon in the power struggles that lie ahead? What are the possibilities of foreign intervention, direct or indirect? In sum, what would be the impact of a weak China—yet one hav-ing nuclear weapons—on the Asian and global scene? Looking in the opposite direction, what if China's march toward power withstands internal challenges and comes under the direction of younger, militantly nationalist leaders, dedicated to putting the imprimatur of China on greater Asia? What would be the impact of a strong China in the decades ahead?

On the surface at least, the Soviet Union seems a more stable political society. Here too, however, a transition is at hand, with older leaders soon to give way to younger generations. And if on the one hand, political institutions—including the Communist Party—seem stronger in Russia than in China at present, on the other hand, the Soviet Union also seems a more porous society, more available to external influences. Moreover, the momentum of change, including higher living standards, now appears to be affecting the interest group infrastructure in the Soviet Union more profoundly than is yet possible in China—with differences in political cultures also making their contribution here. Thus, in Russia too, the tides of change are rising. At some point in the coming decade, is it not possible that the conflict over priorities may become more acute? May not the newly emerging classes of the Soviet Union who have glimpsed the vision of a better material life join forces with the older xenophobic elements of Russian culture to insist that the focus of attention—and resources—turn inward? In sum, will not the major expansion of Soviet commitments abroad undertaken in recent decades come into increasing conflict with the growing demands of the Soviet people for a more rapid tempo of internal development?

Radically different alternatives in foreign policy can thus be posed for the major actors of the Continental Center. A China beset with multiple internal problems might continue—even intensify—its emphasis on "self-reliance" and hold to a minimal, low-posture foreign policy, basically defensive in nature. But, in contrary fashion, this massive society, surmounting or learning to live with its developmental problems, might continue to augment its power and expand its role, particularly in Asia. Similarly, the exclusivist features of Russian culture, always powerful, might reassert themselves, abetted by the yearning for rapid material improvements, in such a manner as to forward policies both nationalist and self-centered. Such policies might find their expression in lowered international commitments, although there are other possibilities. If the advanced Western world falls into serious disarray, for example, the temptations to pursue a "forward" international strategy will be increased. To the implications of these alternatives we must turn shortly.

Southeast Asia

Few regions of the world illustrate more graphically the problems of creating unity out of diversity than does Southeast Asia. The range of ethnic representatives, cultural patterns, and economic and political institutions comes close to covering the gambit of human experience. Among the nearly three hundred million people of this region, one finds most of the world's major religions represented, and many of the great cultures. At the same time, scattered through the interior mountainous regions and jungles are some of the most primitive people surviving into the twentieth century. Nor is this merely a juxtaposition of extremities. Innumerable gradations exist between sophisticated and Stone Age man. Moreover, a fairly rigid economic hierarchy accompanies cultural diversity. Thus, these are plural societies in many senses.

Under these conditions, the task of nation-building in Southeast Asia has been extraordinarily difficult, and in no instance is it complete. It is appropriate, indeed, to ask which governments of this region have acquired sufficient authority to warrant the term *nation?* Some "nations," here as elsewhere, are largely fictional, creatures of small elites and capitals, scarcely acknowledged by the masses of inhabitants, for whom political authority is more immediate and personal, private concerns far outweigh public ones, and national institutions, political or otherwise, do not figure into the patterns of loyalty. Using such measurements, Southeast Asian states lie along a continuum, with the city-state of Singapore paradoxically having acquired the highest degree of nationhood, Laos probably the lowest—but with many states remaining at this point toward the lower end of the scale.

In the effort to create nations, both traditional and modern institutions and techniques have been employed. In Thailand, for example, monarchy has been of great utility, although its survival capacity is still being tested. In other instances, such as Malaysia, the sultanate system was skillfully integrated with electoral politics to ease the path of transition. Even in states where traditional institutions were abandoned or drastically altered, the behavioral patterns of the new political elites provided a sufficient linkage with the past to sustain a considerable degree of continuity. Indonesia and Burma are cases in point.

The global crisis in political leadership, however, extends to this region. The first generation of leaders, intensely political, often charismatic, and carrying the label "Father of Country," is now gone. Unfortunately, in many cases, it left a sorry record in economic affairs. Gradually, a second generation has emerged, usually less colorful, sometimes more pragmatic. A few of the current leaders have demonstrated substantial ability—men like Razak of Malaysia and Lee Kuan Yew of Singapore. Generally, however, present leaders show neither the qualities that draw the citizenry to their cause nor the capacity to handle the complex problems confronting their societies. It is an age of mediocrity.

Finally, as is well known, deep ideological and political fissures run through this region. Every government in Southeast Asia except Indonesia and Laos currently faces at least one active insurgency. Burma and the Philippines must contend with several. The most formidable guerrilla operations are usually under Communist control, although several separatist movements such as that of the Islamic adherents in the Philippines and the Karens in Burma must be accorded real importance. In many cases, guerrilla warfare has sapped the energies of the societies concerned for decades. Moreover, external assistance in varying amounts has been tendered such movements, from the massive involvement of North Vietnam and the two major Communist powers throughout Indochina to the less conspicuous aid given by China—notably in Burma but also to most other Southeast Asian Communist parties. The United States has also been heavily involved, generally on the side of the established governments. Thus, political conflict within the region has come to be internationalized to an extraordinary degree, with resulting high costs and risks.

In contrast to the deeply troubled political scene, the economic potentialities of Southeast Asia are great. This is a region rich in natural resources and fertile land. With a few exceptions (Java, for example), it does not face the problems of massive overpopulation endemic to China and South Asia. In recent decades, moreover, most states have acquired a growing pool of experienced administrators and skilled technicians. Consequently, there is every reason to assume that under conditions of peace and political stability, rapid economic development could ensue. The problem, of course, is peace and stability.

Given the circumstances of Southeast Asia, it is not surprising that all of the major powers of the Pacific-Asian area have had a deep interest and substantial involvement here in recent decades. Thus, the issues governing the future fall into two broad categories, those centering on the status of the region itself and those relating to the external forces.

In the former category, the critical questions are these: Can socioeconomic and political problems be resolved or contained in such a fashion as to strengthen the legitimacy and authority of the governments in power, thereby bolstering the stability of the region? And is it possible for forces holding to radically different ideologies or possessing significantly different cultures to work peacefully together or, at a minimum, coexist without bloodshed? Can a meaningful regionalism emerge in Southeast Asia, one conducive to both economic and political progress? Or, on the contrary, will weakness and division be the predominant political expressions of the future? And will coercion and internecine warfare continue to flourish, with victors prepared to vanquish the defeated totally?

Closely related are questions relating to the second category: Can Southeast Asia be "neutralized" insofar as the major powers are concerned? United by a common interest in seeing no single power achieve hegemony, can these big states cooperate in working out suitable policies pertaining both to direct involvements and to indirect ones, namely, those taking the form of military and economic assistance? Or will major power struggles continue to be reflected sharply in the Southeast Asian region? And will one or another outside nation seek to achieve hegemony or overweaning influence, its protestations to the contrary notwithstanding?

Whatever the answers to these questions, it is clear that peaceful coexistence faces its most critical tests in this region. Moreover, given the commitments, past and present, the results will have an impact beyond Southeast Asia. Major power relations here will continue to be both a reflection and a harbinger of such relations elsewhere. Similarly, in its indigenous trends, this region will suggest the nature of the larger developing world in the decades ahead. Thus, the questions posed here must be explored further from the perspective of the major societies, as we shall shortly do.

South Asia

No part of the Pacific-Asian area has undergone greater political-strategic changes in the past decade than South Asia. Gone is the time when India and Pakistan seemed sufficiently matched in power to warrant external efforts at sustaining the peace via a military equilibrium between these two states. Some would say, of course, that the potentiality never really existed. In any case, India is the dominant power of the subcontinent, today and for the foreseeable future.

Consequently, developments throughout the region hinge to a very considerable extent on trends within India—both as these pertain to domestic politics and foreign policies. What will be the shape of India's political and economic institutions a decade hence, and the nature of its leadership? Will the experiment in political openness on the part of this, one of the world's most underprivileged societies, succeed or fail? Can viable economic policies be found and sustained?

Of equal importance are India's policies toward its neighbors. South Asia is composed of fragile states today, some which have a highly uncertain life expectancy. The Himalayan societies, perched precariously between two large, hostile powers, must hope that internal problems can be so contained and external relations so balanced as to preserve their independence. But recent developments with respect to Sikkim illustrate what can happen when failures on either of these fronts ensue. On India's flanks lie Pakistan and Bangladesh, divided portions of a state once united under Islam. Perhaps from the beginning, that union was doomed. Certainly, religion alone was not a sufficiently binding force. Now, one has split into two, and both new states face serious problems. These problems, moreover, could impinge directly on India. The disintegration of Bangladesh, for example, would have immediate repercussions on West Bengal, already one of the most troubled sections of India. Nor would it be in India's interests to see Pakistan further weakened or dismembered, for this would almost surely increase the general power of the Soviet Union in the region as a whole, a power already significantly high. Yet neither of these possibilities can be totally ruled out.

To the south lies Sri Lanka, still another state in trouble. As is true throughout South Asia, Sri Lanka lives with unresolved communal problems that periodically threaten to erupt into large-scale political disturbances. Naturally, these are exacerbated by a persistent economic malaise. And once again, these are problems, especially the former, which can directly affect India.

Intervention, we were informed during the era of Western imperialism, is often an unavoidable act. Circumstances, not desires, dictate expansionism. Thus, it was necessary for the

British to acquire control or predominant influence over Afghanistan and Burma to ensure their Indian empire, and to extend their influence into the Himalayan area and Tibet as well.

Do these reasons still hold? Will the logic of Bangladesh and Sikkim be repeated? Is an Indian drive for hegemony over the subcontinent implicit in the circumstances of the late twentieth century, or do these circumstances dictate another course? But if it is to be hegemony, at what point might other major powers see their own interests jeopardized?

At present, both Russia and China have substantial commitments in South Asia, primarily as a part of the larger balance-of-power politics in which both are engaged. Moreover, the United States, after a period of low posture, is showing signs of an increased interest in the region. Naturally, the involvement of the major powers has had its impact on states within the region. As India moved toward power, it moved away from nonalignment. Indeed, the Soviet-Indian alliance has had a profound influence on Indian domestic as well as foreign policies, although signs of uneasiness have now appeared. Meanwhile, China has retained its close ties with Pakistan as a counter to this alliance, while at the same time seeking to foster relations with the small states on India's peripheries. China's military power in this region, however, cannot match that of India when backed by Soviet guarantees, and thus China must hope that the political and economic tides within the region are favorable to its cause.

Viewed from most perspectives, those tides seem ominous at present. Among all of the world's regions, it is this one to which the term *hopeless* is most often applied. Population growth is still largely out of control. Most critical resources are in short supply or beyond reach in sufficient quantities because of costs. The food problem threatens to grow steadily worse under current conditions.

In the face of these problems, what is being done by the

leaders of the region? With few exceptions, far too little. Corruption and inefficiency combine to hobble the public sector. Yet most of these governments, proudly proclaiming themselves "socialist," inhibit the private sector sufficiently to render it impotent. Meanwhile, the vast rural areas remain backward because of inadequate incentives and capital investment, except for a few regions where the Green Revolution has broken through.

Unfortunately, South Asia gives strong evidence of a disturbing negative interplay between democratic politics and economic growth. In order to attain and hold power, the politician makes populist promises which cannot be fulfilled, the most expansive of which is to pledge welfarism before sufficient production exists. Then, to camouflage failure, gimmickry is pursued, with nationalization being a favorite move, for it carries with it the aura of egalitarianism. In fact, however, the bureaucracy to whom new power is given invariably proves completely unable to carry out the assigned tasks. There follows an aimless wandering, with political motivations far exceeding economic ones, and basic reforms continuously postponed.

It is not surprising, therefore, that serious observers are now asking some very sober questions relating to aid for this and similar regions. Does it make sense to provide food and other forms of humanitarian relief that may save a few hundred thousand lives if this serves to allow the governments concerned to continue their procrastination and mismanagement, with the result that several million lives are at stake a short time later? How can external assistance become a stimulus rather than a deterrent to change? Is it not necessary at times to cut loose from governments that show neither the ability nor the desire to remedy affairs under their jurisdictions? Such issues can no longer be dodged, and South Asia is a logical arena on which to focus the discussion.

We have now explored briefly the basic character of each of

the major regions into which the Pacific-Asian area is divided, and thereby posed many of the central issues confronting the area as a whole. It remains to examine how these issues affect each of the major powers, and what alternatives are posed to them in their mutual relations.

Chapter 2

JAPAN: What Balance between Continuity and Transition?

In the mid-1970s, Japan faces a new set of challenges, problems largely unanticipated and for which solutions remain elusive. Will these problems be surmounted through the proverbial Japanese ingenuity, or do bleak, troubled years lie ahead? Predictions must be guarded, but two facts are clear: urgent economic requirements will retain a priority in Japanese foreign policy at least equal to that of the past, and in broad terms foreign policy will be subordinate to domestic issues.

As Japanese politics are in a relatively fluid state, one must ask: What are the chances that the dominance of the Liberal Democratic Party—unbroken for almost the whole of the post-1945 era—may end and, if it does, will this produce a significant change in Japanese foreign policy?

Neither part of this question is easily answered. There can be no doubt that the Japanese conservatives are in trouble. Their percentage of the vote has declined in recent years, standing now at about 44 percent of the electorate. Losses in the great metropolitan areas have been especially pronounced, reflective of the enormous problems of inflation, pollution, housing, and similar matters. More disconcerting for LDP adherents, conservative management of Japanese politics seems more inept, the capacity to anticipate issues less acute. In sum, Japan is very much a part of the global crisis in leadership. This fact is recognized even within the LDP, giving rise to a vigorous Young Turk movement. Whatever the future, changes in conservative leadership that will at least have an influence on the style, if not the substance of Japanese politics would seem to be at hand. The elevation of a noted exponent of reform, Miki Takeo, to the prime ministership might be regarded as a first step even though he belonged to the older generation.

If the economic crisis now confronting Japan is both severe and prolonged, a progressive shift away from the moderate conservatives would seem inevitable. The danger is that extremities of both "Left" and "Right" would gain most from such a situation. Yet one must be cautious in predicting sweeping changes. The so-called Left has benefited most from conservative weaknesses and the conditions in which Japan finds itself thus far. In particular, the gains of the Japan Communist Party have been substantial, although it still garners only 10 percent of the total Japanese vote, substantially less than its showing in nations like France and Italy. The Communists, moreover, are the most dynamic force within the Japanese Left at present. They have recruited young leaders of considerable ability; their appeals are shaped around domestic issues of immediate concern to the electorate; their Diet representatives do their homework, enabling them to be effective interrogators; and they have now established an "independent" image with strong nationalist overtones, having cut the apron-strings of both Moscow and Peking. All of these developments have helped the Communists, even in certain rural districts. At the same time, a suspicion understandably remains among many citizens that this new pragmatism is essentially tactical, with the ideological commitment to dictatorship still intact.

The Communists are likely to gain additional seats in the Diet in the near future. Like other members of the opposition, however, a ceiling in Communist strength will be reached, one considerably short of putting them into national power. The more critical issue is thus whether a broader "Left" coalition encompassing Socialists, Communists, and members of the Kōmeitō (Clean Government Party) could emerge as joint holders of power.

The obstacles to a leftist coalition government in Japan remain formidable. The Socialists continue to be plagued with weak leadership, serious internal divisions, and a strongly ideological stance that reflects an old-fashioned Marxist position virtually unchanged since the 1920s, but one not conducive to close interaction with the Communists. Cooperation has been achieved on special issues and candidacies, but the general atmosphere is invariably cautious, sometimes hostile. Indeed, as the Communists have gained in strength (and challenged Socialist dominance in such organizations as Sōhyō, Japan's largest labor federation), an increasing number of Socialists have begun to exhibit a fear of their rivals, and any effort at a closely knit union would almost certainly split the JSP badly.

The Kōmeitō also is a party of many inconsistencies—"conservative" in certain respects, "progressive" in others. It too is highly competitive with the Communists, for in some degree it must seek votes from the same segment of the Japanese electorate.

Despite the favorable political and economic climate, therefore, the prospects for an all-leftist coalition are not as promising as one might assume at first glance. If such a development were to take place, however, what impact would it have on Japanese foreign policy?

Japanese Foreign Policy under the Left

Let us first assume that the current statements and promises of leftist spokesmen were translated into policies. In that case, Japan would officially join the ranks of the "nonaligned," but with a tilt toward the socialist and third worlds. Self-defense units would be kept intact, but would probably not be expanded, and Japan would abrogate the Mutual Security Treaty now in effect with the United States at the earliest opportunity. Although the special security and political ties with Washington would be severed, however, the new leaders would hope that this would not affect the Japanese-American economic relations so crucial to Japan's health. Thus, the effort would be made to achieve a Treaty of Friendship and Commerce with the U.S., as well as multilateral agreements pledging nonaggression and designating the region a non-nuclear zone.

Policies toward the People's Republic of China and the USSR might well remain complex, assuming that Sino-Soviet relations continued on their present course. Paradoxically, ideological and political differences might be of greater import in Japanese relations with Moscow and Peking under a leftist government than with the conservatives. Certainly, the new regime would not be a client state of either Communist giant, although the willingness to expand cultural and economic relations would probably be more in evidence, especially toward the Soviet Union. By the same token, however, such matters could prove to be the cause of serious fissures within the Japanese Left, as they are now.

A leftist coalition government would surely seek a more "Asian" stance, at least initially. Nationalism would be featured as an antidote to "excessive Western influence," particularly American influence. Anti-Americanism, indeed, would become a more prominent feature of the political landscape in Japan.

In the broadest sense, this would be government that sought to minimize conventional balance-of-power politics, staking Japan's prosperity and the regime's survival on being able to achieve maximum access to markets and resource needs under conditions whereby international power or leadership was openly eschewed, thus gambling on a world that posed no threats and few obligations to Japan.

Is there not reason to doubt, however, that the long-held positions of the Left would be translated intact into politics? Admittedly, the current gap between the Japanese "conservatives" and "progressives" is far greater than that which prevailed between such political forces in Great Britain or West Germany prior to the shifts in power there; the situation is more analogous to France or Italy. Nevertheless, any government in Japan, under present conditions, cannot expect to ignore certain basic facts of life and survive. Vital economic ties to the United States and, in a larger sense, to the advanced world require some degree of political as well as economic cooperation. Moreover, whatever the ideological proclivities toward the socialist world, the socioeconomic and political institutions which the new regime would inherit, barring a total revolution, would work in an opposite direction. Nor would the Left be unified on policies, if the coalition of forces envisaged here were to come to power. The voice of the "Left moderates," indeed, might be more powerful than at present within this camp, given the strong conservative elements that would remain in the political arena, available to assume power again.

Nevertheless, a leftist coalition government in Japan would inaugurate or accelerate trends in the directions sketched here. However, such a government is not in the offing, at least immediately, as we have noted. A more likely change would involve a coalition of a different type: a combination of the LDP and elements of the opposition, notably the Democratic Socialists, the Kōmeitō, and possibly some "rightist" portions of the JSP. Such a coalition, formal or informal, would be conducive to the same general trends as a leftist coalition, but on a more moderate, variegated pattern.

Japanese Foreign Policy under the Conservatives

Another possibility exists, namely, the continuance of the Liberal Democratic Party in power, with certain changes taking place *within* that party. At the moment, this possibility must be accorded slightly greater weight than the others, with the international climate as it affects the Japanese economy probably being the most crucial variable. Assuming this occurrence, what are the likely trends in Japanese foreign policy?

For some years, Japan has lived with a growing anomaly. It has become an economic giant. Indeed, Japan and the United States constitute the world's only universal economic powers in terms of the scope of their operations and concerns. Yet as recent events have illustrated so clearly, Japan is an uniquely vulnerable giant. Its dependency on resources and markets external to its own territory is extraordinarily high. In this sense, more than any other major power, Japan requires an open, peaceful international environment. It cannot afford the policies of self-reliance.

On the other hand, Japan's voice in shaping international trends, or even its capacity to defend those interests which Japanese leaders may consider crucial, remains limited. What other major society has such a slight political role, both regionally and on the global stage? In military terms, moreover, Japan cannot be compared with the other important powers, including its near neighbors, the Soviet Union and the People's Republic of China. Japan even has less overall military capacity than Taiwan and North or South Korea, making it the weakest state in Northeast Asia from a strategic standpoint.

Inevitably, these conditions give Japanese foreign policy an aura of impotence and dependency. On the economic front as well, vulnerability now vies with power in such a manner as to bring into question the force of Japan's economic weapons.

Naturally, this situation has been productive of mounting frustrations. One result has been an increase in nationalist sentiments, manifesting themselves in a variety of ways, but generally pointing toward the desire for a more independent foreign policy on the one hand and greater international recognition for Japan and respect for its interests on the other. To date, however, this new nationalism has made itself felt in actual policies only in limited degree. Its influence has been primarily a negative one: a decline in enthusiasm for most if not all foreign nations and a renewed quest for identity as a people and nation; a corresponding downgrading of foreign ties; and a certain turning inward, sometimes with Pan-Asian as well as Japan-centered overtones.

The current mood is consonant with some of the deepest wellsprings of Japanese culture. In essence, the Japanese are introspective and introverted—a private people. Burdened or blessed with intense commitments to the small groups, familial and otherwise, which form the nuclei of their culture, the broader and vaguer commitments that comprise international relations do not come naturally. Most internal Japanese relations, moreover, are hierarchical in nature, making international ties based on equality exceedingly difficult to fashion and maintain. Superiority or inferiority and, above all, aloofness from the unknown come more easily.

Yet the present mood, together with the forces that sustain it, are challenged by the realities that underlie the new Japan and its relationship to the world. In the midst of this basic conflict, Japanese foreign policy has recently been characterized by drift and uncertainty. Psychological and political support for the policies of the past has waned. But basic alternatives to those policies have seemed either unfeasible or unduly hazardous. To appreciate this dilemma, let us examine more closely the most fundamental factors shaping Japanese foreign policy, including the central issues with which that nation must cope.

The Historical Context

First, there are the geopolitical facts of life as these manifest themselves in the late twentieth century. Japan, like Great Britain, is a small island nation lying off the coast of a major continent. Historically, the most crucial issue was aloofness from or involvement with that continent. The Japanese response varied with the times. On occasion, the contact was intimate, stormy or otherwise, and productive of much that went into the making of Japanese culture. During other periods, aloofness prevailed, and that too had its impact.

Connected with this issue was another: alignment versus independent action. Despite its cultural proclivities for separateness, Japan in the course of modernization found that ties out of Asia supported policies in Asia. Thus, alliances were consummated, first with Great Britain, then with the Axis nations, and in the postwar era with the United States. Perhaps it is not surprising, therefore, that one basic cleavage within policy-making and political circles remains that between the "Asianists" and those prepared to place their priorities on the West.

Meanwhile, in recent decades, new complexities have made themselves felt, illustrating the fact that geopolitical considerations are no more static than other variables influencing foreign policy. Prior to World War II, Northeast Asia—indeed, all of Asia—was a vacuum of power except for Japan itself. This single fact contributed mightily to Japanese expansionism, especially because in the midst of weakness two tempting targets presented themselves—Communism and Western imperialism. Both fired Japan with a sense of mission, not merely for itself, but on behalf of all Asians. Today, however, Asia is far from being a power vacuum. On the contrary, Japan finds itself surrounded on three sides by great powers: to the near north, the Soviet Union; to the near west, the People's Republic of China; and in the more distant east and south, the United States. In an age when strategic power is held by continental-mass societies, Japan finds itself in the center of a region where the three most formidable such societies come into close interaction. Assertiveness in such a setting is not easy.

Meanwhile, if communism has become too powerful to be challenged in the old manner, colonialism, at least in its classic forms, has been replaced by independence. Asia is free, even if Asians by the millions are still unfree, wearing the bondage of ignorance, poverty, and servitude to governments indigenous but also imperious. To free Asia today is scarcely within the capacities of any single external source, whatever aid it may render. From whence, then, can come a new sense of mission or perception of role that might constructively counteract the exclusivist currents now running strongly?

The Economic Imperatives

Presumably, this must come from within the economic sphere, and indeed it is here that Japanese self-interest and enlightened internationalism find their most logical nexus. What will be Japan's primary economic needs in the period ahead, and what policies will be most conducive to achieving these? Most conservative leaders join with spokesmen for the Left in acknowledging the need to shift the emphasis from high growth rates to raising living standards and improving the quality of life. If the challenge confronting the conservatives is to be put in its most simple form, it is to modify its image in the direction of human welfare, lowering the priorities on increases in the gross national product. This challenge, however, comes at a time when the phenomenally high growth rates of the past could not be sustained under any policy.

For the foreseeable future, Japan will live with three conditions limiting growth: rising resource costs, an increased scarcity of labor, and the need to take further measures to protect the environment. Even under these conditions, the current plan as projected by the Ministry of Industry and International Trade (1974) is to maintain economic growth at an average of 6 percent over the coming decade, down from the 10 to 11 percent of the recent past, but still sufficient to make Japan one of the most rapidly developing nations in the world. It is not assumed that inflation can be halted—only slowed, with wholesale prices rising at 7.6 percent until 1980, 2.2 percent from 1980 to 1985, consumer prices rising by 8.5 percent until 1980, 3.9 percent between 1980 and 1985. These increases would be more than offset for the average Japanese, according to the plan, by wage increases of 16 percent in 1976, 12 percent in 1977, and 10 to 11 percent annually from 1978.

At this point, it is not possible to predict whether such a plan can be realized, partly because much depends on the international environment, as has been repeatedly stressed here. If it is achieved, energetic activity on the part of both the Japanese government and people will be required, however, in addition to ample cooperation from international developments. Speaking to the former factor, what is the current Japanese program of action? The first requirement is the fullest possible access to those raw materials and energy sources essential to the Japanese economy, and on the most favorable terms possible in an era of ever more intensive competition and mounting scarcities. The premium will be on the widest possible diversification of sources, with special emphasis on those states that are least vulnerable to radical fluctuations. As ocean resources will become increasingly vital, moreover, the settlement of maritime jurisdiction and specific territorial issues in Northeast Asia with due regard for Japanese interests assumes an importance almost totally unrealized a few years ago. At the same time, research and development with respect to resource substitutes such as solar energy must be given a high priority.

Resource needs, of necessity, underline the significance of Japan's relations with the emerging world, although if the plans outlined here are to be consummated in their entirety, cooperation with the "advanced" nations is equally important. The same complex requirements pertain to other portions of the economic plan. The transferral of Japanese heavy and chemical industries abroad on a large scale is now contemplated, so as to bring these close to resource bases, and to alleviate the labor and environmental problems connected with further expansion at home.

Foreign investment of a different character will be expected to continue at a substantial rate in the developed nations. Already, Japanese investments abroad total some U.S. $10 billion, up from a mere U.S. $710 million at the end of 1967, with 25 percent of that total in the United States, most of it in commerce and services. Within Japan itself, the shift increasingly will be to high-technology industries, and to the services, an accommodation to growing Japanese affluence.

Expansion of trade is scheduled to accompany investment advances, with the premium once again on tapping as many sources as possible. The principal agencies underwriting economic exchange among industrial nations, the International Monetary Fund (IMF) and the General Agreement on Trade and Tariffs (GATT), have been in considerable disarray, with rejuvenation through reform badly needed. Certainly, no nation stands to profit or lose more than Japan from the state of health among the advanced nations and in the economic institutions through which they interact.

It is equally clear, however, that if Japanese economic plans are to be realized, receptive environments encompassing both the "emerging" societies and the major Communist states are vital. As noted, Japanese projections for the future take diversification as a primary goal; no opportunity, however small, is to be neglected if it serves the broader purpose. In a certain sense, this argues for equidistance in foreign policy. But it is also obvious that some regions and nations will continue to be far more critical to Japan's economic well-being than others. For example, 22 percent of Japan's total trade, as well as total foreign investment, is with the United States at this point.

Political Values

One other basic factor must be considered in exploring the alternatives for Japanese foreign policy, namely, the contemporary character of political institutions in that society. Japan is a remarkably open society, one in which all forms of political expression are permissible, and parliamentary institutions, underwritten by a full range of political parties, operate with as much effectiveness as elsewhere. Japanese democracy, to be sure, has its own unique attributes, and in addition, a number of weaknesses—some of which it shares with similar systems. Standing on the outer frontiers of freedom, it must tolerate abuses to freedom from many quarters, risk the disunity that goes with uninhibited popular rights.

The dramatic post-1945 political revolution in Japan has at this point left a substantial impact not merely on the politics of the nation, but on its culture in the broadest sense—on art, literature, the theatre, and also on the life style and values of younger generations who now far outnumber those coming to maturity under the old order. Japan is thus Asian with a difference—and that difference weighs against close identification either with the rigidly authoritarian states or the slowly emerging ones that people the area. It is always possible that Japan might undergo a retreat from freedom, but in any case the problems as well as the achievements of this nation couple it politically with the more advanced industrial societies. This must have some influence on foreign policies, even in an era of realpolitik when ideological considerations have subsided.

The Alternatives Available

What, then, are the broad foreign policy alternatives available to Japan? We have already briefly discussed the "neutralist-pacifist" option in conjunction with the possibility of a shift toward the Left. Let us now explore the prospects under an assumption of "moderate" political rule.

Perhaps the possible alternatives are more narrow than is commonly conceived. Let us first explore an oft discussed scenario, that of a Japan strongly assertive in the international arena, practicing high-posture diplomacy by adding military and political weight to its economic capacities. Pursuing this policy, Japan would shift from the present strictly defensive military posture to one of offensive capacity, including nuclear weapons. It would speak with increased insistence at regional and international councils, defending Japanese interests vigorously even when these conflicted with those of other large nations. Such policies might be undertaken either with some degree of alignment (presumably with the United States) or, more logically, under conditions where the aim was for "friendly" but relatively equidistant relations with the other major powers. In any event, a new emphasis would be placed on ties with select Third World countries, notably those having special economic significance for Japan.

A High-Posture Policy?

The sketch just presented is one of a Japan powerful in the classical sense, and therein lie its fatal flaws. For Japan, there can be no return to the era of the 1930s. First, as we have noted, Asia has changed fundamentally. The continent is no longer a vacuum of power. On the contrary, Japan is surrounded by nations far stronger in military terms than it is. Indeed, this is an era when such power is held most naturally by societies larger in territory, states containing the greater part of their resource needs within their own boundaries. Empire in the classical sense is passé. What nation can protect its overseas markets or investments today by direct political rule or the application of overt military power?

At present, the military forces of Japan, numbering slightly over two hundred thousand men and furnished with highly modern, but overwhelmingly defensive weaponry, are capable of strictly limited operations. They are equipped to engage in interisland movement, but not in any overseas campaign. Even with respect to defensive capacities, the present plan calls for Japanese forces to be able to hold out for approximately ten days in the highly unlikely event of a land invasion of Japanese territory (with the Russians generally presumed to be the hypothetical enemy). If one posits a more likely form of external military challenge, namely, a military blockade, what would be required to offset such an action? Such a blockade could be undertaken either in the near vicinity or many thousands of miles distant, in the Indian Ocean or near the Malacca Straits, for example. In either case, to meet such a challenge militarily would seem far beyond Japan's capabilities alone unless it were prepared for a truly herculean military drive. Even then, the extreme vulnerability of this nation to nuclear warfare and the difficulty involved in mounting a credible second-strike capacity raise additional questions about the feasibility of any effort to become a formidable military power. Presumably, the concentration would have to be on mobile facilities such as Trident-type submarines. One can assume, however, that nuclear weapon developments of any type on the part of Japan would provoke early responses from that nation's neighbors, especially the Soviet Union and China. Quickly, nuclear missiles would be trained on logical Japanese targets, raising security issues far beyond the capacity of the Japanese to meet.

An extensive military effort would also have serious psychological and political repercussions throughout Asia, and possibly beyond, threatening that primary goal: an environment receptive to Japanese markets and investments. Even with power limited to the economic sphere, the Japanese have discovered recently how deeply seated are the old antagonisms and suspicions. Premier Tanaka's visit to Southeast Asia was the occasion for festering hostilities to boil over, although indigenous issues were contributory causes to the rioting, particularly in Indonesia. If to Japan's economic capacities was added extensive military-political strength, tensions might well be increased to the point where Japan's entire economic game plan was jeopardized.

There is another type of threat that could be envisaged, namely, an internal insurgent movement—one either seeking to generate its own resources or obtaining some external assistance. Admittedly, Japan's separation from the continent and the relatively small space in which such a movement could operate make it difficult to conceptualize a large-scale Japanese guerrilla force. Nevertheless, of all types of threats that can be ·conceived, it is this one for which the present Japanese defense forces are best equipped to deal, without external aid.

Thus far, no reference has been made to such internal considerations as Japanese public opinion and recent political trends. Clearly, these pose additional obstacles to high-posture diplomacy. In every poll taken in recent years, the Japanese public has voiced its strong opposition to extensive rearmament, and most particularly to the acquisition of nuclear weapons. A majority do support limited rearmament for defense purposes only.

In considerable part, current opinion rests on the conviction that Japan faces no threat. Indeed, it is the absence of any perception of threat that leads to the belief by many Japanese that the Mutual Security Treaty and, more particularly, the American bases in Japan are not primarily for the defense of Japan but for the larger purposes of the United States in Asia. Because the linkage between these two considerations is not widely accepted at present, bases are seen as an annoyance—and in themselves, a threat, possibly involving Japan in conflict—by a sizable number of Japanese. We shall return to this matter in discussing U.S. policy. However, it should be noted here that pressures from the Japanese public have placed LDP governments on the defensive over the base issue periodically, especially when an emotional issue emerges, such as the assertion that certain American warships carry nuclear weapons into Japanese ports. Even under conservative governments, these pressures could conceivably reach a level making further modifications in current defense agreements not merely desirable but essential. Needless to say, the Left spearheads the attack on bases. At the same time, however, it would strongly resist any form of high-posture diplomacy by a Gaullist Japan, at least under present circumstances.

The inability to achieve consensus on Japanese foreign policy has not proved to be a critical problem in the past, because those policies have been essentially passive and pragmatic. Japan has pursued with single-minded dedication the route suggested by its economic interests, reacting rather than acting, and taking the most minimal risks possible. Less than one percent of the GNP has been expended in the military realm, and even with respect to economic-technical assistance Japan's programs have been strongly oriented toward facilitating its markets.

Under these conditions, the Japanese Left has found it extremely difficult to get a handle on governmental policies, and hence it has been forced to resort largely to abstract ideological attacks carrying little weight with the Japanese public. However, if Japanese foreign policies were to become higher in priority and visibility, with costs and risks greatly increased, the fissures in this society would soon come to the fore in a more serious way. Internal stability itself could be threatened. Only under very great provocation is any Japanese government likely to risk such a trail of events.

Internal political considerations, however, have not been the crucial determinants for top policy-makers. Rather, the inability to conceptualize any form of high military-political posture that would enhance security or the protection of vital interests has been the decisive consideration. "Final" decisions on this matter were made only after extensive internal debate and serious studies by those most concerned with defense and related matters. These decisions *were* made, however, several

years ago, and they are encompassed in the Fourth Defense
Plan as well as in various other governmental programs. No
significant changes in the defense structure are contemplated,
with such monetary increases as have been requested primarily
destined to meet inflationary pressures; modest sums are intended to replace outdated equipment with more modern
military hardware. Even this latest plan, however, is jeopardized by the high rate of inflation.

The thesis that Japan ranks seventh in military power, incidentally, is both inaccurate and misleading. First, it is based
on cost calculations, but a number of countries support a larger
military establishment much more cheaply. Second, it does not
take into account the fact that almost all of Japan's neighbors
are more powerful militarily—and likely to remain so.

If there are no current indications of a shift in basic military
posture, neither does Japan seem likely to embark on a major
political offensive. In the quest for an expanded role, Japanese
leaders have sent up certain trial balloons such as the proposal
for a Pacific Conference. From private sources have come other
ideas: Japan as the leader of the "middle powers," or the initiator of disarmament proposals. Given the present state of the
world, and of Japan, none of these schemes seems very realistic,
and most of them fall into the "what can we possibly propose?"
category. Any initiatives in the political realm worth undertaking involve the risk of alienating important forces in the
global arena, and that is precisely why low-posture diplomacy
has been assiduously pursued. Japan's most logical initiatives
lie in the economic and technological realm, and although these
are by no means divorced from politics, at least here Japan can
lead from both strength and need.

If the foregoing analysis is correct, the odds against high-
posture diplomacy are very great. Given the uncertain state of
the world, however, it behooves us to outline those circumstances that would create the greatest temptations to move
toward such a course. Let us first assume the continued general

weakness of the international order and, further, a serious, prolonged economic crisis—or series of crises—centering on the "advanced," industrial nations. Accompanying such conditions might well be a deterioration of Japanese-American relations, punctuated by periodic peaks of tension, as competition in the economic arena became more acute, the climate for cooperation less promising. At the same time, circumstances, including domestic politics, would completely undermine the credibility of the United States as a protector of Japanese security. The American presence in Asia, indeed, would become a minimal one, forcing all allies to operate increasingly on their own, unless other protectors were available.

Let us now assume that our gloomy picture is further complicated by the emergence of a serious crisis involving Japan with another state. Possibly the issue would be a jurisdictional one, or events affecting the lives and properties of Japanese citizens. Such a crisis might involve one of the major powers, but it could also involve South or North Korea, or Taiwan, among others. If the issue were sufficiently grave, anger among the Japanese people might mount very rapidly, together with a demand for action. In the absence of reliable allies, would attitudes toward rearmament quickly change? Might a strong "rightist" movement ensue if the "Left" had not already taken advantage of conditions to establish its own preeminence? Even a "leftist" nationalism can be envisaged, in the pattern of contemporary China.

Admittedly, these are the most logical circumstances, with other variants conceivable, under which basic foreign policies might shift toward high-posture diplomacy. Almost certainly, if all of these circumstances were to come to pass, the repercussions on Japanese domestic politics would be profound. Japanese democracy would be in deepest peril, with the centrist forces losing ground to the extremities of Left and Right. Guerrilla warfare, or at least a prounounced increase in political violence, could not be ruled out. It is less clear, however, that even under these conditions Japan would resort to a high military-political posture on the international front. None of the massive obstacles to the success of such a course would have been removed by the events which we have posited. To be sure, mistaken or illogical actions on the part of a desperate leadership and people can never be ruled out. But neither can they be made the basis for future projections of policy.

A New Alliance or a Modification of the Past?

What, then, is the most likely course of action for Japan in the years ahead?

It is always possible at this point to project the availability of new allies, notably in the form of the People's Republic of China or the USSR. We have already suggested the problems making such a move unlikely. Barring.a major political shift in one of the two nations, the interests which Japan has in common with China lie largely in the economic sphere, and even here elements of potential competition or friction vie with those of cooperation. The great developmental differences between these two societies, which now amount to cultural differences of the first magnitude, combined with the peculiar differences in each state's strength and weaknesses, will remain such as to make the concept of a Sino-Japanese alliance a romantic myth, albeit one alluring to a number of Japanese. These considerations are more compelling in any contemplation of a Soviet-Japanese alliance. The trends which we have sketched might well be conducive to an accelerated movement toward equidistance in external relations and a growing emphasis on self-reliance, but an effort to substitute a new alliance for a faltering one seems less likely.

Subtle shifts from the policies of the past, with the primary goals left basically intact, are the most logical developments for the near and middle-range future. Given its economic game plan, Japan can benefit most by seeking to retain certain special ties with the United States. It is only through the United States, for example, that the opportunities for reversing the tides of economic nationalism among advanced states and establishing workable monetary, trade, and investment policies on the international level are in the least promising, granted that the prospects are uncertain. Japan's economic health, moreover, will still depend heavily on American policies and attitudes, no matter how successful the economic diversification program now contemplated.

If Japan is not yet prepared to take the risks of unarmed neutralism, given the troubles and diversities of the world around it, the American nuclear umbrella will continue to be of value. At the very least, it helps to rationalize low defense expenditures and in other respects reduces the intensity of the debate that would otherwise exist over security questions. In the Japanese circles that count, moreover, the United States will probably remain credible—at any rate, sufficiently credible . to deter those who might seek to challenge Japan over some matter of consequence,—although recent trends and events make this hypothesis challengeable.

The true effectiveness of past American deterrence is overlooked when one concentrates solely on its military, more particularly, its nuclear aspects. It has been the combination of a specific commitment to Japan and a network of other commitments involving a substantial military *and* political-economic presence throughout the region that has lent both credibility and effectiveness. Thus, deterrence is closely connected with Sino-American and Soviet-American détente, and also with the roles that the United States plays with respect to such small yet important nations as South Korea and Taiwan. In the absence of some truly acceptable and enforceable international order, why should Japan give up the benefits of this order, if it continues? For the moment, of course, we are merely considering policies from a Japanese standpoint. The United States at a minimum may want additional quid pro quo or burden-sharing, issues raised by it periodically in the past, and conceivably may opt for an entirely new set of policies—issues to be discussed later.

Japanese interests do dictate efforts to defuse the explosive issues still existing in northeast Asia, especially those relating to divided states. Events on the Korean peninsula or in Taiwan are of great consequence to Japan. If a lasting peace for the region is to be brought closer, several basic principles will have to be accepted. These include the recognition of existing de facto states and the insistence that their mutual relations evolve without a resort to force. Both of these principles require the cooperation of all of the major powers, as well as of the parties most immediately concerned. Unilateral Japanese political initiatives, however, are unlikely to be helpful, even when one grants the sizable Japanese stake in the outcome. General policies already being pursued, namely, the separation of economics and politics, are basically in line with the needs of northeast Asia at this point, however, and thus a Japanese contribution may flow from these policies. Economically, Japan can interact with benefit to every existing state in the region. Any Communist program of unification by force, whether applied to Korea or to Taiwan, is clearly adverse to Japan's interests, but it could probably do little to prevent such actions by itself.

In sum, Japan can live with the status quo in northeast Asia quite comfortably, and in a limited but possibly important sense it can help to support that status quo. Nor would an evolutionary development between Communist and non-Communist sectors of the type marking West-East German relations harm Japan. Any effort to upset the prevailing order by the use of massive military force would constitute a threat, one possibly having profound, long-range repercussions—but this is one of the many contingencies beyond the control of the Japanese unless they are prepared to take truly major risks.

Meanwhile, efforts to normalize and advance relations with

the Soviet Union and the People's Republic of China will undoubtedly go forward, as will the attempt to keep these two
relationships somewhat equal in character. Here, equidistance
does have very real meaning for Japan, given the deep
animosities currently operating between the two Communist
giants. But equidistance is also a policy impossible to achieve in
any absolute sense, here as in other settings. China and the
Soviet Union come before Japan with quite different attrac-
tions—and blemishes. At the moment, the tilt is in favor of
China, not merely for complex historical and cultural reasons,
but also because of more recent developments. Despite the
monumental changes now driving them apart at an accelerated
rate, China and Japan have a cultural legacy in common. Of
greater significance, the Japanese still perceive the Chinese as a
people they can understand more easily and with whom they
share certain attributes as Asians. Furthermore, a guilt complex exists in some Japanese circles toward China as a result of
World War II, although this factor has been overemphasized.
Finally, a number of Chinese presently holding high political
posts studied in Japan in their youth.

These factors together have provided China with an access
to Japan unmatchable by most other nations. This is not an
unalloyed advantage to be sure, for it can lead to charges of undue influence, or interference in Japan's internal affairs. On
balance, nevertheless, it has thus far proved to be a considerable asset.

China's economic cards in bidding for Japanese attention
remain obscure at this point. After normalization, Sino-
Japanese trade shot up, and it continues to increase at a more
modest rate. The unresolved questions are these: What general
course will the Chinese economy take, and more specifically
what policies will a post-Mao government follow with respect
to foreign trade and investment? Will the PRC allow Japan to
expand its share of China's trade beyond the 20 to 25 percent it
currently holds? And most importantly, will the People's

Republic find in oil and other commodities the necessary sources of foreign exchange whereby to pay for its imports on an expanded scale? Recently discovered petroleum deposits appear very promising, and Chinese leaders have been quick to use oil politically, including pledges to Japan to furnish ever-increasing amounts, in an effort to forestall Soviet-Japanese collaboration. In 1974, China furnished Japan 4.9 million tons of oil, a very small fraction of Japan's current yearly requirements, but according to some accounts, the PRC hopes to raise its production to some 300 million tons per year by 1980 and to sell Japan 40 to 50 million tons, approximately 7 to 9 percent of estimated Japanese needs of that period. This could be highly significant, both for China and Japan. Still, both the economic policies and the resources of China remain unsettled matters at this point. Whatever promise future developments may hold, Japanese enthusiasm for the prospects of economic relations with the PRC has been tempered by recent problems.

The Russians have few historical or cultural assets to be parlayed into gains with Japan. To the Japanese, Russians are very foreign and, on the whole, suspect. The history of Japanese-Russian relations, including the era after 1945, is replete with tension, toughness, and betrayal. Even recent Soviet policies toward Japan involve many actions that seem to contravene Russian interests. A whole people has been unnecessarily alienated by the almost unalleviated elements of harshness and intransigency characterizing Moscow's Japan policies. The current refusal of the Russian government to concede on the issue of four insignificant islands off the shores of Hokkaido—arguments concerning the precedent that might be set notwithstanding—are but the latest example.

Nevertheless, Siberia beckons to a resource-starved Japan, and the Russians are now deeply interested in the rapid development of this vast territory for both economic and strategic reasons. Such development could most easily and quickly be undertaken with foreign technical and economic assistance, and Japan is a logical source. Thus, in the near and middle-range future, the Soviet Union has an economic potential for Japan probably greater than that offered by China. Emphasis, however, must be on the word *potential,* because a variety of factors intervene to make the future of Soviet-Japanese relations as uncertain as Japan's economic relations with the PRC.

To date, the Russians have not made such a major proposal as the Tyumen gas and oil field development economically attractive. Given the strategic implications of this and similar projects, moreover, the Japanese regard American participation as crucial, partly to offset Chinese pressure. American intentions, however, remain unclear. Thus, while some Siberian projects involving Japanese participation are getting underway, the degree to which Japan can and will participate in Siberian development remains unclear. Meanwhile, there are points at issue between Japan and the USSR other than the northern islands. The fishing problem is a perennial one, and it leads into the whole complex and unresolved issue of maritime jurisdiction, certainly not a bilateral issue exclusively, but one in which Japanese and Russian interests are deeply involved. With or without Japanese aid, moreover, the Soviets will expand their Pacific military installations. Increased numbers of Russian ships and planes will operate out of the eastern Siberia region. This too cannot leave Japan unconcerned.

Despite these problems, the Sino-Soviet cleavage, on balance, has been of great benefit to Japan. In some degree, Japan has been sought, and will continue to be sought, by both Communist giants in their competition for position and influence. At the very least, each will seek to deny the other the full weight of Japan's skills and power. It is primarily for this reason that neither the USSR nor the PRC have been interested in seeing Japan's security ties with the United States disturbed. Clearly, a Sino-Soviet war would be destabilizing to Japan as it would be to all other countries in Asia, although

Tokyo could probably avoid direct involvement. But a restoration of close ties between Peking and Moscow would also constitute a threat, as it would liberate a sizable amount of the military power now concentrated in Central Asia, making it available elsewhere. More broadly, it would enable each of the major Communist states to pursue a more flexible policy toward other nations, and it might encourage more forceful policies toward neighboring states of whatever political type. But a case can be made that certain benefits could flow from Sino-Soviet détente, especially if it were of limited nature. For example, some agreement on arms limitations might result. The current pressures which Japan feels from one party to the quarrel when it seeks betterment of relations with the other party might be removed. In general, however, it is logical for Japan to feel apprehensive about any dramatic changes in the Sino-Soviet relationship, whether for the better or the worse.

An element of greater independence has already entered Japanese policies as these relate to the Third World. This independence, however, expresses itself in reactions rather than initiatives. To a greater extent than previously, Japan has begun to accommodate itself to attitudes or policies generally reflective of dominant Third World positions, or at a minimum abstain from any actions that could antagonize this force. At the same time, Tokyo continues to be concerned about Washington's feelings. The shift is thus a cautious one. Its positive manifestations, moreover, invariably take economic forms, with Japan offering assistance of new types, extending its technology to areas previously overlooked. If Japan's economic circumstances (and those of the world) permit, this trend will undoubtedly continue.

A Balance Sheet on the Future

In sum, the foreign policy of Japan is probably not destined to undergo massive changes in the years immediately ahead. This will be a source of frustration both to certain

Japanese and to certain foreigners, but that frustration is built into Japan's unique situation. Despite the ties that have bound Japan and the United States so closely together for nearly three decades, most Japanese do not consider themselves to have been involved with Americans in any intimate or special way. A sense of isolation, indeed, has permeated Japanese consciousness throughout the whole of the modern era. This is understandable. As we have noted, the Japanese are a very private people, not given easily to personal commitments and the costs which they exact. Moreover, Japanese political culture does not lend itself easily to international relations among equals. Beyond these considerations, however, the very facts of Japanese development have set this nation apart. It is in, but not fully of Asia. Its problems as well as its progress align it naturally with the "advanced West," and particularly with the United States, yet the sense of mutual identification on both sides is significantly weaker than one might presume.

The element of uniqueness present in this situation can be exaggerated, of course. In very few nations do the people have a strong international consciousness. In many parts of the world, it has been difficult enough to implant nationalism as a primary value. Where successfully installed, moreover, nationalism tends to preempt other forms of political identification, localist and internationalist alike. The current global crisis reflects this fact in no small measure. At a time when the need for workable international institutions has never seemed greater, nationalist currents everywhere are mounting. The Japanese as a people must be included in this trend, but Japan as a government has now come to the realization (some would say belatedly) that an effective international order, especially in the economic sphere, is essential to its well-being. A paradox thus ensues: a people whose proclivities are for aloofness and a government whose commitments are for greater integration.

Commitments, moreover, are not the equivalent of action. Japanese spokesmen emphasize the limited degree to which

Japan can influence other nations in the direction of a new internationalism. Once the recurrent theme was "Japan is poor," a refrain that dominated Japanese thought long after it ceased to be a fact. Now the theme is "Japan is vulnerable—and being vulnerable is impotent to serve as catalyst and initiator of a new economic order." Perhaps this too will pass, but low-posture diplomacy is both safe and a proved success. It served as the protective cloak under which Japan became an economic giant. Thus, there is no reason to expect an assertion of Japanese leadership in the near future. The Marxian thesis that military and political power inevitably follows economic prowess, like so many nineteenth-century concepts, is not necessarily correct when applied to the late twentieth century.

In all probability, Japan will do what comes naturally, what is implicit in the delicate balance of socioeconomic, political, and psychological factors that comprise its domestic setting, and the imperatives that govern its foreign policies. With government and the private sector working closely together, Japanese economic and technical assistance, singly and in consort with others, will operate to advance the tempo of development in various countries. Ideological differences in themselves will not be a critical determinant. The effort to separate economics and politics will be accelerated in this era of détente. The vital issues will be these: Can the Japanese input, unilateral or otherwise, be of significance in meeting the formidable socioeconomic problems confronting much of the world and especially Asia—or is the environment insufficiently receptive, the timing too late, the amount too little? Can the input serve as the basis for much broader, indigenous transformations, increasingly of a self-generating character—or will it hew to the old, self-serving orientation?

Japan can also make a contribution at another level. In company with their counterparts elsewhere, Japanese science and technology will be harnessed to meet those challenges that are going to determine the nature of man and society in the twenty-first century: new forms of energy; new types and sources of food; the planning of births and the extension of life; and the management as well as the expansion of resources. Having long been a borrower in the field of advanced technology, Japan is in a position now to become a lender.

Meanwhile, in the construction of new economic institutions at the regional and international levels, Japan can be expected to play a cooperative, if largely subordinate role. No bold international initiatives are to be expected from Tokyo. The leadership must come from others. Japan's primary contributions will come in the form of an increasing receptivity to all forms of economic interchange. Even those structural elements of the Japanese economy such as the distribution system that have long abetted exclusivism will gradually yield to greater openness. At the regional level, Japanese initiatives, both planned and unintended, may well be of greater consequence. There is a good chance that economic regionalism in many parts of the world will be the most dynamic development of the next few decades. In the Pacific-Asian area, Japan almost certainly will play a key role in any such trend.

The contributions outlined here are certainly not insignificant. But, they are also not fully satisfying, either to some Japanese or to some of the other actors on the international stage. Unfortunately, ours is still a divided and quarrelsome world. Cleavages based upon cultural, developmental, and ideological differences abound, and there is no indication that they will quickly disappear. As a result, violence is endemic in this era, at every level of human interaction. No adequate international institutions exist either to adjudicate issues or enforce the peace. We thus continue to be dependent upon that self-enforcing mechanism, a political-military equilibrium that keeps the risks of war for any party very high.

To maintain such an equilibrium is costly, especially to nations centrally involved like the United States, the Soviet Union, and China. Viewed in this light, Japan's current international contributions seem quite minimal (especially from an American perspective), and taking purely economic forms as they do, their influence on the global order appears to have greater long-range than immediate potentialities.

When our times are seen in this perspective, both the foreign resentments over Japan's "privileged position" and the restiveness among many Japanese themselves, unhappy with their nation's image and role, can be appreciated. After the major alternatives have been fully examined, however, they prove to be either unfeasible, undesirable, or both. Hence, Japan as a nation and the Japanese as people are more likely to live with their frustrations than to undertake any major shifts in foreign policy and role.

Chapter 3

CHINA: Emerging Nation and Regional Power

The People's Republic of China is now twenty-five years old, and on the verge of a major transition. Whenever the commanding figure of an era passes from the scene, important changes are set in motion, although these often come in stages. In the case of China, it is not merely Mao Tse-tung but an entire generation of leaders who are now approaching the end of their active political and military careers. Sometimes it is forgotten that these individuals had spent another quarter of a century or more in political activities before they attained final power. They were already middle-aged men when the Communist flag was finally planted over Peking, men seasoned by years of hardship and revolutionary experience.

The Domestic Setting

When the Communists first came to power, they displayed a remarkable 'unity. It had not always been so. The early Chinese Communist movement was strife-ridden, and the final battles for party control were fought as late as the 1941–1942 period, in the course of the *cheng-feng* (Rectification) Campaign. At a considerably earlier point, however, Mao Tsetung had already been recognized as *primus inter pares*. With final victory in 1949 came an impressive display of solidarity. Even among those who had once opposed Mao, a number were reincorporated into the Party (at lower levels).

Nor did there appear to be any serious divisions over issues. In the realm of foreign policy, Mao himself set forth the basic guidelines when he declared that the People's Republic of China would be a loyal member of the socialist bloc "led by the Great Soviet Union." Russia reciprocated by giving vital economic and technical assistance to the new government, enabling it to undertake a major program of industrial rehabilitation and expansion. This aid, as well as the general conditions of the period, strongly influenced the Chinese in the direction of the Soviet economic model.

The rhetoric displayed on the international front was radical, although it was rarely accompanied by action of a similar nature. China offered itself as a revolutionary example to the Afro-Asian-Latin American world in the struggle against "imperialism and reaction." Toward the United States and a number of other Western states, Peking's leaders were contemptuous, treating the "capitalist world" with the scorn which victors reserve for the vanquished.

Twenty-five years later, some extraordinary changes had taken place. The Soviet Union was still the focal point of attention, but as enemy not ally. The official rhetoric, both in the domestic and foreign arenas, was still radical, but the policies were complex and in considerable degree paradoxical. Many of them were also in dispute. The unity with which the Chinese Communist Party had commenced its era of control was now gone. A host of issues, some of them fundamental in character, had arisen after the mid-1950s to divide the top leadership. Inextricably connected with these issues was the emergence of factionalism and an ultimate struggle for power turning old comrades into bitter enemies. If we may believe Communist chronicles, even murder crept into the hearts of men who had worked together intimately for four decades or more.

Thus, Mao and his colleagues leave the political scene at a time when China's political institutions bear the scars of strenuous in-fighting. The Party itself, from which all power is supposed to flow, has been greatly weakened by recent events. Meanwhile, important figures—both old and new—vie for role and authority. Some have lengthy service records, and a host of protégés, in a system where seniority can still command respect. Others are protected and advanced via their close connections with Mao or Chou En-lai, the two seemingly unbreakable men of this era. Still others, coming from the younger ranks, are climbing or leaping upward, propelled by a variety of factors.

The cominbation of weak institutions and strong personalities does not augur well for the future political stability of China. And because both issues and personalities, intertwined, bear heavily on foreign as well as domestic policies, we must examine them as a prelude to exploring China's international role.

At the outset, one point should be emphasized. In taking careful note of the aura of uneasiness that currently surrounds Chinese politics and the probability that political instability will be a recurrent factor for the near future at least, it is not necessary to predict disintegration or a new "warlord" era. Although possible, these latter eventualities do not seem likely. First, the New China has concentrated on a powerful nationalist campaign, one reaching hundreds of millions of citizens and being emphasized especially in front of the political-military elites. The message is simple. China must be made rich and strong. Everyone must be prepared to sacrifice his own personal gain, material or otherwise, to that goal. And anyone who would risk China's unity by factional activities, challenge the policies of Chairman Mao and the Party, is a potential traitor. Among the younger generations particularly, this message —and the program accompanying it—must have had a substantial impact.

Meanwhile, the power of the center has been greatly increased both as a result of actions specifically directed to this end and as a product of general development. Communications have been extended and improved; large military forces can now be moved quickly to any potential troublespot. The allocation of resources and manpower has been centralized, as has the planning process itself. Although some elements of decentralization exist, the truly critical decisions continue to be made in Peking. The military structure also appears to be much more highly centralized, with the Party now very alert to the need to control the gun as a result of the Lin Piao affair.

Collective Leadership—Reality or Fiction?

There is still a question as to whether political instability in China can be contained at elitist levels, or whether it will spill over, affecting productivity and the public order. Such a question cannot be answered, given the data at hand. We can, however, examine the type of issues that bear on it. Unity itself, as we have already indicated, is the supreme issue of the moment. The pledge is for collective leadership, and it is clear that Mao has hoped in recent times to put together a "three-in-one" coalition, with senior statesmen, middle-aged veterans, and tested youth combining to provide China with the full advantages of three-generational rule. This is more easily said than done. The fierce political struggles of the last decade and a half have left the senior ranks deeply divided, with death now taking its rising toll. The impact of those struggles on the middle ranks may have been even more serious, for the burdens of the immediate future will fall largely here. With a few notable exceptions like Wang Hung-wen, youth still stands in the wings, awaiting its cue after adjustments at the higher level have been completed.

The difficulties involved in reconstructing a unified Party can be discerned from the evidence furnished by the PRC itself. The Ninth Party Congress, coming in April 1969 at the close of the Great Proletarian Cultural Revolution, was intended to launch a new Party, one cleansed of the sins of Liu Shao-ch'i-ism and more broadly representative of the masses. Subsequent developments were to show, however, that this congress merely captured the kaleidoscopic events for a moment, after which they rushed on. Soon a number of leading Party figures including the heir-apparent, Lin Piao, were swept away in the aftermath of what was officially described as an abortive military coup d'état in September 1971.

Nearly two years passed before the Tenth Party Congress could be held, in August 1973. The extraordinary secrecy and brevity of this congress, moreover, left numerous mysteries in its wake. Then another lapse of time occurred until the oft-postponed Fourth National People's Congress was finally convened, January 13–17, 1975. In the interim, extensive efforts were made to end or patch over the political divisions that ran through the Party, from the center to the provincial and local levels.

The Fourth NPC was initially heralded by many observers as victory for the "moderates," headed by Chou En-lai, and an indication that China's transition to a post-Maoist era could be smooth. Such interpretations were reasonable on the basis of the data available and suceptible to measurement. If Chou is to be considered a "moderate," and the moderate-radical dichotomy is meaningful (both of which concepts can be challenged), the key administrative appointments went to men closely associated with the seventy-seven-year-old premier. It was probably more accurate, however, to consider the Fourth NPC a holding operation. The "moderates" confirmed or reconfirmed in office ranged in age from a youthful seventy (Teng Hsiao-p'ing) to eighty-nine (Chu Teh), suggesting that this is indeed a transitional period. Soon, moreover, prominent ideologues like Yao Wen-yuan were writing major articles that seemed designed to keep the "Left" Line alive and forceful.

The post-Mao era is coming in stages. At eighty-one, and in fragile health, Mao himself is already removed from day-today matters, and although his imprimatur appears to lie on the events of January, he attended neither the congress nor the second Plenary Session of the Tenth Central Committee, a session which approved a new constitution and elevated Teng Hsiao-p'ing to the standing committee of the Politburo. Similarly, Chou En-lai—present at both meetings—is nonetheless both aging and ill, scarcely capable of sustaining his pace of a few years ago. Thus, the two men who have towered over the political scene for decades are being forced by health and age to turn over power to others. The fact that both still live, however, is of vital importance to the succession issue at this point in time. Ill or not, they can continue to play the dominant roles in picking those whom they wish to succeed them.

Even so, clouds obscure the precise shape of the coming order. It would now appear that two men are destined for key administrative and party roles, Teng Hsiao-p'ing and Chang Ch'un-ch'iao. Teng, in disgrace only a few years ago as a cohort of Liu Shao-ch'i, has not only been rehabilitated but now seems firmly in line to succeed Chou En-lai as premier when the latter finally departs. The rising star of Chang Ch'un-ch'iao, however, is worthy of careful attention because, not yet sixty, he now holds the second deputy premiership, next to Teng, as well as being on the standing committee of the Politburo and quite possibly secretary general of the Party—or its functional equivalent. Chang, from Shanghai and once regarded as a member of the "radical" Shanghai group, reportedly has long been close to Mao and his wife, but he has also been regarded as "moving toward the center," and thereby making himself acceptable to others.

If the futures of these two men (subject to unexpected upheavals) appear bright, however, powerful elements of uncertainty still hover over Chinese politics. What of Wang Hung-wen, widely reported to have been picked by Mao personally and undergoing a training period preliminary to taking over party leadership? Wang, still in his late thirties, has been seen as the representative of the ideal man from a Maoist perspective: of proletarian background, but with military experience; youthful and filled with the idealism of his youth; and combining toughness with the type of "radicalism" that came from his Shanghai setting. Is Wang still destined for great power? Are his positions, which include vice-chairmanship of the Party, member of its standing committee, and third-ranking position next to Mao and Chou, still valid, and are they meaningful?

And Chiang Ching, Mao's wife, what of her? This formidable woman has parlayed her position as wife of the chairman and his communications channel into a role of great significance. She too is a latecomer to high politics, her prominence coming only in the 1960s. Her debut, moreover, was made in the cultural and educational field, and this remains the area of her primary interest. Her general role in the Party and government, however, have been extensive since the Cultural Revolution—and controversial. Some foreign observers believe that she is actually Mao's choice as his true successor, and that he is hoping to bolster her power base by building up the Shanghai group. Others expect her political demise to follow shortly after Mao's death, whatever the chairman's hopes.

The very term *Shanghai group* is subject to uncertainty. Generally, the key figures from Shanghai have been considered "radical," because their rise was associated with the campaign launched by Mao and his wife from Shanghai to topple the "power-holders" of the Center in Peking. It is true that from Shanghai have emanated many of the boldest experiments since the mid-sixties, and some of the most extravagant rhetoric. It is also this municipality which has appeared to have the strongest civilian cast to its politics, raising questions about the relation between its representatives and those of the professional military. Moreover, Shanghai, given its productivity capacities, is of vital importance to the whole of

China—economically, hence politically. It is by no means clear, however, that "the Shanghai group" today is a unified body, operating in coordinated fashion.

Meanwhile, from the military comes another element in the coalition presently governing China. At the center stands the venerable Yeh Chien-ying, now in his mid-seventies, symbol of the politicized military man long separated from active command. Yeh, confirmed at the January 1975 congress in the position of defense minister, a position he had been holding since Lin Piao's downfall, must certainly be regarded as a transitional figure. The other military men who have risen high in party ranks would include Ch'en Hsi-lien, elevated to a deputy premiership, concurrently member of the Politburo and commander of the all-important Peking Military Region; and Li Teh-sheng, previous head of the General Political Department of the army, commander of the critical Shenyang Military Region fronting on the Soviet border to the north, Party vice-chairman and currently full member of the Politburo. Nor are these the only professional military men of political importance. Hsü Shih-yu, commander of the Canton Military Region, and Wang Tung-hsing, long close to Mao and involved in the security field, both occupy Politburo seats, in addition to such a ceremonial figure as Chu Teh.

The presence of these individuals at the very top of Party as well as key military posts is reflective of this Communist Party's guerrilla traditions as well as the roles which the army was called on to play during the 1960s in China's domestic politics. No problem has worried Mao more in recent years than the threat of military dominance over the Party. Strenuous measures have been adopted in the aftermath of the Lin Piao affair to reduce military influence. In January 1974, eight of China's thirteen military regional commanders were shifted to new posts and divested of their provincial Party and administrative positions. This was an obvious effort to subordinate the military to Party authority at the subnational level and reduce the problem of "mountain-topism" or excessive local autonomy. Those men holding Politburo or Central Committee posts at the center, however, retained such positions.

Meanwhile, a new emphasis on the people's militia is being voiced, with the suggestion of expanded functions encompassing internal security and defense. This could be construed as an effort to reduce the army's power—and to raise old, thorny issues. At the same time, Party organs are full of articles proclaiming the critical importance of having the Party command the gun and seeking to illustrate that point by insisting that it was Chairman Mao and the Party, not Lin Piao, who won China's "War of Liberation" against the Kuomintang.

The military itself undoubtedly has factional problems as a result of the purges of the recent past—and the fact that many of those purged remain alive. Here, as elsewhere, personal loyalties run strong, some of them connected with the close working relations established in earlier decades, some a product of the Communist era. Thus, when a top leader is purged, his subordinates may be in trouble. For example, a number of Lin Piao's associates went down with him. One may assume that those who remain alive bide their time, hoping for rehabilitation, or even revenge. Naturally, this problem goes far beyond the military, affecting the Party and the state administration as well, and at lower as well as at upper echelons. It could well be at the root of current factional difficulties, and it is not the type of problem to be resolved by the stroke of a pen or the issuance of an order.

How great is the threat of the military, even if it be a divided military? One of Mao's favorite sayings, as is well known, is that power comes out of the barrel of a gun. His own experience taught him at an early point to make certain that he was always close to that gun, and this as much as any single factor accounts for his survival, personal and political. In the event of any serious power struggle after his demise, the gun will surely be important. It cannot be a case of army versus Party, but rather of some civilian-military (or military-civilian) coalition overcoming its opposition and gradually sorting out the true power-holders from those who will fall by the wayside. All will be done in the name of the Party and probably in the name of Mao.

In sum, a working coalition does exist today at the top of the Chinese political system. It has a certain balance among Party, state administration, and military elements; and also among the old, the middle-aged, and the young. Yet its character has been very much shaped by Mao and Chou. Thus the question emerges, can it survive their departure, and for how long? And the fact that no single representative group within the coalition is itself monolithic does not alter the fact that the Party, by doctrine entitled to supreme authority, faces two persistent competitors for power. One of these is the bureaucracy. By virtue of the fact that communism is above all an intensively and extensively bureaucratic system, this challenge is always present. Even—or perhaps especially—the subordinate bureaucracy has repeatedly shown its capacity to alter, thwart, and negate Party orders. Hence, the endless campaigns against bureaucratism. There is every reason to believe, moreover, that whether in the Party apparatus or in other structures it is the compromises hammered out within the bureaucratic framework that account for much that comes forth as policy, domestic and foreign.

The second competitor, as we have noted, is the military. A signal difference between the Chinese and Soviet Communist Parties at this point lies in the fact that in the Soviet Union the military essentially constitutes a pressure group on the Party at the top, whereas in China the military is a vital element *within* the Politburo, that small powerful body that determines policy in the Party's name. This distinction cannot be waved aside with the comment that all Communist military men are different from other military men, especially the men of the

PLA, being highly politicized and fully integrated into Party rank. The cases of P'eng Te-huai and others illustrate the fact that functional specialization can easily carry with it a propensity for policy bias.

The degree of unity that accompanies the next stages of Chinese modernization, together with the type of leadership that emerges, are variables that will surely influence Chinese foreign policies and China's role in the world. So will decisions taken with respect to certain substantive issues currently confronting Chinese decision-makers. In the economic sphere, as has been noted, the exhortations are for continued individual sacrifice so that China can become rich and strong. In 1975, the Chinese claim major gains in agricultural production. More muted are the claims for industry, with signs that once again a political campaign (anti-Lin, anti-Confucius) had a depressing effect in early 1974.

In any case, if certain leaders have their way, consumption will be curbed, with the emphasis on capital accumulation for both economic modernization and military expenditures. In this, one hears strong echoes of Meiji Japan.

The question of self-reliance also figures prominently into current Party discussions. Although the PRC has recently turned outward in some degree in its effort to utilize the technology and products of the advanced industrial societies (as well as their food), the continued demands that self-reliance be practiced to the maximum extent possible, voiced in official organs, suggest that Peking's present leaders want to combine both approaches. Considerable indecision exists, however, concerning the precise mix. The ultimate trends in this regard will obviously have far-reaching repercussions on other policies.

These issues and others that could be mentioned point to one central conclusion: in many respects, China is an emerging society, confronting problems similar in nature to those faced by other such societies, irrespective of their economic and political systems. In general, these problems are conducive to weakness, hence to cautious foreign policies, ones normally subject to severe domestic constraints.

At the same time, however, China is more than just another "late developing country." The People's Republic has standing military forces numbering approximately three million men, plus large auxiliaries in the form of people's militia. It is developing a considerable conventional naval and air capacity. Moreover, its ballistic missile program is progressing slowly and reportedly with setbacks, but by the beginning of the 1980s it should have an ICBM capability. Thus, China easily has the greatest military capacities of any Asian state—the Soviet Union excepted. By virtue of its size and commitments, both military and political, it is a power of at least regional consequence, particularly when juxtaposed against the small nations on its peripheries. Moreover, Peking hopes to parlay its ideological-political stances into a position of substantial global influence, especially in relation to the Third World. It is obvious, therefore, that the People's Republic of China must be treated as a major element (but not a major power) on the international stage. Its uniqueness lies in the particular combination of weaknesses and strengths which it exhibits, and in its present style of international politics.

The Foundations of Chinese Foreign Policy

With this complex picture in mind, let us explore current Chinese foreign policies and the alternatives available for the future. As noted earlier, China's image of the world has changed dramatically in the last twenty-five years. Once there were essentially only two camps, the socialists and the capitalist-imperialists. Neutralism or nonalignment, in Chinese eyes, could be neither a meaningful nor a permanent position.

One either joined the world's "progressive" forces or their enemies. Today, as far as Peking is concerned, the socialist world is moribund, at least in its original form. The Chinese have written off the Soviet Union and its closest allies as socialists. Only internal revolutions can bring them back into the fold. Meanwhile, China identifies itself with another force, the Third World.

Accompanying this monumental shift is a new conceptualization of today's international order or, as Peking prefers, disorder. At present, the world is divided into three component parts: the superpowers; the second intermediate zone; and the Third World. In the first category come the United States and the Soviet Union, defined respectively as the forces of imperialism and social-imperialism. Western Europe and Japan comprise the second category, representing national bourgeois states subject to superpower pressures, hence susceptible to nationalist appeals. The Third World represents the vast majority of the globe's population, the peasant and proletarian forces of Asia, Africa, and Latin America with whom China not only identifies but whom it hopes to influence and lead.

This image is heavily laden with familiar ideological overtones. In essence, it is the application of class concepts to national categories, an approach pioneered much earlier, when the advanced capitalist states were seen as the urban centers to be surrounded by a global countryside comprising the peasant-proletarian forces of the non-West. The new themes, moreover, bear a strong resemblance to the Chinese Communist tactics of the late 1930s, the period of the Sino-Japanese War. To oppose the primary enemy, Japan (the USSR), an alliance of convenience with a secondary enemy, the Kuomintang (the U.S.), was undertaken. These united front tactics were further strengthened by a broadly gauged appeal to China's national bourgeois forces (Western Europe and Japan) as well as to the peasantry and proletariat (the Afro-Asian-Latin American world).

The Superpowers: Russia

Although the ideological and tactical antecedents of current policies are clear and relatively simple, the policies themselves are both complex and, at points, paradoxical. Let us first look at Peking's approaches to the superpowers. It comes as a shock to find that in this period of Sino-American rapprochement, cold-war rhetoric still abounds in Peking's treatment of the superpower issue, with the United States subjected to attacks only a few decibels in intensity below those directed against the Soviet Union. Indeed, the gap seems to have narrowed in recent months. The United States has been publicly accused of wide-ranging crimes in Indochina, the Middle East, and Latin America. Even American policies in Europe are described as "economic imperialism in its purest form."

The choicest epithets, however, are reserved for the Russians. In his report to the Tenth Party Congress, Premier Chou En-lai summarized Soviet inequities in a manner that still portrays accurately the official Chinese view:

Over the last two decades, the Soviet revisionist ruling clique, from Khrushchev to Brezhnev, has made a socialist country degenerate into a social-imperialist country. Internally, it has restored capitalism, enforced a fascist dictatorship, and enslaved people of all nationalities, thus deepening political and economic contradictions as well as contradictions among nationalities. Externally, it has invaded and occupied Czechoslovakia, massed its troops along the Chinese border, sent troops into the People's Republic of Mongolia, supported the traitorous Lon Nol clique, suppressed the Polish workers' rebellion, intervened in Egypt causing the expulsion of Soviet experts, dismembered Pakistan, and carried out subversive activities in many Asian and African countries. This series of facts has profoundly exposed its ugly features as the new czar and its reactionary nature, namely, "SOCIALISM IN WORDS, IMPERIALISM IN DEEDS." The more evil and foul things it does, the sooner the time when Soviet revisionism will be relegated to the historical museum by the people of the Soviet Union and the rest of the world.

As if this bill of attainder were not enough, a variety of added changes relate to Soviet-American "collusion." Here the pattern was set in the late 1960s over the nonproliferation treaty—that the two superpowers, intent on preserving their exclusive control, are committed to secret diplomacy designed to force all other states to concur in agreements in the drafting of which they have played no part.

More recently, similar charges have focused on the Middle East, with heavy emphasis on "the dirty deal" to ease restrictions on Soviet Jewish emigration to Israel. This and other acts are cited as evidence that Russian-American collaboration is dedicated to "the destruction" of the Arab cause.

Finally, Peking has regularly sought to put multilateral issues such as maritime jurisdiction, population control, and food into a superpowers-versus-the-world framework, with polemics often dominating the stage.

Has this behavior advanced China's cause with the Third World or other Communist states? Some observers think that the results have been largely negative, with the propaganda too crude and self-serving to be effective. Yet an attack on the superpowers will always strike a responsive chord among many of the small and weak states, especially when it is couched in stridently nationalist tones.

Surveying Peking's numerous pronouncements on the superpower threat, one must thus ask: what part political game, what part genuine fear? Granting the possibility that Peking sees this attack as a means of garnering political strength, there undoubtedly remains an element of genuine concern. Weak as it is in comparison with either of its defined enemies, China under Mao and Chou finds it vital to prevent any sweeping Soviet-American détente. Recently, China has asserted repeatedly that war between the United States and the USSR is inevitable, returning to an earlier theme with renewed insistence. To keep détente between the superpowers as limited as possible and make it costly to other Soviet relationships, to put the superpowers on the defensive vis-à-vis the rest of the world, to align China itself loosely with all nonsuperpowers—all this is part and parcel of China's reliance on balance-of-power politics to protect its national interests.

Is there also a fear of imminent war, of a Soviet nuclear strike? Many Americans, official and otherwise, believe this is to be the case, and after a visit to China one could easily hold that view. In the recent past, Peking has been at great pains to emphasize the continuing danger of a Soviet attack. The foreign guest is shown one of the air-raid shelters being constructed throughout the land at great cost. He is repeatedly told that a million-odd Russian soldiers and vast amounts of military equipment menace China to the north and west. No effort is made to hide from him the anti-Soviet campaign that permeates schools, work places, and all other outlets—a campaign that seems to be aimed in part at steeling the populace against any and all Soviet actions.

This evidence notwithstanding, a strong case can be made for the thesis that the primary concern of the men who govern China today is not the threat of imminent war but the possibility—indeed, the inevitability—of the reemergence of the Russian issue in domestic Chinese politics. In the recent past, a number of articles "using the past to serve the present" have drawn lessons from ancient Chinese history that could not be more precise in their implications for today and tomorrow. Various Confucianist traitors, it is asserted, favored capitulationist policies toward the marauding Huns of the north. They argued that the policies of confrontation would lead to national extinction, and that to maintain a large standing army was to rob the people of consumer necessities and keep them poor. They made no distinction between just and unjust conflicts, and insisted that territory was useless. They even claimed that bad relations with the Huns were a product of "a few troublemaking ministers." Their proposals were to reduce China's armed forces, proclaim a ceasefire, dismantle defense installations, and "use large sums of money" to make peace with the Huns.

Before seeking to analyze these remarks further, let us assess current Soviet policies toward China. The Russians appear to be saying to Chinese leaders, "If you insist on confrontation, we will make it as costly as possible. But if you—or those who come after you—want some accommodation, we are prepared to be reasonable." Under present circumstances, the pressure is kept on, but periodic signals are given that relations could be significantly improved. Thus, the Russians have mobilized men and equipment in huge quantities along the 4,800-mile Sino-Soviet frontier, including nuclear weapons and all types of modern conventional hardware. But if recent reports are correct, they have engaged in some reduction of forces. On several occasions, moreover, Brezhnev has proposed a nonaggression pact with the PRC and indicated a desire for the "normalization" of relations.

These policies amount to a classic carrot-and-stick approach, and currently the Russians carry a very big stick and possess a correspondingly big carrot. In some respects, their position resembles that of the United States in the 1950s and early 1960s. At times, tensions are heightened, deliberately or otherwise. At other times, offers—or gestures—of conciliation are advanced. The Russian hope is obvious: although Mao is regarded as beyond salvation, the leaders who follow him may decide that it is in China's own national interests to seek at least limited détente with the USSR, thereby relieving the risks and costs of the present policy.

What are the perspectives of Mao and those now making Chinese foreign policy? It would be surprising if the Russian issue did not cause apprehension, and as we have noted the evidence that this is the case is now incontrovertible. Although many of the details remain obscure, Soviet policy has been the subject of repeated discussions, debates, and divisions within the Chinese ruling circle for at least fifteen years. Careers have been made or broken over this critical issue. Every key argument and prediction must have been indelibly engraved on the minds of the leading participants. This type of issue does not go away.

There are strong reasons to believe that Mao and a number of others have long since crossed the Rubicon on Soviet policy. Mistrust, even hatred of the Russians for them may be largely a product of events that took place during the first decade of Communist rule, but it is also deeply embedded in the traditions of China. Indeed, a strong element of xenophobia exists in Chinese political culture pertaining to all foreigners. This serves to support Mao's recent policies toward the Soviet Union.

Some advantages accrue from the present state of affairs which should also be noted. It is helpful, possibly even indispensable, to have a foreign enemy—both to induce the sacrifices demanded of the Chinese people in this spartan era and to preserve the elitist unity so important in an initial nation-building stage. Moreover, to foreign nations, the Soviet threat explains, even sanctions, China's unrelenting drive to become a major military power, one armed with an array of nuclear weapons—so that this drive does not arouse the fear and hostility it otherwise might. For these purposes, Russia now plays the role earlier occupied by the United States.

On the other hand, the current policy of confrontation involves heavy costs and risks. At a minimum, it requires that a crash program directed toward nuclear and conventional weapon development continue, a massive armed force be maintained on the Sino-Soviet frontier, and various other defensive preparations be forwarded—expensive activities for a society still groping its way from backwardness. But in addition, the present level of confrontation canalizes Chinese foreign policy in general, blurring the desired image and accentuating certain contradictions. It also engenders deep, costly divisions within Communist and revolutionary movements everywhere, weakening the political front on which Peking once counted so strongly. All in all, the costs of confrontation are formidable.

Thus, although Sino-Soviet rapprochement is far from inevitable, the issue will continue to be debatable—and debated. It is precisely this fact, not the imminence of war, that probably most concerns Mao. He and those who oppose "concessions" to the Russians in exchange for détente must realize that at some point in the future certain figures within the top elite will once again argue that China's national interests would be better served by a policy of limited rapprochement with Russia. It will not be necessary to push for any return to the old alliance—only to reduce tensions and begin a process of step-by-step normalization, making possible the reallocation of some of China's resources and a greater flexibility with respect to other foreign areas. It is most important to note that if American power and presence in Asia declines in a striking fashion, the strength of the accommodationists' argument will be enhanced. Then reliance on the U.S.—and the benefits to be derived from détente here—will have been misplaced.

It is possible, moreover, to conjure up a somber setting for such a debate. In the event of a serious internal political crisis, might not one of the factions involved in the struggle for power take this position and, in addition, turn to the Russians for active support? Presumably such assistance could take any one of a wide range of forms: from the furnishing of arms to direct intervention; from encouragement given to autonomous or secessionist efforts, possibly involving border regions, to support for a new coterie of central leaders. Indeed, whatever the precise facts, the Lin Piao affair is being presented as one illustration of this general threat.

It is thus the potential interaction between the Soviet issue and Chinese domestic politics that has recently concerned Peking's leadership in these twilight years of rule by first-generation revolutionaries. Concrete indication of this fact is to be found in Chou En-lai's Tenth Party Congress report. On both domestic and foreign policy issues, that report was relatively hard-line, suggesting either the need to fend off some continuing "Left" opposition to present policies or another Mao-directed swing of the pendulum. The present international situation, Chou declared, was characterized by great disorder. This would continue, and it was good for it threw the enemies of the people into confusion and division. Collusion between the two superpowers was temporary, contention was absolute. Both of the superpowers were accused by Chou of a desire to "devour" China, a nation saved because it was too "tough even to bite." His indictment of the USSR has already been cited. But the most interesting section of Chou's report dealt with the problem of internal subversion and the purported Soviet link. The Brezhnev group, proclaimed Chou, remained unreconciled to the downfall of men like Liu Shao-ch'i and Lin Piao, men who had worked "under the baton of Soviet revisionism." The Chinese premier then asserted, "Enemies at home and abroad all understand that the easiest way to capture a fortress is from within." And he continued, "Lin Piaos will appear again and so will persons like Wang Ming [once Secretary General of the CCP but since the 1950s an exile in the USSR, who died in the spring of 1974], Liu Shao-ch'i, P'eng Te-huai, and Kao Kang." A bleak prospect this, and presumably not the type of disorder desired by Chou.

Since these words were uttered in August 1973, there has been limited if any movement in Sino-Soviet relations, and sharp Chinese attacks on Soviet policies and leadership continue unabated. In early November 1974, on the occasion of the fifty-seventh anniversary of the October Revolution, the Chinese did propose a nonaggression pact, thereby seeming to respond to repeated Soviet urgings in this direction. Peking's message asserted that China had consistently maintained that "the differences of principle" between the PRC and the USSR should not hamper the normalization of relations between the two states on the basis of the five principles of peaceful coexistence. The proposal, however, contained the proviso that there be a military disengagement of both sides from the areas of dispute.

Speaking nearly three weeks later in Ulaanbaatar, Brezhnev flatly rejected the offer, asserting that although at first glance it appeared that the Chinese leaders were coming out for a normalization of relations with the USSR, their words were divorced from their deeds. He indicated that the USSR could not accept any pullback of Soviet forces under present conditions and that no Soviet border regions were "disputed territory."

Two interpretations of Peking's action are possible. Was it merely a tactical maneuver, an effort to counter politically the various Soviet proposals of recent years, and not to be taken seriously? Or should it be seen as the first signal that China wants to establish a policy of equidistance between the United States and the USSR, and that even under Mao some policy revisions are possible? Any further analysis of these vital questions, and of Chinese foreign policy options pertaining to the two superpowers, requires that we first explore the status of Sino-American relations.

The Superpowers: America

U.S.-Chinese relations must be viewed as a part of a triangle including also the Soviet Union. From its beginnings, the new era in communications between Peking and Washington was a product of the steady deterioration in Peking-Moscow links. Although the Nixon administration's indications of a serious interest in improving relations with the PRC were important, the basic changes in attitude and policy came from China. As early as March 1961, in the opening months of the Kennedy administration, the United States had signaled its desire to improve relations, offering a group exchange of journalists and the sale or gift of grain to a China in extreme need. The response had been swift and unequivocal. No improvement was possible until the Taiwan issue was settled. Clearly, to Peking the latter condition meant an American abandonment of all commitments to the Nationalists.

What caused the dramatic changes in Peking's policies a decade later? No doubt several factors were involved, but the principal one was a deep and growing fear of the Soviet Union. Whatever the situation later, Peking's leaders were greatly concerned in 1969–1970 that Moscow might launch a massive attack on China, one involving nuclear as well as conventional weapons. There was considerable reason for this fear. Czechoslovakia had occurred. The Brezhnev Doctrine had been issued, a doctrine proclaiming that no state was free to leave socialism (as defined by the Soviet Union), and Mao had already been declared a false Marxist in official Soviet pronouncements. Finally, rumors had been planted by Soviet sources that if the Chinese continued to be intransigent regarding the border issues and conflict ensued, the Russians would not consider themselves confined to the use of conventional weaponry. If the purpose of this rumor was to force the Chinese to the bargaining table, it succeeded. But it may also have been the final straw in determining Peking on a new course.

At the close of the Cultural Revolution, the People's Republic of China was almost totally isolated. The inanities practiced toward foreign states and persons during that revolution, and the withdrawal of Chinese ambassadors from all countries except Egypt, had reduced China's foreign relations to a bare minimum. In such a condition, it was impossible to negotiate—or fight—from any degree of strength. The key to a new policy was the United States. Only through some détente with Washington could admission into the United Nations be assured, improved relations with Japan and Western Europe be guaranteed, and the general visibility of China on the international stage be correspondingly enhanced.

It is vitally important to realize that from a Chinese perspective, the limited détente with the U.S. which came into being at this time was based on China's need of the United

States, first as a counterweight to the Soviet Union, and second as the means whereby a shift from isolation to international participation could be undertaken. The new policy was thus based on the premise that the United States would continue to be a major and credible power in the Pacific-Asian area and on the global scene. The new ties were not produced out of any ideological or political convergence, nor were they the result of agreement on such specific issues as Taiwan, Indochina, or Korea. At best, such agreement as existed pertained to much broader considerations: the avoidance of war, the prevention of any single power achieving hegemony in Asia, and a mutual concern over Soviet intentions and actions. At root, however, China's limited détente with the United States stemmed from Peking's commitment to balance-of-power politics.

All of this was explained rather candidly to the cadres. In confidential speeches and statements directed toward Party workers, Peking spokesmen insisted that the new relation with Washington did not represent any abandonment of principle. It was intended to offset the threat of a near and rising power, and as the United States was in some respects a declining one, it represented a smaller menace.

As in the case of the 1930s, it was essential that a united front be formed against the primary foe of the moment. That did not require a lessening of commitment to the causes previously supported, nor any loss of independence. Had not the united front with the Kuomintang resulted in ultimate Communist victory? Indeed, it was argued, this was an appropriate time to take advantage of developments in the Pacific-Asian theatre. The United States, defeated in Indochina, would not undertake military intervention again in the near future. Progress on the Taiwan issue could and should be made while Chiang Kai-shek still lived, whatever his crimes, for he remained a symbol of One China. A new relation with the United States would undermine the independence movement there. It would also be conducive to normalization of relations with Japan on China's terms.

These facts must be fully understood in order to appreciate China's complex, evolving policies toward the United States. The first major milestone came in the form of the Shanghai Communiqué, issued at the conclusion of President Nixon's visit to China in February 1972. After several years of public signals and highly secret private negotiations, many of them carried on via intermediaries, a new era in Sino-American relations was proclaimed. The American effort to contain the People's Republic of China by isolation was now to give way to an era of détente, with the pledge that each party would work toward eventual "normalization" on a full scale. Trade and cultural exchanges would commence immediately. On the highly sensitive issue of Taiwan, both sides made concessions. China dropped its long-held position that a settlement of this issue was the *sine qua non* of any improvement in relations. The United States acceded to a statement that it understood that "all people" on both sides of the Taiwan Straits supported the principle of One China, with Taiwan being an integral part of China. As this was patently untrue and served to undermine the Taiwan independence movement, it represented an American concession that was undoubtedly regarded as significant by Peking. Yet, the issue—and most specifically, future American policies—remained unresolved.

Despite assurances of the type noted here, the impact of these developments on the Chinese people—and China's closest allies, such as the North Koreans—must have been substantial. A man previously described as "the chieftain of the foremost imperialist power" was pictured throughout China smiling and shaking hands with Chairman Mao. Once again, Americans were climbing on the Great Wall and visiting other striking monuments to China's past. Sports competitions, starting with ping pong, got underway first. Soon even an American philharmonic orchestra was permitted to play Western music in a land where the leaders had long proclaimed most such music to be decadent bourgeois rubbish. Reflecting Mao's comment that representatives of the "Center" and "Right" as well as the "Left" should be permitted to visit the New China, a stream of Americans of varying political persuasions undertook the long-forbidden pilgrimage. Trade also began, with China commencing purchases of both food grains and high-technology products such as aircraft.

By the spring of 1973, an agreement had been reached to establish liaison missions in Washington and Peking, despite the fact that only a few months earlier important Chinese had made private statements to the effect that as long as the United States tendered diplomatic recognition to the Republic of China on Taiwan, no Peking officials could set foot in Washington. Secretary Kissinger, moreover, continued to make periodic visits to the PRC where consultations on a wide range of issues took place.

Only the naive, however, saw these developments in simple, uncomplicated terms. Pursuing an historic adage, "Fight, fight; talk, talk," Chinese leaders continued to follow policies that encompassed both conflict and accommodation with the United States. On the one hand, intercourse of various sorts began, and on some crucial issues, such as Vietnam and Korea, China rendered limited private assistance, primarily in the form of refraining from certain actions and undertaking some private counseling. But on the other hand, as we have noted, the public attacks on American foreign policies continued in many forms, and the PRC policies on such issues as Indochina, the Koreas, and Taiwan as officially proclaimed remained inflexible.

In mid-1973, moreover, a harsh reading of Sino-American relations was provided by no less a personage than Chou En-lai in an extraordinary passage in his report to the Tenth Party Congress. There is a distinction, he asserted, between the "necessary compromises" between revolutionary countries and imperialist countries and the sinister compromise between "Soviet revisionism" and "U.S. imperialism." Quoting Lenin,

"One learns to distinguish between a man who gives bandits money and firearms in order to lessen the damage they can do and facilitate their capture and execution, and a man who gives bandits money and firearms in order to share in the loot." Such a position falls somewhat short of all-out friendship with the United States.

Peking's continued willingness to play contrapuntal themes was indicated by the joint Sino-American communiqué of November 14, 1973, which came at the end of a five-day visit by Kissinger to Peking. It referred to talks with Mao conducted in a "friendly atmosphere," a phrase always used purposefully by the Chinese; promised frequent consultations on concrete issues; and pledged increased exchanges and trade as well as expanded functions for the liaison missions.

Yet by the end of 1974, many signs indicated a deterioration in Sino-American relations, the only questions being the causes, extent and duration. Communist spokesmen themselves signaled unhappiness with respect to trends involving Taiwan, and a campaign got underway to increase pressure on the United States on this issue. American organizations involved in exchange and trade promotion were told that their attitude on the Taiwan issue would be an important factor in determining Peking's policies. Cultural exchanges were kept to a relatively small number, with Americans having limited success in achieving the type of balance in these exchanges that reflected their interests. Chinese interference in the selection of American delegations made its appearance. Meanwhile, trade failed to reach earlier expectations. Finally, the Kissinger visit to Peking that followed the Vladivostok Summit produced little of substance except the announcement that President Ford would visit China in 1975. But this latter agreement could be interpreted as additional pressure on the United States to show "progress" with respect to the Taiwan issue prior to that visit.

Whether recent trends in Sino-American relations are defined as merely a dip in what was always destined to be a zigzag process, or whether they are seen as the beginning of a more fundamental shift, the evidence of a cooling off is too strong to be ignored. Nor would the causes appear to be confined solely to the Taiwan issue, although that is the most immediate and overt factor. The recent anti-Lin, anti-Confucius campaign carried with it the same chauvinistic, xenophobic themes recurrent in Chinese history and in that of other modernizing societies. A pendulumlike swing from periods of "excessive borrowing" or "intensive fraternization" to periods of reasserting indigenous values and condemning "slavish copying" has often been noted in such societies, especially in northeast Asia. In recent times, the attack in the PRC on Western culture and the insistence on self-reliance have been labeled as "leftist," but they are a part of a very old tradition.

If this represents one element underlying the present Chinese mood, another more important consideration may relate to a reevaluation of the superpowers, both as threat and as source of support. At root, as has been noted, the dramatic Chinese volte-face toward the United States was based on two factors: a deep fear of the Soviet Union and the belief that the United States would remain a credible power in Asia. There are increasing indications that the Chinese fear of a Soviet military attack has declined. At the same time, it is very possible that doubts concerning American presence and credibility in Asia have grown. The combination would be conducive to an exploration of policy alternatives.

The Superpowers: Policy Alternatives
What broad alternatives are available to the People's Republic of China in its relations with Russia and America? Three "pure" alternatives would appear to exist. Put in simple terms, these are: continued confrontation with the Soviet Union on an extensive scale, with or without armed conflict; the restoration of "friendly" relations with the USSR to an extent permitting cordial Party as well as state relations; the improve-

ment of state-to-state relations with Russia sufficient to permit movement toward equidistance between the two superpowers, but stopping considerably short of any reestablished Sino-Soviet alliance.

These alternatives have been phrased with primary reference to the Soviet Union, but each has its clear implications for Sino-American relations. If the first alternative were to prevail, a high premium on closer relations with the United States would continue, for only Washington could serve as a counterbalance to the Soviet threat, not even excluding the possibility of military assistance. The disadvantages of this alternative from a Chinese perspective have already been suggested. Its costs and risks are high. Current evidence suggests that instead of closing the security gap, the PRC has run into problems in perfecting its nuclear systems, and meanwhile the Russians have made major strides in improving the accuracy of their missiles. Thus, China may actually be more vulnerable in the coming years than in the recent past. Moreover, a confrontation policy limits greatly the flexibility in general foreign policy available to China, and vastly complicates its relations with certain other states. Finally, such a policy involves a greater reliance on the United States than may be warranted, taking into consideration all current factors.

The second alternative would appear to run counter not merely to the thinking of Mao and many other Chinese leaders, but also to the course of recent history and the deeply rooted traditions of both societies. Given the force of nationalism now manifest in both Soviet and Chinese societies, the geopolitical circumstances in which these two states find themselves, and the significant differences in their stages of development, the reestablishment of a close-knit alliance must be accorded a low probability. At the very least, it would require a monumental change, both of personnel and of policies, in one of the two societies.

The third alternative, however difficult of attainment, is the

most logical from a Chinese perspective. Lessening the costs of
confrontation with the USSR, it also reduces the risks of
dependency on the United States. Ideally, it permits China to
be in the envied position of playing one superpower off against
the other, while at the same time avoiding the unpleasantries of
alliance. Thus, it caters to the spirit of nationalism, the mood of
self-reliance, now so strongly in vogue. This alternative,
moreover, becomes more appealing if on the one hand the
Soviet Union seems less disposed toward military conflict, and
on the other hand the United States seems less reliable as a
Pacific-Asian power.

The Second Intermediate Zone

Prior to any final assessment of future trends, however, let
us examine China's relations with the Second Intermediate
Zone and the Third World. Following the limited détente with
the United States, the PRC's relations with Japan underwent a
rapid and equally striking change. Peking's attacks on Japan as
an incipient military power, successor to American imperialism
in Asia, ceased. Cordiality toward the Tanaka government
replaced bitterness toward the previous Sato administration,
with the Chinese meanwhile redoubling their efforts to reach
the Japanese people through a variety of channels.

On balance, the results have been very favorable from
Peking's viewpoint. China's primary objective, the containment
of Japan in northeast Asia, has apparently been successful. To
obtain normalized relations with Peking, Japan was forced to
break diplomatic ties with Taiwan, and its overall relations
with the Nationalist government there have continued to
deteriorate, although economic intercourse remains very important. Nor have Japan's earlier suggestions that it had a vital
interest in the security of South Korea resulted in any commitments. On the contrary, here too, political relations have
worsened despite the importance of economic ties. Thus,
although Japan's stake in future developments in both Taiwan

and South Korea remains high, its political relations with these states are poor. In this sense, Japan is more isolated within the northeast Asian region than was the case a few years ago. To ensure that this continues, until recently at least, Peking has been prepared to urge that the Mutual Security ties with the United States be maintained, at least temporarily. In a communiqué issued after the visit of the Japanese Socialist Party delegation, on May 12, 1975, however, Peking's leaders for the first time in many years supported the scrapping of the Mutual Security Treaty. Is the PRC signaling a change of policy on this matter?

Chinese policy is also directed toward keeping Soviet-Japanese ties minimal. Here too, preliminary successes have been scored, due in part to Soviet policies. In an effort to neutralize the economic benefits from Japanese investment in Siberia, Peking has indicated its willingness to provide Japan with ever-increasing quantities of oil in the years ahead, as indicated earlier. There remain various imponderables in the Sino-Japanese economic relationship. At what rate will the Chinese economy grow, and to what extent are Chinese leaders prepared to turn outward in quest of economic and technical assistance? How great a dependency on one nation will Peking accept? Will it restrict Japan to approximately one-quarter of its total foreign trade, with Japan already being within this range?

When a balance sheet has been drawn up, as indicated earlier, the odds are strongly against a Sino-Japanese alliance. The elements of potential competition are at least as strong as those of cooperation, and they exist in many areas: maritime jurisdiction; the problems of the divided states; influence in Southeast Asia; and involvement in the internal politics of each society. However, China can be expected to continue to aim at these primary objectives with respect to Japan: restricting Japanese power to the economic sphere; seeking to utilize that power to China's benefit; thwarting close Soviet-Japanese ties and, in the long run, weakening also the American-Japanese relationship.

With respect to Western Europe, China's interests are more limited. But here too, interesting changes have taken place. A decade or less ago, this region was largely ignored or denounced as a capitalist enclave of U.S. imperialism. Only France was cultivated, largely because of de Gaulle, who was correctly perceived as a thorn in the American side. Now Peking sees all of Western Europe (along with Eastern Europe) as a region that can be separated from the superpowers and caused to play an independent role. Via some combination of nationalist and community sentiments, the Second Zone in Peking's eyes can make a significant contribution to a global balance of power benefiting China. Nonetheless, certain immediate priorities modify, even contradict, this strategic view. In particular, an American military presence in Europe is not only acceptable but desired to the extent that it makes Western European defense against the Soviet Union credible. At this point, in sum, China is prepared to sustain the American military role in the Second Intermediate Zone where it is directed primarily against the Soviet Union, even as it attacks American economic and cultural interactions.

The Third World

It remains to examine China's relations with the so-called Third World, present and future. In recent years, the Chinese leaders have repeatedly proclaimed themselves a part of that world, stressing the common interests in nation-building and economic development, and emphasizing also the common threat that comes from superpower efforts to achieve global hegemony. For these purposes, the Chinese have a slogan endlessly repeated on official occasions: "Countries want independence, nations want liberation, and people want revolution."

In its combined Third World and liberation movement

policies, the People's Republic once again lives with a number of contradictions. Here the ideological quotient remains highest, but it is also here that pragmatic individual policies are displayed most strikingly. In one aspect, the Third World is treated as a unit by Peking, and its multiple diversities and internal conflicts minimized or ignored. By definition, it is regarded as a revolutionary unit, being disposed against the status quo and also against the affluent, advanced, and powerfully entrenched states. Still bearing the deep psychological scars of her own recent past, China—the world's largest society—now seeks to speak in a voice consonant with those of the small and weak.

In part, this is an ideological and psychological necessity for old first-generation revolutionaries who held for decades a commitment to internationalism via the Communist cause alone. With that commitment rudely shattered by events, on what other sources can one's identification with internationalism now rest? Where are susceptible proletarian-peasant masses to be found? How, in short, can one exhibit one's Marxism-Leninism in the late twentieth century except through union with the Third World?

At the same time, China's current Third World policies are based on hard-headed political considerations, being in major degree a reflection of her relations with the USSR and the United States. If successful, China's alignment with and influence on this group of states would strike a serious ideological as well as political blow at the Soviet Union. Russia too acknowledges the Third World as possessing revolutionary potential and proclivities for socialism. Thus, if the "first socialist state" were to lose out in the competition for influence here, its legitimacy as the logical leader of "the progressive forces of the world" would be further and seriously undermined. Similarly, these policies are a form of competition with the world's most powerful open society, the United States—a competition that runs minimal costs and risks, and to some extent offsets the charge that Peking's leaders have sold out to Washington.

How well is the People's Republic doing with respect to the Third World? On balance, Peking has reason to be relatively pleased with current developments. The resolutions and speeches in various recent international conferences and United Nations sessions testify that on many matters Peking is on the same wavelength as a number of African, Asian, and Latin American states. Indeed, on occasion, both the Soviet Union and the United States have been placed strongly on the defensive, and not infrequently have found themselves—singly or together—in a minority position.

On the global scene, in truth, China is credible as a developing nation, facing problems common to others and constituting no appreciable threat. Having had a record of limited involvement, moreover, her policy legacy is largely clear of the blemishes, errors, and failures characterizing the record of major actors. Only occasionally—and primarily in Africa—have the Chinese been heavy-handed in areas outside of Asia. As has been noted, moreover, China is now calling for nationalist, not Communist revolutions. This is exceedingly wise, for effective Communist comrades in the Third World, especially in Africa and Latin America, are rare indeed.

From China's strengths in dealing with the Third World also stem her weaknesses. To the extent that these states and movements require concrete military, economic, and technical assistance, the People's Republic is of limited utility. Peking's foreign aid programs, although generally cost effective in both economic and political terms, can only be small when measured against the vastness of the needs. Thus, nations once strongly wooed by China, notably Cuba and Egypt, must continue to depend on the Soviet Union—or the West. Cultural links between China and much of the Third World are also tenuous; problems of language, custom, and outlook abound. It is not easy for the Chinese, long self-sufficient and inward-looking, possessors of a great cultural legacy, to exhibit the traits associated with fraternity, egalitarianism, and internationalism. For many within the Third World, even among those who admire them, the Chinese remain exotic and indisputably foreign.

It is not surprising, moreover, that the steadfastness of Peking's revolutionary zeal is being questioned in some quarters. Who would have believed a few years ago that the leaders of such nations as Greece and Iran would be going to China as state guests? If these states are members of the Third World, they are scarcely "progressive" elements. In truth, of course, in her effort to counter Russian containment policies, China has logically paid special attention to those states on the periphery of the Soviet Union irrespective of their political coloration. Realistic balance-of-power considerations thus compete with,. even submerge on occasion, ideological commitments. And suitable complexities have inevitably accompanied China's movement in status and role from international rebel to active participant in such institutions and patterns of multilateral politics as the current world affords. In these respects, the People's Republic of China is simply exhibiting the traits of an important society.

These various factors are graphically illustrated by Chinese policies toward the small states of Asia, a region where China is already accepted as a major power. Here, tradition as well as the forces of nationalism and ideology come into play. Historically, in meeting the problem of the "barbarians" on their borders, the rulers of China pursued a carrot-and-stick policy. Those who behaved "correctly" were invited to the Chinese capital as guests with gifts exchanged and cultural contacts established, enabling the Chinese model to be appreciated and adapted. Toward those who misbehaved, sanctions or threats of sanctions were applied.

The current leaders of China have repeatedly and emphatically made it clear that the People's Republic has special interests and responsibilities in Asia. What does this mean? Aware of a reduction in the American commitment, various states of Southeast Asia are now seeking to find out. Malaysia, for example, has established diplomatic relations with the PRC, and other states including Thailand, the Philippines, and Singapore have been engaged in discussions, formal and otherwise, looking toward some form of relations. Certain of these states are also attempting to discover whether Chinese support to guerrilla movements confronting them can be ended or reduced. That support has been of three types: China has allowed clandestine radio stations purporting to be the voice of the Free Malaysians (Thai, Burmese, and so forth) to operate from locations within China, broadcasting in the indigenous language in an effort to cultivate the climate for a Communist revolution; she has also invited as guests, and on occasion given long-term asylum to various Communist leaders of the area, with the presumption that periodic discussions of concrete tactics and strategy take place; finally, some training and military-economic support have been given to guerrilla groups.

Thus far, Peking has taken an ambiguous position when these matters have been raised. Questioners are either told flatly that China does not interfere in the internal affairs of other states, or that a distinction must be made between the Chinese state and the Communist Party of China—hence that the Party cannot be expected to sever all fraternal ties with fellow parties on the establishment of state-to-state relations. These are scarcely satisfactory answers, and there can be little doubt that most Southeast Asian leaders from Burma to Indonesia are worried about China's future role in this region. It is possible that this concern extends to Hanoi as well.

Almost certainly, China's minimal demands on these states will include the proviso that they not be closely affiliated with any "threatening" major state, or be members of a potentially hostile military bloc. Ideally, the People's Republic would probably prefer to deal with small, discrete political units in the region. Hence it is questionable whether Peking would actually favor a Hanoi-controlled Indochina, though perhaps equally questionable whether it would be prepared to take positive steps to prevent such an occurrence. There can be no doubt, however, that China remains concerned lest the Soviet Union play a larger role in this part of the world. Could this along with other considerations induce Peking to accept the neutralization of Southeast Asia, and work toward making the five principles of peaceful coexistence operational here? A cautious exploration of these possibilities is now underway, with views ranging from moderate optimism to deep doubt being expressed in the region.

Whatever course prevails, it is extremely unlikely that China will totally abandon those Communist movements of the area which have been closely affiliated with Peking. To do so would risk cleavages within China herself, and would also leave the People's Republic extremely vulnerable to a Soviet counterattack. The mix, however, can and quite possibly will be changed. As the emphasis on state-to-state relations rises, comrade-to-comrade relations can be made more discreet and lower key. The Chinese might also encourage a shift in Communist tactics, with greater attention to legal and quasi-legal activities, urban-centered. Such a trend would be less embarrassing to Peking, and possibly less demanding. In any case, the People's Republic could be expected after the establishment of formal diplomatic relations to behave with great circumspection insofar as its official staff was concerned, fully aware that its activities were being closely watched. Peking has now taken a strong official stand against dual nationality for the Overseas Chinese, and urged that even those electing to remain Chinese citizens abide by the laws of the countries in which they reside. It is fully aware of the liabilities which the Overseas Chinese represent for the PRC in the quest to establish closer ties with the indigenous peoples of Southeast Asia.

Nevertheless, most current governments of this region remain nervous about China's intentions, and not without reason. China continues to render support to such guerrilla movements as the White Flag Communists in Burma—despite Ne Win's efforts to practice neutralism. Whatever the official PRC position, the sizable body of Overseas Chinese in Southeast Asia constitute a worry, for they have legitimate grievances against the governments (and people) of their adopted lands. A guerrilla communism proclaiming its allegiance to Maoist principles, moreover, still represents a potential threat in some areas, a threat that is almost certain to grow in the aftermath of Communist victories in Indochina. To date, Peking's attitudes and actions have been insufficient to reassure most Southeast Asian leaders. Viewed from Bangkok, Singapore, Rangoon, or Jakarta, China appears as something more than just a developing state, and the crucial tests of peaceful coexistence may well take place here.

Toward the one big state of the Third World, namely, India, China continues to show no interest in improving relations, although at some point this attitude could conceivably change. To date, Peking has regarded Mrs. Gandhi's India as a part of the Soviet Union's containment policies. It has also believed that South Asia is fundamentally unstable, and that time is on its side. Hence, its policies have been devoted to balancing the Soviet-Indian entente through whatever means are available—including staunch support for Pakistan and overtures to all of the small states on India's peripheries. It is possible, however, as we shall later indicate, that at some point China might seek to woo India, thereby weakening its ties with the USSR.

It can thus be seen that although the rhetoric applied to China's Third World policies is simple, the policies themselves are complex, extraordinarily varied, and susceptible to change—with East Asia a special case. If there is a broad trend, it has been toward accommodation with the existing order from country to country, working on a state-to-state basis to support perceived Chinese interests.

An Overview

Let us now seek a summary and projection of Chinese foreign policies. In many respects, China resembles all other major societies en route to power and prestige. Although her policies contain strands of tradition and ideology, the dominant element is clearly nationalism—in the modern sense of that term. As this is so, China's present foreign policies are vastly more complex and also more contradictory than in the past, but equally they are more suited to China's interests. China today has regional power and global presence. In both settings, she manipulates state-to-state, people-to-people, and comrade-to-comrade relationships, with the current emphasis on the first two of these. The old ideology continues to be enshrined as ritual and recited as dogma, but it is increasingly separated from the dynamic processes of Chinese society, in foreign as well as domestic policies.

Yet the ideological quotient in Chinese policy must still be reckoned with. As we have seen, the image of a world divided into three basic elements is rich in ideological connotations, albeit ones different from those advanced by Marx. There *is* still an international proletariat, with peasant and national bourgeois allies, but now these are states, not classes! Moreover, in one part of themselves, the current Chinese leaders, it must be emphasized, *are* deeply ideological, and it is always possible that circumstances, at home and abroad, might produce another swing to the "Left," bringing rhetoric and policy into closer alignment.

As the Mao era comes to a close, the essence of the struggle lies precisely here. A satisfactory synthesis rather than a constant struggle between theory and practice may ultimately evolve, but it is not yet in sight nor is it implicit in the Maoist style.

Only the present trend is clear. Progressively, Chinese foreign policy has become state oriented. And within this orientation, the most immediate, crucial relationships are those contained in the China-U.S.-Soviet triangle. Denunciations of hegemony and attacks on the two superpowers are the natural responses of the weakest member of the triangle. To date, however, China has leaned to one side. In the opening years, the leaning toward the Soviet Union was pronounced, and it had a signal effect on both institutions and policies. In recent years, there has been a more modest but nonetheless distinct tilt toward the United States, not out of ideological or political affinity but because of the perceived need to offset the Soviet threat. The People's Republic, like other major societies, has been drawn into balance-of-power politics in an era when no other means of protecting its interests and security exists.

What of the future? As indicated earlier, from its standpoint, the optimal policy for the PRC would be that of approximating equidistance between the United States and the USSR, and through this position endeavoring to play one off against the other. To establish such a policy, however, will not be easy. First, Sino-Soviet relations are now enmeshed in deep emotional bitterness, with the elites on both sides cultivating, consciously or unconsciously, the strong racial antagonisms that have always been latent and periodically overt in the relations between these two peoples. Geography, moreover, dictates that these states must coexist in close proximity. Under these conditions, interference in each other's internal affairs becomes easier, more tempting—especially as both claim adherence to Marxism-Leninism, an international creed.

These same factors make any restoration of the Sino-Soviet alliance even more difficult, and looking ahead to the next decade, that course of action seems very improbable. The nationalist tides in both Russia and China are now running swiftly. Indeed, in China particularly, they seem to dominate all else, producing appeals for sacrifice on behalf of power, un- wavering patriotism, and a commitment to self-reliance that stand in strident contrast to traditional Marxist inter- nationalism. That any group of Chinese leaders would consider subordinating themselves and their nation once again to a more powerful, more advanced (and still demanding) Soviet Union seems most unlikely.

On the other hand, as has been stressed, Chinese Com- munist leaders are fully aware that a major conflict with Russia would be disastrous. Although China—and even an indigenous Communism—might survive, the hard-won gains of recent decades would be wiped out, and the resulting internal chaos would resemble that which ended Kuomintang rule. Even short of war, the costs and risks of the present level of tension have caused serious debate within the top ruling circles of the PRC. Certain key figures, with fragmentary evidence suggesting that many of them have been military men, have argued privately that a lowering of tension and some degree of normalization are in China's own interests.

Current Soviet policies are skillfully aimed at encouraging the latter argument. As noted earlier, the Soviet Union now carries a big stick—and possesses a big carrot. Its present hope is that Mao will be replaced by "more reasonable men," and that through an evolutionary process China will once again gravitate in the direction of Russia, economically, politically, and ideologically. It does not anticipate a restoration of the Sino-Soviet alliance in its old forms, but it believes that a relationship similar to that between the USSR and Yugoslavia is possible.

In this situation, the United States may well prove to be one of the most critical variables. As has been strongly emphasized, the new Sino-American relationship, from Peking's perspective, was based on considerations of power, not of identity. Its basis was tactical more than strategic, although tactics can come to influence strategy. One vital issue within the PRC's top leadership today is whether the United States will continue to be a major credible force in Asia. Doubts on this score are already being translated into a greater caution with respect to the American relationship. And if the ultimate decision in Peking is that the United States is withdrawing from the Pacific-Asian area, the pressures to reach an accommodation with the Soviet Union will be much greater. Then, balance-of-power policies will no longer possess their former validity.

Already, the basic alternatives in Sino-American relations have been suggested. The extremity of either alliance or war is not probable in the decade ahead. Major differences of policy and dissimilarities of values preclude the former, and the great disparity of strength, together with the impossibility of "victory," rule out the latter. The meaningful alternatives lie closer to the middle range, and in considerable measure, as we have noted, they are both interactive with and partial determinants of the alternatives in Sino-Soviet relations.

The most probable developments are these: On the economic front, trade will increase, with the major variables being the health of the two economies and policy decisions in Peking regarding basic economic policies. This trade, however, will not be crucial to either state. In the cultural field, progress will be slow, with the Chinese interest being primarily in exchanges from which China can benefit either in developmental terms or politically, and with the United States pressing for greater reciprocity.

Politically, a number of issues, in Asia and elsewhere, will continue to separate the PRC and the United States. China will certainly continue its pressure to get Washington to abandon its commitments to Taiwan, but it is exceedingly unlikely that Peking is prepared to pledge that this issue will be resolved peacefully. On the contrary, influential spokesmen like Teng Hsiao-p'ing have recently gone to some pains to indicate that the PRC is not ruling out the use of force, if necessary, to secure

Taiwan. He has also implied that the creation of an internal guerrilla movement with mainland support is one of the possible routes of "liberation."

Nor do policies on the Korean issue appear to be converging. On the contrary, since the Indochina debacle, the PRC appears to have drawn even closer to North Korea. On April 26, 1975, the joint communiqué issued in the name of the two nations after an eight-day Peking visit by Kim Il-sŏng (which included a "most significant meeting" with Mao) coupled the reunification of Korea with the liberation of Taiwan as objectives both critical and warranting mutual assistance. In mentioning Chinese support for the *peaceful* reunification of the Korean fatherland, it was made clear that this could only be accomplished via Kim Il-sŏng's program, a set of policies bearing the strongest resemblance to the liberation program of North Vietnam, so recently triumphant. For the time being at least, the combination of Communist successes in Indochina and the long-standing Chinese desire to keep this strategic area away from the Russians appears to have brought Peking and P'yongyang into increased alignment.

In Indochina also, Chinese and American positions remain widely divergent despite earlier signals to the Vietnamese Communists that China's national interests took precedence over those of Hanoi—a pattern that may reassert itself under other circumstances. At no point did Peking provide evidence that it would throw its active support behind solutions giving the non-Communists of this region a good opportunity for political survival. Even Sihanouk, a long-time Chinese protégé, can only be a figurehead in the fashion of Soong Ching-ling if Peking's scenario for Cambodia is realized. Compromises in Indochina thus hinge at present on a new balance of forces *sans* American power or credibility and Peking's assessment of its broader interests.

In sum, although the extremes can be ruled out, the precise nature of future Sino-American relations remains uncertain.

Present trends are not encouraging from an American perspective. The indications are that some reexamination of its posture and policies vis-à-vis the superpowers has commenced, with the current movement toward greater equidistance, propelled by a diminished fear of war with Russia and growing doubts about American capacities or will.

In its relations with the Second Intermediate Zone, as we have noted, China will continue its efforts to contain Japan politically and militarily while making selective use of Japanese economic and technical capacities. Even if Sino-Soviet relations improve, it is doubtful that Peking will want to see a close Soviet-Japanese relationship unfold. Hence, efforts to influence Japan via promises (and delivery) of oil will continue, as will the recurrent campaigns to influence key interest groups in Japan via "cultural relations." The China factor in Japanese politics will thus remain a very important one.

Relations with Western Europe will also reflect the prevailing state of Sino-Soviet relations. As long as the cleavage remains deep, China will continue to encourage the Western Europeans to unite against a Soviet threat, even to the extent of seeking continued American guarantees. China would certainly not object to a return of the cold war in Europe so as to relieve pressure on her. But should Sino-Soviet relations improve dramatically, the tendency would be for a return to the spheres-of-influence understanding between Russia and China which operated in the early days of the PRC, with Moscow assuming primary responsibilities in Europe, Peking in Asia.

Finally, there can be little doubt that China intends to be a major power in Asia, the restrictions being essentially those imposed on it by the circumstances of backwardness. Thus, the small states of the region will have to find ways of accepting Chinese interests as a permanent part of the considerations governing their behavior and policies. Under optimal conditions, this will promote the effort to maintain independence through policies of equidistance, a trend now growing in

Southeast Asia. Under less advantageous circumstances, it may require a choice of protectors in the fashion of the People's Republic of Mongolia, or possibly at a later point a more meaningful regional security structure, backed by multilateral guarantees.

Chapter 4

INDIA: The Trauma of Openness

Like China, India faces the formidable combination of massiveness and serious underdevelopment, as this term is used in the late twentieth century. It is also a society characterized by significantly greater heterogeneity than its large neighbor to the north. Having taken the democratic path until recently, moreover, Indian leadership has had to contend both with deeply implanted traditions not easily uprooted by persuasion—or law—and a wide range of dissidence.

It is not surprising, therefore, that India represents yet another nation beset with multiple domestic problems, with an uncertain prognosis for its political future. Perhaps the miracle here lies in the sheer fact of survival for nearly three decades. Now, however, democracy in India is in jeopardy.

Until the events of the recent past, India was regarded as a state that could combine political openness and economic development successfully. Thanks to the Green Revolution, wheat production had shown spectacular increases, and overall food production was keeping well ahead of population growth. The dominant party system provided a considerable measure of stability while at the same time permitting open debate and a meaningful opposition. In sum, the perimeters of the Indian political system were sufficiently wide to allow dissidence to take lawful, legitimate channels. Despite the enormity of certain problems, therefore, no revolutionary movement of significance emerged, with the possible exception of the persistent Naga struggle in the highly sensitive northeast frontier, a typical minority protest.

The pendulum may have swung too far in the direction of pessimism regarding India's future at this point. It is obvious now, however, that serious domestic problems exist, and as they bear on the alternatives available in the foreign policy realm, we cannot ignore them. Once again, the questions must be posed: Is this nation likely to experience grave political instability in the decade ahead, and what type of political change would affect its foreign policies? Is the increased authoritarianism now exhibited by Mrs. Gandhi temporary or permanent?

The Influence of Domestic Factors

As in the case of other major Asian states, the variables — both external and internal — are so numerous and complex that prediction is rendered extremely hazardous. Given India's massive economic and social problems, the chances for political instability must be considered high. On the other hand, for reasons shortly to be considered, a very limited correlation between the extent of socioeconomic crisis and the potentialities for political change has existed in the past. Most of the political elite, moreover, have had a strong commitment to the prevailing political institutions, and for this reason among others those institutions showed remarkable resiliency until recently, especially when one considers the strains imposed on them. One of the key questions, therefore, relates to possible changes in the political commitments of current and succeeding elites.

Historical Antecedents

To appreciate these factors, one must examine closely the political history of modern India. The force which has provided indispensable continuity and direction to Indian politics, first as independence movement, subsequently as governing body, has been the Congress Party. In many respects, that party remains a movement, one deeply factionalized yet able to coopt a sufficient number of diverse elements to dominate the political scene. If there has been continuity of party, moreover, there has also been continuity of leadership. To a very appreciable extent, top leadership in this party—*and most other parties*—has come from an urban intelligentsia, upper class or caste in background, predominately Indoaryan. In the case of Congress, there has also been a goodly admixture of rural landed representatives at secondary levels.

The traditions of this party can be depicted through two men. Jawaharlal Nehru and Mahatma Gandhi. Nehru combined in his person Indian Brahminism, a British elitist education, and a strong commitment to Fabian socialism. In these respects, he was more than an individual; he was representative of the class that has played the major role in India's postindependence politics. The deep impact of both parliamentarism and socialism on first-generation Indian leaders testifies to the influence of several streams within British political culture. The British institutional model, to be sure, had to be adapted to India's circumstances. A federal system based on states having considerable autonomy puts this nation in the same broad category as other continental-mass societies. In its commitment until recently to democracy, however, including the protection of civil liberties and genuine political competition, India had become increasingly unique in Asia.

Mahatma Gandhi also left his imprint on Indian politics, but contrapuntally to that of Nehru. Gandhi's major contribution was that of *satyagraha,* a form of peaceful, nonviolent protest. It was a technique shrewdly chosen with respect to time and target, and it has continued to be a part of the tactics of Indian dissidence. Gandhi's concern with the Indian peasant and his strong emphasis on cottage industry were often equated with an antimodern, anti-Western bias, and in fact these themes were supported by a curious medley of individuals in other parts of Asia, some of them devotees of traditionalism, cultural purity, and Pan-Asianism. But Gandhism might also be regarded as a precursor to other experiments in nonurban development.

On the surface, it is difficult to find Gandhi in contemporary Indian politics except through such protest movements as that of Jayaprakash Narayan. Gandhi had an affinity for his society, however, that was often lacking in the Cambridge-trained intellectual, and elements of Gandhism remain integral to the culture. Will a new generation of Indian leaders, divorced from the socialization provided by British education, proclaim themselves adherents of a more indigenous political course, Gandhian or otherwise? Indeed, is a new path, product of protest and reaction, already en route?

Congress and Its Opponents

To date, the strength of the Congress Party has lain in the fact that it has been able and willing to encompass many diverse socioeconomic elements, thereby preempting the political field from its opponents. Congress has lived with heterogeneity and contradiction. It has been "radical" in the cities, "conservative" in the countryside. What it has lacked in consistency, it has gained in power.

The controversial women who now leads the Congress Party, Mrs. Gandhi, daughter of Nehru, illustrates these qualities. Indira Gandhi, a shrewd politician and a mediocre student of economics, has responded instinctively to the most immediate pressures, the most obvious challenges—those within the party and in the larger political arena. Her first accomplishment was the elimination or reduction in power of the Congress old guard, the men of her father's generation whose political techniques and economic instincts were moderate to conservative. For these purposes it was expedient to fashion an alliance with the "Left," and this was to have a pronounced influence on both domestic and foreign policies. Now, she has launched more sweeping attacks upon opponents of all types, including the media—supported by her bloc.

The alliance between the Congress Party and the Communist Party of India (CPI) was more easily consummated than would have been possible elsewhere in Asia or in most other parts of the world. The CPI was a product of traditions similar to those of Congress in terms of the background and socialization of its leaders. The Communists were already working within the parliamentary system, albeit with signs of restiveness from their "left wing."

From Mrs. Gandhi's standpoint, this alliance had major political advantages. It isolated the Congress "Right," split the Communist "Left," and enabled the party to approach the urban centers as a "progressive" political force without disturbing its conservative rural underpinnings. It also made easier and more natural a turn toward the Soviet Union, not merely in defense matters, but in economic affairs as well. The men around Mrs. Gandhi, coming predominately from the "left wing" of the Congress, were in some cases especially receptive to this course.

As is well known, policies can also be strongly influenced by highly personal considerations. Like her father, Mrs. Gandhi has a deep, ineradicable bias against the United States, product of her familial and social environment. Thus, it has been easy to combine the tilt to the "left" with an anti-American stance that has sometimes taken bizarre and petty forms. As we shall see, however, this has not prevented the prime minister from seeking (and obtaining) American aid in times of crisis.

It should now be easier to understand one of the important idiosyncrasies of the current Indian political system, namely, the limited correlation between socioeconomic crises and political instability. The Congress Party still represents a national movement, although the long-term effects of the present repressive policies upon it remain to be measured. This party alone has had a mass base on a national scale. Some moderate or conservative opponents have had strong regional bases, but they have not been a national symbol or force. The "radical" opposition, represented by the Communist Party of India—Marxist (CPIM) and the Naxalites, has also been essentially local or regional in its strength and led primarily by urband, middle-class intellectuals. Its organizational strength is limited, its ties with the masses weak. Hence, its leaders can easily be coerced. And the government has once again shown itself willing to use coercion as well as cooption with regard to its opponents, especially when it considers them to be challenging the authority of the state in an illegal manner.

Thus, even in a period of multiple crises, the prospects for toppling Mrs. Gandhi's alliance seem doubtful—at least immediately. One must presume, however, that if economic conditions remain bad and political repression drives deep wedges into the elite, some type of political upheaval could follow. What is the economic situation? India starts with a number of serious handicaps relating to population, resources, and deeply ingrained traditions. In major degree, however, blame for the present grave situation must be placed on the central government. That portion of the Indian bureaucracy which has been given responsibility for industrial management and production, as noted earlier, has proved to be both inefficient and corrupt. Its record, with limited exceptions, has been abysmal, yet little attention has been given to basic changes. The private sector, meanwhile, languishes for want of approval and support. Manpower training is haphazard, and the entire higher educational system is drastically in need of reform.

It is in the vital agrarian sector that the conservatism of Congress and the government dominates the scene, underwritten by the dependence of the party upon the more affluent segment of the rural population. Thus, land reform, credit, and a number of other badly needed measures fail to materialize. Developments in agriculture have produced a steadily increasing number of middle- and upper-middle-class rural residents, and some regions of India can be considered relatively prosperous. It is the lower one-half or one-third of the peasantry—many of them landless tenants—whose condition is so deplorable. Similarly, in urban areas, new middle and upper classes are growing, encompassing a high portion of the bureaucracy and intelligentsia as well as the commercial-industrial and professional classes. Again, it is those on the bottom rungs of the urban socioeconomic structure that live on the margins—many of them refugees from the countryside.

In one sense, the growing middle class probably augurs well for political stability, especially if a foundation can be put under the lowest classes to prevent degradation. It should be remembered that the Kuomintang was making progress in China in a somewhat similar fashion in the early 1930s, with an opposition weak and fragmented—until a prolonged, devastating war gave the Communists their chance for victory. There are, however, some uncertainties that pertain to the middle class as well as to the lower echelons of Indian society. As yet, Mrs. Gandhi's government has failed to grapple in any satisfactory manner with the most elemental issues affecting minimal, and population increases continue to run at least 2.2 percent per year. Management of the public sector, as noted, remains inefficient, and corruption at high levels of the bureaucracy is prevalent. Given the situation operating in the private sector, foreign investment there has been minimal. Meanwhile, the impact of the oil crisis has been extremely serious for India, driving prices up in such a fashion as to augment inflation, reducing vital fertilizer supplies (thereby adversely affecting food production), and underlining India's resource deficiencies. Mrs. Gandhi's current efforts to combine populism with repression testify to her awareness of these problems.

Thus, although the circumstances and issues are different, we must ask of India the same basic question put concerning

China and Japan. Could fundamental changes occur, evolutionary or revolutionary, bringing to power new forces, be they derived from parties, bureaucracy, or the military? We have already indicated that the chances of toppling Congress, and replacing it with a national government headed by another party or coalition, seem minimal even in this period of troubles.

Political Disintegration?

Is it possible, however, that India will have its own form of "warlordism"? Could events—prolonged economic crises coupled with continuing issues derived from India's multilinguistic, multicultural setting—eat away at the power of the center and lead to a steady rise of state autonomy, with different political forces in power at this level? This has always been a threat—or hope—depending on one's perspective. Regional differences have been preserved and in some cases enhanced through politics. The Congress has witnessed a loss of power in certain states, sometimes for a protracted period of time. Political, social, and economic policies have varied considerably from state to state, unlike the situation in either China or Japan. In recent years, moreover, a new type of leader has emerged from within Congress itself—an individual coming to the center with strong local or regional ties, as might be expected of a second- and third-generation political elite.

Given the extraordinary nature of our times and the particular features of the Indian polity, one cannot rule out the possibility of centripetal developments producing a weak center and increasingly assertive and diverse states. Carried to extremes, this trend could lead to collapse and civil war. On the other hand, several well-known factors reduce the likelihood of such an occurrence. First, the force of Indian nationalism should not be depreciated, intense sectoral and regional commitments notwithstanding. Several generations of younger Indians have been schooled to think in national terms and take pride in their Indianness.

Some indication of nationalist power can be seen from the

general support given such major activities in the foreign arena as the opposition to China, participation in the Bangladesh War, and on the local scene the explosion of a nuclear device. But Indian nationalism has not been cultivated with the same intensity, or commitment to uniformity, as has characterized the policies of the People's Republic of China. Nor does India come from the same background of cultural homogeneity as Japan. Hence, nationalism here should be regarded as a more fragile weapon with which to resist fragmentation. It is not negligible, however, especially as it affects the Indian elite.

The more concrete barriers to disintegration relate to financial and coercive power. As in the case of other federal systems, the Indian central government retains far-reaching fiscal controls and powers of allocation. It has exercised these powers effectively in the past, determining even such important matters as the location of industrial development. These powers can work sacrifices on the wealthier states and benefit the poorer ones. They can also be turned to political purposes. In any case, however, they tend to bind the states to the center, willingly or unwillingly.

New Delhi has also built up major military and paramilitary forces. The national military services comprise one million men, with very modern equipment. Auxiliaries are also available, particularly for domestic use. The evidence thus far would indicate that these forces will obey the center's command. Nor is there any doubt that the national government is prepared to use the military if necessary. Any seccessionist movement could not overlook these facts.

A seizure of power by the Indian bureaucracy is a very different type of issue. As in all modern states, the bureaucracy has already acquired a significant amount of power, especially when juxtaposed against popularly elected legislators. On the advice of key leaders, it drafts basic policies and legislation, and then administers the laws enacted. To the average Indian citizen, it *is* the government, and from its officiousness, inefficiency, lack of responsibility, and corruption stem many of his grievances. Nevertheless, under the Indian political system, the role of the political leader in setting basic policy remains the critical one. Unlike Japan where the dominant party until recently was generally led by ex-bureaucrats, the Congress Party has few such individuals in its top ranks. Unlike China where the political system serves to distinguish sharply between the professionals in politics (be they Party or bureaucratic cadres) and the citizenry at large, the Indian system permits a certain flow of amateurs into the political arena. Some even reach the top. The role of the Indian bureaucracy in decision-making will continue to be a major one, but this force, dispersed and disparate, will not be the commanding one.

The Role of the Military

The military represent more of an enigma. To date, their leaders have been strictly in the Sandhurst tradition, eschewing political involvements and performing on command as professional soldiers. Although India as a state never practiced Gandhism, either at home or abroad, the aura of pacifism connected with Gandhi and one prominent wing of the Congress movement did serve to restrain the prestige and status of the soldier. The humiliating defeat suffered at the hands of China in 1962 did not add to Indian military laurels. Yet the response of the Indian citizenry to the successes of the Bangladesh War and the explosion of a nuclear device indicate that public sentiment (and professional *esprit de corps*) can change rapidly.

The yearning for effective leadership is no less in India than in many other societies currently undergoing crises. At best, Mrs. Gandhi only partially satisfies that yearning, and only for a certain segment of the people. Indeed, her popularity had slipped badly prior to her recent militant actions. In the event of her political demise—whatever the cause—is her successor likely to be drawn from military ranks? Could India possibly join those states exchanging civilian for military rule?

The most likely scenario for such a development would appear to be this: The economic and political crises in India worsen and are prolonged. They are accompanied by rising social disturbances, requiring repeated use of military and paramilitary forces. Initially complacent top military figures become disturbed, partly because of a growing resistance to this role from within military ranks. Martial law, moreover, requires a progressive involvement of the military in policy-making. From these circumstances, a coup takes place, with men of the rank of major and colonel playing the central roles, but using certain generals as shields.

Such a scenario cannot be ruled out as impossible, but even under current conditions, it seems improbable. Like many other Indian institutions, the military represent a hetero-geneous force, being composed of men of widely differing castes, regional origins, and linguistic-cultural groups. The type of unity necessary to an effective coup or rule on a na-tional scale would be enormously difficult to achieve at this point, especially if it were attempted against a leadership and party carrying the traditions of the Indian national revolu-tion. One important variable, however, is insufficiently under-stood. Little is known about the attitudes, cohesion, and po-tential capacity for action of the Indian army's middle-level officers. Unlike their superiors, these colonels are not products of extended British training. In some cases, moreover, they are known to be disgusted with the ineffectiveness of civil ad-ministrators and politicians. Under present circumstances, therefore, they become a group to watch.

Changes in Congress?

The most probable alternative, however, remains to be in-troduced, namely, a transition within the Congress Party itself. The "Independence" or first generation of Indian Congress leaders are now rapidly passing from the scene. Mrs. Gandhi herself, still potentially available for a number of years, represents a second generation. Already, however, a number of third- and fourth-generation leaders are emerging, especially at the state levels. Although personal loyalty to Mrs. Gandhi remains a critical factor in one's rise to prominence and has produced an uncommon number of party hacks, some elements of these newer generations show traits significantly different from those of their elders.

To attempt a precise prototype would be dangerous, for differences are at least as important as similarities. Nonetheless, some trends are discernible. The highly Westernized, urban intellectuals appear to be giving ground to those who come from provincial towns, educated in local schools, and having some rural or quasi-rural connections. These individuals first achieve prominence in local politics, and retain important local roots. In some cases, at least, they seem less wedded to Western-style parliamentarism and less averse to direct action, particularly if it is conducive to the results they seek. Do Mrs. Gandhi's current policies reflect their influence already?

It is yet too early to assert with confidence that this type of leader will come to dominate the Congress Party, or even to play a meaningful role in collaboration with older colleagues in the next decade and beyond. One suspects, however, that the first two generations of Indian leaders cannot be duplicated whatever the circumstances, and that although their influence will leave its mark on the politics of the future, new indigenous elements will emerge represented by forces more closely connected with the roots and branches of Indian society. Such a development, as can now be seen, will not be conducive to the strengthening of civil liberties or parliamentary politics, but it might foster a more forceful and effective approach to domestic problems.

In sum, the current odds favor a continuance of the Congress Party in power, with alterations over time in the nature of its upper levels of leadership. Even under the present leadership, however, critical policy decisions lie ahead, decisions affecting the basic nature of India's political and economic institutions. In the recent past, the Soviet model has exercised substantial influence on certain aspects of Indian planning and economic policy. Will this continue, or—as in the case of China, but involving a different route—will India seek a more indigenous path? Is New Delhi prepared to turn outward with respect to both the public and the private sectors, seeking foreign assistance on a mutually attractive basis? Can productivity be raised via improved management, new incentives, and increased state investment, particularly 'in agriculture? Unquestionably, the greatly elevated oil prices will continue to have a depressing effect on Indian development. Is it to be an open or closed system—economic and political? More precisely, if, as now seems probable, the tilt is toward authoritarianism, how far will the pendulum swing?

Foreign Policy Alternatives

Against this pattern of problems and uncertainties, let us explore the alternatives in foreign policy available to India, noting first those basic historical and geopolitical factors that have influenced policies in the past. Until the early modern era, the South Asian subcontinent was relatively isolated, surrounded by lofty mountain ranges—and bleak lands beyond—to the north, impenetrable jungles to the east, and vast deserts to the west. India's position enabled it to develop a highly distinctive culture, albeit one with numerous variations. On the other hand, like China, India was subject to a series of invasions from the interior. From earliest times, more "advanced" or more powerful forces penetrated the subcontinent, sometimes with sustained effect on the society they found. Indeed, as in the case of the Moghuls, foreign influences on India were probably more pervasive than those on China in the course of its interaction with "barbarians."

The Evolution of Indian Foreign Policy

With the advent of the modern era, the threat to India shifted. Now it was from the sea, and from the industrializing West, that the conquerors came. Once again, the parallel with China is an interesting one. But whereas the Chinese managed to cling precariously to independence, the Indians came under a long period of British rule. The degree to which this shaped modern Indian politics has already been indicated. It is also possible that the colonial experience, while it bred a strong nationalism, was partly responsible for the general absence of xenophobia, especially among the political elite—in strident contrast to the situation in Northeast Asia. A flexibility and receptivity to change, together with a genuine cosmopolitanism, have been hallmarks of the modern Indian elites.

During the British era, India had no foreign policy, as policy was British. Nor was a great interest in the Asian environment cultivated. Most educated Indians looked to Europe or America, generally with mixed love-hate emotions. Once again, Nehru typified for his generation the trauma and the ambivalence of the upper-class colonial. It is thus not surprising that in the post-1945 period Nehru shaped India's domestic institutions after the British model but foreign policies on the basis of Asianism and nonalignment, twin symbols of the newly won independence.

There is ample evidence that from the very beginning of this era Nehru hoped to reduce the role and power of the West in Asia by reaching agreements with the major societies of the area. It was for this reason that he sought close relations with China, first via the Kuomintang, subsequently via the Communists. In this course, Nehru naturally depreciated ideological or political differences, preferring to emphasize the common nationalist interests in combatting Western imperialism. This led to certain "concessions," notably on Tibet, which could not have been prevented but which were later to be regretted. The Indian policies of this period also masked the fact that Asian societies confronted a new era scarcely knowing one another. Geographic isolation and foreign dominance had interacted for centuries to keep their mutual relations minimal, with the primary attention of their elites focused elsewhere. When the first emotional upsurge attending the relations among newly independent states had subsided, the importance of cultural and political diversities (frequently accompanied by economic similarities) had to be faced.

Nonetheless, Pan-Asianism continued to hold a broad attraction, as the Bandung Conference of 1954 was to indicate. It was in connection with this conference, moreover, that the most substantial effort to create meaningful principles of peaceful coexistence was made. These principles, five in number, centered on pledges to avoid interference in the affairs of another nation, accept differences of political and social systems, and acknowledge the equality and sovereignty of each nation-state. Bandung represented the high point in the post-1945 Pan-Asianist movement. Some six years later, India and China were moving toward confrontation, and Nehru's dream of close Sino-Indian relations was shattered.

In a sense, however, Pan-Asianism was expanded during this period to encompass the Third World. The effort was to find a basic unity, or commonness of purpose, among the ex-colonial and underdeveloped societies. Nehru himself envisaged this grouping not as an alliance or a monolithic bloc, but as an independent, loosely associated third force capable of alleviating the tensions of the Cold War. His concept of non-alignment was that it did not preclude India or others from taking firm positions on specific issues. It was not equivalent to neutralism. Rather it represented the avoidance of permanent commitment to one force or bloc. In his own way, Nehru hoped to serve as balancer and mediator in international affairs.

As one looks back on this period, a curious irony can be perceived. At the outset of the postwar era, India had broad contacts with other Afro-Asian societies and considerable political as well as moral authority. China, on the other hand, was generally isolated from the Third World (including Asian) states and, after the advent of the Communists, strongly tied to the Soviet Union both for defense and economic reasons. Some two decades later, the situation was almost precisely reversed.

In retrospect, India's international influence during the first years after World War II can be seen to have rested on fragile foundations—the prestige of one man, the tolerance of the great powers, the still unfolding nationalist revolutions. By the time of his death, Nehru was deeply disillusioned, especially toward China (and the disillusionment was mutual). Indian foreign policy, without abandoning old shibboleths, was undergoing major changes.

The Advent of Regional Priority

For more than a decade, Indian attention has been focused almost exclusively on the region of which it is a part. Attendance at such international gatherings as those of the non-aligned states continues, but India does not pretend to play a leading role or set the moral tone, as was once the case. Meanwhile, however, New Delhi has advanced its position in South Asia in a fashion that might well have startled Nehru. Today, India is a dominant power of the subcontinent, and it has given ample indications that it does not intend to be reticent in wielding that power when it is adjudged necessary in terms of Indian national interests.

It can be argued that Indian dominance was always implicit in the political configuration of South Asia. Nevertheless, the question of whether peace and the status quo in this region might not be sought through an internal balance of power between Pakistan and India was not finally resolved until the 1971 Bangladesh War. The defeat and division of Pakistan as a result of this war ended such a possibility. At present, India's minimal request from those within and outside the subcontinent is that they accept the new order, namely, Indian superiority in this region. To a considerable extent, this has occurred. Even Pakistan gives strong evidence of acknowledging the superior power of India, at least in private, while other South Asian states follow suit, willingly or begrudgingly. Among the major external powers, only China holds back from such recognition. The USSR professes itself enormously pleased, and the U.S. accepts the realities without overt emotional display.

Thus, some of the most important foreign policy issues that lie ahead relate to India's role as a regional power. Newly acquired strength is not an unmixed blessing. With power comes responsibilities and difficult decisions, some of which defy the professions of purity so easily given at a time of impotence.

Like the Russians, Chinese, and Americans before them, Indian leaders are in the process of completing and seeking to protect their own contiguous empire. In the process, they are encompassing some peoples—directly or indirectly—who have no desire to fall under Indian control. How far will this process go? What are to be the perimeters of Indian rule—and beyond this, predominant Indian influence? As mentioned earlier, certain classical principles would appear to be operating, ones that pertained to British policies in the subcontinent a century or more ago.

Security involves not merely the capacity to defend one's territory to its furthermost boundaries, but some type of buffer system that serves as defense in greater depth. With the advent of the intercontinental nuclear age, perhaps the buffer concept is obsolete, or should be. Recent history, however, could not persuade the Indians on this score. The wars fought—and those that continue to be feared—involve near-neighbors, Pakistan and China. Thus, if an effective buffer system is difficult, even impossible, to achieve, it remains highly desirable.

Pakistan

During the first two decades of independence, India's major foreign policy decisions—as opposed to its broader ideological stance—were made primarily in response to the Pakistan issue. Accusing Pakistan of aggressive intentions, India strongly and, on occasion, bitterly opposed efforts by external forces to see that the two states received balanced military assistance. The hope, of course, was that such a policy would produce a political-military equilibrium in the subcontinent conducive to peace. It was this issue that created the most serious problems in Indo-American relations.

Pakistan has not ceased to be a matter of concern, but for the time being at least it is not considered a formidable military opponent. Indeed, India must now consider the possible impact of a further disintegration of Pakistan, and for most Indian policy-makers this possibility is not welcome. Chaos on India's western flank would almost certainly mean the closer presence of the Soviet Union either directly, or indirectly through Afghanistan. As there is already a growing uneasiness over the heavy Indian reliance on Russia, such prospects can only be disconcerting. India's self-interests are best served, therefore, by having Pakistan preserved in its present form and reasonably stable, albeit without new stocks of sophisticated weaponry.

China

China probably represents a deeper concern at present, although the feeling has grown that the PRC has neither the will nor the means to challenge India in the subcontinent militarily, and no doubt the special ties with the USSR have strengthened that feeling. The Bangladesh War, in an immediate sense at least, was a tremendous boost to Indian morale and self-confidence, not least because the biggest loser apart from Pakistan was China and the limitations on Chinese power in this region were graphically revealed.

Nevertheless, the 1962 debacle has not been forgotten, nor the fact that the People's Liberation Army mans the northern frontiers in considerable force. Because New Delhi is now interested in seeing the status quo maintained in South Asia, it has recurrently sought an improvement of relations with China on this basis. As pointed out earlier, its overtures have thus far been ignored. Peking's attitude toward New Delhi has been that of contempt mixed with anger. It has regarded the leadership as ineffective and incorrigibly "bourgeois." Nor has it had any respect for Indian military prowess. Even the news that India had conducted a successful explosion of a nuclear device evoked no Chinese public concern, for the official position of Peking is that nuclear proliferation does not constitute a problem. (Privately, Peking could not have been pleased.) The Chinese have seen India as a lackey of the Soviet Union, an integral part of the Soviet containment policy directed against China. Until recently, at least, as we have indicated, they have been confident that the political-economic situation in South Asia is fundamentally unstable, and susceptible to dramatic change. Hence, they have seen no compelling reason to take initiatives for change. China's main thrust has been to cultivate the states peripheral to India, including Pakistan, attempting wherever possible to forward its own containment policy.

As was also suggested earlier, however, Chinese policies could undergo alterations at some point. Peking undoubtedly knows that New Delhi is uneasy—and somewhat dissatisfied—with its reliance on the Soviet Union. A chance exists to further weaken those ties, and Peking might well move in that direction, especially as Indian predominance in South Asia now appears a reality not likely to be overturned.

The Himalayan States

Even were Sino-Indian relations to improve, however, India would naturally continue to be concerned with the politics of the Himalayan states. At a minimum, it demands nonalignment; preferably, it wants a client relation, including a receptivity to Indian military presence and policy direction. Thus, in the case of Nepal, the largest of these states, nonalignment has been reluctantly accepted, with the fairly sizable anti-Indian forces held in check by the presence of available alternatives in the form of Nepalese political exiles living in India. As the perimeters of permissible policies on both sides have gradually been established, Indian-Nepali relations appear to have stabilized, and that may continue. The Nepalese government has carefully fashioned its own policies of equidistance between China and India. But if the internal political situation in Nepal were to become seriously troubled, it could have immediate repercussions beyond Nepal's borders.

The extent to which the domestic politics of the Himalayan states can become a critical variable is well illustrated by Sikkim, the ministate east of Nepal. With some justice, the Indians claim that their recent annexation of Sikkim was involuntary, a necessity imposed on New Delhi by virtue of the breakdown of political stability within Sikkim itself. India could not afford to have a chaotic political situation here, one susceptible to the possible manipulation of external forces, in so strategic an area. Indian and Chinese forces still face each other on Sikkim's northern and eastern borders.

Whatever the merits of the Indian position, and they may be considerable, it is precisely the same position as that taken by nineteenth-century British rulers in explaining or defending their policies toward such peripheral areas as the northwest frontier, Afghanistan, and Tibet. Then too, a buffer-state system surrounding the Indian heartland was regarded as critical, given the perceptions of Russian and Chinese interests in this general region.

Whether the situation in Sikkim warranted the drastic action taken is debated even by Indians. India's position in this tiny country was already paramount. There can be no doubt, however, that a Sikkimese nationalist movement disturbing to the Indians had been fostered by the royal family and particularly by the American wife of the Chogyal. Sikkimese politics have long been complicated by the fact that Nepalis outnumber Sikkimese, making democracy a dangerous experiment for the latter group. Indeed, the Indians have held this fact over the head of the Sikkimese aristocracy for some years, as an inducement for cooperation. When growing political problems caused the Indians to end such Sikkimese autonomy as had previously existed, however, they sought to justify their actions as in line with Sikkimese aspirations, using a collaborationist figure to bolster such claims. No one, least of all the Indian leaders themselves, was misled by this line.

Sikkim provides an illustration of the close correlation between domestic politics and Indian responses along her highly sensitive frontiers. Bhutan, the third Himalayan state, has thus far managed to maintain general control over internal affairs by accepting an extensive Indian military presence and consultation on many matters, particularly those relating to security and foreign affairs. Sporadic political intrigues, generally centering on the throne, and such actions as Bhutan's entry into the United Nations have disturbed the Indians, but not disrupted the prevailing relationship.

India's relations with the Himalayan states have some similarity to Soviet-Outer Mongolian and Chinese-Tibetan relations. In the latter case, incorporation with autonomy has been followed by increasing demands for political compliance amounting to Sinicization. A formidable Chinese military presence has been required for internal as well as international reasons, for like most other minority peoples of Central Asia, the Tibetans did not submit to the controls imposed by a major power voluntarily. In the case of the People's Republic of Mongolia, formal independence has been achieved in exchange for full reliance on Russian military power and a political system which, together with its economic support, reflects the pervasiveness of Soviet influence.

To some extent, we are witnessing a reversion to a more traditional type of international relations on the Asian continent, one characteristic of the pre-European era. This type found its fullest expression in China's historical relations with peripheral peoples. Western concepts like equality and sovereignty were foreign to these relations. Suzerainty and the sophisticated application of techniques like the tribute system, policies involving a wide range of rewards and punishments, were central to the practices of these times. The international order could thus encompass infinite gradations of dependence-independence, intimacy-aloofness, friendliness-hostility.

The prominence accorded Western political and legal concepts may have obscured the degree to which similar relations have in actuality applied elsewhere, including the "advanced" West. Nevertheless, the differences were important, as the repeated confrontations of the nineteenth century illustrated. For a time, the West imposed its own order throughout Asia, abetted by Japan—a nation adhering to Western norms. Now, with the retreat of the West from Asia, and in the absence of any coherent international order, an element of traditionalism is returning, albeit one operating alongside more "modern" techniques and radically changed sociopolitical and geopolitical circumstances.

Bangladesh

India's most complex regional problem of the near future, however, may not be relations with the Himalayan states, or even with Pakistan, but the troublesome problem of Bangladesh. Once again, the close interaction between domestic and foreign policies is graphically illustrated by developments here. Indian intervention in the Pakistani civil war was essentially a product of heavy domestic pressures and particularly the serious complications generated in the adjoining Indian state of West Bengal. Millions of refugees from what was then East Pakistan poured into an area of India that was already a depressed region. As the people on both sides of the border are Bengali, sharing a common language and culture, it was doubly difficult to prevent events on the Pakistan side from having major repercussions on the Indian side.

Unfortunately for India, this situation will continue. Bangladesh could thus cause India far greater problems as an independent state than when it was a part of Pakistan. In the initial period, Bangladesh owed its very existence to the Indian army, and in many respects it occupied the position of client state. Swiftly, however, attitudes changed. By mid-1974, India had become the chief scapegoat, blamed for a wide variety of ills, from smuggling to insufficient aid. Many of the charges were unfair, but they illustrated the volatile nature of Indian-Bangladeshi relations and the dangers that loomed ahead.

Can India avoid further deep involvement if the political and economic system of this new nation collapses? In a region of desperation, Bangladesh is the most desperate. Combining a huge population and meager resources, that country currently appears to have a most dismal future. Economic conditions are terrible, with little prospect of significant improvements. The floods were serious but convenient, as they enabled an appeal for international aid on behalf of a nation that was already bankrupt. Yet external assistance under prevailing conditions can, at best, postpone catastrophe, and in the process of post-ponement enable it to take on greater proportions. The Dacca government as presently constituted sets a new record for in-efficiency, with corruption also running well above the tolerable levels. Disillusionment on the part of the citizenry, and the elite as well, has quickly built up. Even the prime minister, Father of the Nation, had seriously slipped in prestige by mid-1974, prior to his assumption of dictatorial power. Many of the supporters of revolt spoke of "a revolution betrayed."

The issue which hangs over India is clear. What if Bangladesh is threatened with sudden or even creeping chaos, and millions of refugees once again pour into West Bengal? Or what if the political course takes a turn that encourages the greater involvement of a major power from outside the region? Given the already precarious political balance existing in West Bengal, and the multiple economic and social difficulties of this region, can the Indian government look with complacence on such occurrences? The answer is almost certainly in the negative. Hence, Indian intervention, directly or indirectly, voluntarily or involuntarily, remains a distinct possibility.

Sri Lanka

Relations with Sri Lanka to the south are currently quite satisfactory, but here too domestic issues exist which could easily affect bilateral ties. Sri Lanka is a nation that has experimented with the same broad political and economic policies as India, and faces many of the same difficulties. Socialism has thus far failed abysmally, and in the wake of economic malaise, dissidence comes in various forms. Inevitably, the government has felt it necessary to tighten restrictions, although a considerable measure of freedom is allowed, particularly if it is conducted through oral, informal channels. Sri Lanka also has a communal issue of serious proportions. The minority Tamil (South Indians) are unhappy to the point of bitterness with their treatment at the hands of the majority Sinhalese. India has been scrupulously careful not to intervene on this issue, but in the event of a major upheaval New Delhi could scarcely avoid deep concern, given the proximity of Sri Lanka to South India. It should be noted, however, that New Delhi gave prompt and effective aid to the Sri Lanka government at the time of the 1971 uprising there. India is not likely to look with favor on efforts to change the political system by force from whatever source.

The Requirements of Regional Power

Thus far, we have suggested that despite the grave domestic problems to be faced India is likely to survive as an entity and gain in military strength, especially as measured against her smaller neighbors. Moreover, there appears to be no opponent, political party or otherwise, that can successfully challenge the ruling Congress Party now or in the foreseeable future. Leadership within that party will undergo changes, possibly significant changes, in the years ahead, but in themselves these changes are not likely to affect the main course of Indian foreign policy. India has achieved a type of hegemony within the subcontinent, and she has also secured, in one form or another, a broad recognition of that fact. By the same token, however, she now finds herself more seriously affected by and, hence, potentially more involved in the internal affairs of the other states of this region. As a regional power of consequence, India will face new responsibilities and recurrent decisions of critical import.

It is impossible to predict with precision the form which Indian regional policies will take. We have, however, sketched out the major alternatives. These range from annexation to an acceptance of nonalignment. Undoubtedly, specific policies will hinge on a wide range of variables, but there is every reason to expect that India will protect her newly acquired dominance, taking whatever means are regarded as necessary to prevent external developments from impinging adversely on India itself or being conducive to the creation of major-power enclaves in states on her borders. Under these circumstances, India is certain to be regarded with suspicion and wariness by her small neighbors. Clearly, her recent actions in Bangladesh and Sikkim were not conducive to any alleviation of such feelings.

To date, New Delhi's primary concerns have been with India's land frontiers. Recent events, however, have caused attention to turn to that route which the Europeans used in planting their flags on Indian territory, the sea. With the Middle East—and oil—having assumed such vital significance in international affairs, the Indian Ocean has acquired a greatly enhanced strategic importance. If an oil blockade were imposed, for example, this would be one logical locus of action. Suddenly, this ocean has taken on some of the symbolism of a life line, especially for nations like Japan. Among the oil producers themselves, Iran—second only to Saudi Arabia in current production—now looms as a rising power, military as well as economic, in this region.

It is thus not surprising that both the Soviet Union and the United States have shown signs of increased commitment here. For some time, the Russians have been seeking coaling stations and other facilities in South and Southeast Asia for a growing Soviet fleet operating in these seas. The United States has indicated similar interests, focusing most recently on the British-held island of Diego García. These events, and especially the latter, have been increasingly disturbing to the Indian government. To counter them, New Delhi has made repeated private representations and publicly advanced a "peace-zone" concept intended to prevent the Indian Ocean from becoming a region of superpower confrontation. The Indian position is complicated, however, by the fact that it firmly rejects the idea of South Asia being made a nuclear-free zone, a proposal most recently advanced by Pakistan. On this front, India clearly chooses to keep its options open.

It is entirely possible, therefore, that in the decade ahead India will find itself not only involved in developing and maintaining a formidable ground and air force, but also in establishing a substantially larger naval force in an effort to make the Indian Ocean *its* ocean. A host of factors now indicates that the oceans of the world will take on greatly enhanced strategic importance. Here, some of the major remaining resources lie. Here also, a range of tactics short of all-out war can be employed, including blockade and the mounting of an off-shore military presence.

This raises the question of whether India will gradually acquire both an expanding interest in affairs outside its immediate region and a capacity for greater participation. Put simply, will India become an international as well as a regional power? The combination of developmental priorities at home and heavy regional responsibilities would seem to militate strongly against such an occurrence, even if India eventually opts for nuclear weapons. At most, New Delhi might seek to extend its influence politically, as China has done, aiming to recapture some of the moral authority or symbolic prestige of Nehru's time. Success in any such endeavor, however, would require greater domestic achievements and a different type of leadership.

If it is unlikely that India will soon become a global power, this nation will almost certainly have an increased interest and involvement in select regions outside South Asia as well as in certain international or extraregional bodies, particularly those dealing with social and economic issues. Among the regions of importance to India, none will be more significant than the Middle East, both for economic and strategic reasons. India, so adversely affected by the oil crisis, desperately needs petrodollars. Can some form of interaction with the oil-rich nations be achieved? Further, Iran now looms as a substantial military power, with interests in the Indian Ocean and South Asia in addition to the Middle East. Both Pakistan and India can be expected to vie for Iran's support. Indeed, this has already begun, with India scoring early gains and the shah showing an interest in playing a larger role throughout the area.

Under the circumstances, Southeast Asia could also become more important than has been the case in recent years. Negatively, a serious deterioration of political order in Burma, especially if coupled with the increased power of the Chinese-sponsored White Flag Burmese Communists, might further complicate India's security problems on the northeastern frontiers. For some years, small numbers of Naga insurrectionaries receiving training in China have trooped back and forth across Burma's poorly controlled north-central territory. On the positive side, Southeast Asia is another region rich in resources, awaiting peace and more effective governments in order to realize its great potential. When and if these conditions prevail, India might benefit appreciably through economic interaction.

Relations with the Major Powers

It remains for us to explore more thoroughly India's relations with the other major societies of the Pacific-Asian region. In the past fifteen years, no external relationship has been more critical than that with the Soviet Union. In the final years of the 1950s, Russia—already deeply embroiled in controversies with Peking—took the position that the Sino-Indian conflict was unnecessary, damaging to the international Communist cause, and a result essentially of excessive Chinese nationalism. Assistance to India continued, and the breach with China widened. The culmination came with the Treaty of Friendship, signed in 1971.

India insisted that its new relationship with the Soviet Union did not constitute an abandonment of nonalignment. In point of fact, however, India had become aligned, and dependent on Soviet military and economic assistance to an appreciable extent. All alliances in recent times have been less exclusive than in the so-called Cold War period, allowing greater independence and flexibility. Clearly, however, the special ties between New Delhi and Moscow had many of the attributes of an alliance. These relations, moreover, had a growing impact on Indian domestic policies, both economic and political. They were manifest as well in areas of foreign policy, notably in India's stance at Afro-Asian conferences.

Ties with the Soviet Union paid off at the time of the Bangladesh War. Not only did Russia give India its strongest political support in the international arena, but its military shield served as a guarantee against possible Chinese intervention—although the likelihood of such a move under any conditions could be debated. Yet this period may have marked the high tide in Soviet-Indian alignment. Mrs. Gandhi, it might be noted, did not receive unstinting Soviet support in this crisis without strenuous, even angry insistence. Moreover, in New Delhi, there were always qualms about the sharpness of its tilt toward Moscow, a number of leaders regarding this more as an act of necessity than a move to be cheered. The liabilities appeared to grow. Not only did the alignment cast a shadow over India's relations with China and, to a lesser extent, with the United States. It also created an image of dependence harmful to India's standing with many elements of the Third World. Finally, and very importantly, Russian economic and technical assistance proved to be a disappointment in the period of India's greatest need. By the end of 1974, New Delhi had a clear sense of the limitations involved in Soviet aid, granting its continued importance.

Even during the period of greatest dependence, India fended off certain pressures. An enthusiastic endorsement of Moscow's call for an Asian collective security program was avoided, although "interest" in the idea was voiced. Negotiations over the right of Soviet naval vessels to use Indian ports were stretched out, with a decision postponed.

In the recent past, it has become clear that India would like to move closer to a policy of equidistance among the major powers. New Delhi recognizes that under prevailing or likely circumstances, some special ties, especially in the security realm, will continue with Moscow. However, the overtures toward China and the new receptivity toward the United States are genuine. India's hour of greatest need for a Soviet alliance seems past—unless internal trends dictate otherwise. The new Indian position on the subcontinent appears unchallengable, unless India's own domestic troubles intervene. Thus, India could profit from "normalizing" its relations with China on the basis of the status quo and improving its relations with the United States. It must be admitted, however, that Mrs. Gandhi's current domestic policies might increase India's estrangement from both the PRC and the U.S. and heighten dependence upon the USSR.

Equidistance can be considered a new term for nonalignment. As should have become clear, it is a widely shared desideratum in contemporary international relations, in a period when blocs have lost their cohesion and heavy reliance on an exclusive bilateral relation appears both less feasible and less necessary. Yet it should also be clear that equidistance can more easily be a goal or symbol than a reality. In the case of India, one major uncertainty lies in the future attitudes and actions of China. Another pertains to the United States. Exploration of this latter issue will be continued in a later section, but here it must be noted that the question of the importance of South Asia to American national interests has been, and will continue to be, extensively debated.

Obviously, the United States has an interest in seeing a democratic system preserved in a society so large and so influential, even granting its weaknesses. India as a politically open society would help to preserve the broad political-military equilibrium which the United States does, and should, regard as vital in the Pacific-Asian region. Earlier rhetoric, however, about how much the world's two largest democracies had in common was largely meaningless, and the forms of American aid often counterproductive. Given current developments, moreover, American assistance at this point, even on a much larger scale than seems feasible, would not help to move this society toward a resolution or serious tackling of its socioeconomic problems or toward reestablishing democratic rights. The critical variables lie within India.

Strategically, as has been indicated, an increased American interest has been shown in the Indian Ocean, partly as a result of the oil crisis but also because of the presumed increase in Soviet naval activity in the region. However, this entire matter remains highly controversial in American political circles. An increased American military presence in this region, moreover, would be productive of negative Indian responses, as has been indicated, although in the event of another crisis affecting its security India would undoubtedly call on the United States once more for military support. It is doubtful whether under any circumstances the United States would become involved militarily on the Asian subcontinent.

Allowing the Soviet Union and China to play the more critical balancing roles, the United States has deliberately maintained a low posture in recent years, its tilt toward Pakistan during the Bangladesh War notwithstanding. That posture—accompanied by rather modest aid, except in the case of Bangladesh where economic assistance has been considerable—seems to accord with American interests and is not likely to be altered. It is thus doubtful whether India could induce a greatly accelerated American participation or support on its behalf, even if it wishes to do so. As indicated earlier, New Delhi has secured acceptance by Washington of its new dominance in the region. Some other irritants of the past are in the process of being smoothed out. But for the duration of Mrs. Gandhi's government, some residue of the anti-Americanism long present among a portion of India's ruling circle will remain, and be reciprocated in Washington. Moreover, differences on certain issues and on perceptions of national interests will continue to make themselves manifest. Indeed, if the present repression continues, the gap will surely grow wider. In any case, America's primary interests and commitments are likely to lie outside South Asia—frustrating any Indian policy of complete equidistance.

Can relations with Japan be strengthened and extended? The vastness and diversity of Asia is nowhere more tellingly revealed than in the past relations between India and Japan. During World War II, Japanese leaders did seek to cultivate Indian nationalism as a part of their general campaign to enlist Asian colonial peoples in a crusade against Western imperialism. In general, however, these two great societies have scarcely acknowledged and seldom understood each other, separated as they are by huge distances—geographic, cultural, and developmental.

Under certain conditions, Japan could provide India with major assistance in its drive toward economic development. If an open political system and a mixed economy are preserved, that should increase the potentials. Once again, however, Indian policies are the critical variable. Japanese investment has come primarily from the private sector. Will India choose to create the conditions making such investment more attractive? If the Japanese government were to move toward augmented assistance to the public sector, is India prepared to take full advantage of such an opportunity? For the foreseeable future, in any case, the Indian-Japanese relationship will be essentially an economic one, possibly important, possibly peripheral—but available.

Future Probabilities

The outlines of future Indian foreign policy and India's interaction with the other major societies of the Pacific-Asian region thus seem reasonably clear. The chances are strong that India's dominance over the South Asian region will remain firm, and even increase. New Delhi will not be popular with a number of its smaller neighbors, but none can afford to ignore or offend her. Over time, moreover, reasonable accommodations will be achieved in most cases, the important variable being the ability of these peripheral states to keep their own political house in order and avoid frightening India with the prospect of an instability that lends itself either to impingements on Indian domestic problems or the extensive influence of another large state.

India's military power will be enhanced in the course of the next decade, whether or not it elects to develop nuclear weapons. It is unlikely, however, that India will be considered a global power at any point during the period. Rather, expanding Indian interests will display themselves in an increasing interaction with the Middle East, and quite possibly with Southeast Asia and Japan. There will also be a developing interest in select international bodies of a technical nature.

With respect to the major powers, India's goal will be a greater degree of equidistance than has marked her policies in recent years. It is possible that relations with China can be improved, although it is difficult to envisage a situation where relations with the two Communist giants are approximately the same. That would require a series of changes in the international order, including changes in Sino-Soviet relations themselves. Nor does it seem likely that the United States will play a major role, at least in bilateral terms, although modest improvements are feasible. Relations with Japan will be of a very special character. Hence, the tilt will continue to be toward the Soviet Union, and that could be made sharper, depending upon domestic trends.

These projections rest on one major premise, namely that despite the serious problems confronting it, India will remain a viable political entity, able to contain dissidence and successfully alter the recent course so as to achieve a modest but sufficient level of economic development. The current political–economic crises make firm predictions impossible. The probabilities of a more authoritarian India now seem much greater than in the past. A major precedent has been established, and even if democratic rights are restored, it remains available for future use. Thus, at this point, it is the spector of authoritarianism rather than that of dissolution that confronts the Indian polity.

Chapter 5

INDONESIA: Symbol of the Developmental Dilemma

The Indonesian archipelago stretches for some three thousand miles across the lower part of Southeast Asia, its far western portions jutting into the Indian Ocean, its eastern extremities lying in the South Pacific. Its thousands of islands and 120 million people make Indonesia not only the largest state of its region, but also the nation of greatest natural wealth. Its rich resources include oil, minerals, and soil and climate conducive to the production of such important commercial export crops as rubber, palm oil, tea, and coffee. If Southeast Asia is to have a regional leader, Indonesia is the most logical candidate.

Once again, we are confronted with a society facing a number of serious domestic problems. Hence, it is essential to examine the context in which foreign policies must be determined. What are the historical antecedents here, and how strongly do they still govern thought and action? Can this society of extraordinary diversity maintain political stability in the next decade and beyond? Is economic development en route, and in what forms?

The Paths of Indonesian Nationalism

September through October 1965 marked a major watershed in Indonesian policies, domestic and foreign, but the

Sukarno era left its legacy, especially in the form of the negative lessons which it bequeathed. Hence, this era warrants some initial attention. Sukarnoism came to an end with the bloody September 30 coup, a putsch that failed in its attempt to guarantee leftist supremacy in a faltering leader's final years.

Sukarno blanketed Indonesian politics in the years prior to his downfall, and his imprimatur was placed as heavily on foreign as on domestic policies. In many respects, he typified the first-generation Asian revolutionary. Strongly nationalist, Sukarno was imbued with visions of social justice that made him highly receptive to socialism (although this did not inhibit him from pursuing a style and standard of living closely approximating that of a Javanese prince). He was well educated, and he had a penchant for ideology or, more accurately, for concise phrases and slogans lending themselves to acronyms. But he was not truly an intellectual or a theorist. And his knowledge of, and interest in, economic matters was minimal.

Sukarno's contributions to Indonesian nationalism in the late colonial era and to the initial phases of nation-building were major ones, but by any measurement the final years of his reign were disastrous ones for the Indonesian people. Almost the only things moving were population and inflation rates, and they were galloping. Production was stagnant. New investment, foreign or domestic, was in steady decline. At the finale, the economic system was in total collapse.

Nor was the internal political situation better. Ending the experiment with Western-style parliamentarism, Sukarno proclaimed "guided democracy," which turned out in fact to be a type of oligarchic order, with civil liberties for dissenters greatly restricted, and the Leader himself serving as impresario. Sukarno presided over and sought to keep in balance three diverse forces: the Moslems (or one significant element thereof), the military, and the Communists—while heading himself the Left Nationalists.

The domestic economic and political situation certainly influenced trends in Indonesian foreign policy in the late Sukarno era. Rather than turning greater attention to the economic crisis, Sukarno sought to serve certain political interest groups and unify the public via an adventurous foreign policy, and one that became ever more grandiose. As his political order came to depend increasingly on the Left, with the military looming up as the chief potential threat, moreover, his foreign policy reflected this fact. Thus, a poverty-stricken Indonesia found itself engaged in confrontation with Malaysia—labeled by the Sukarnoists a neocolonial state—with the suggestion that a new Malay empire might be in the making.

Meanwhile, Jakarta aligned itself with Peking as well as with P'yŏngyang and Hanoi, moving decisively away from earlier proclamations of nonalignment. Indeed, Sukarno envisaged Indonesia as one of the leaders of a world force to rival that headed by the "capitalist" and "imperialist" powers. Thus, in the name of the Newly Emerging States, he took Indonesia out of the United Nations and, with Peking's support, laid the foundations of a building that would house the rival international body. For all of the non-Communist states of Southeast Asia, not Malaysia alone, these developments were profoundly disturbing. The prospect was of a Peking-Jakarta alliance operating in pincer fashion against the region, spawning as well as capitalizing on internal problems.

It was only by the narrowest of margins that a Communist-Left Nationalist coalition failed to seize power in the fall of 1965, but fail they did, and the aftermath was an extraordinarily bloody one for them and for Indonesia. Those killed numbered in the hundreds of thousands, most but not all individuals identified as Communists or leftists. Tens of thousands of others were imprisoned, including most of the surviving Sukarnoist era leaders associated with the old coalition. The Communists who survived were primarily those who had been traveling or studying abroad at the time of the abortive coup, and they became permanent exiles in Peking or Moscow.

A few elements managed to avoid detection, and there have been rumors of a Communist underground, but nearly ten years after the event the Indonesian Communist Party remains shattered and divided—a disorganized, furtive force of little political consequence.

Political retirement came not merely to the Communists and the Left Nationalists but to most of those forming the political elite of the old era, and to the front groups which they had organized and led. The new leaders were military men (few of them with any political experience except as they had garnered it in earlier administrative roles), served by a small cadre of trained technicians, mainly economists. As might have been expected, initially the new government received enthusiastic support across a broad political spectrum—from social democrats and liberals, some of whom had to be released from jails; from students and workers who hoped for an economic upswing; and from a public grown weary of empty rhetoric and unfulfilled promises.

The New Era

The new regime made its own promises, to be sure, most of them low-key and somber. Pragmatism would replace utopianism, with the premium on hard-headed policies that would end rampant inflation and economic stagnation. The cult of personality would no longer be the basis of the political system. Institutions would be built, political institutions molded to Indonesia's needs and permitting the participation of the citizenry. First, however, a period of tutelage and exploration would take place, during which civil liberties would be restricted.

From the outset, Indonesia's new military leaders also made it clear that drastic changes would be effected in foreign policy. The era of adventurism was over, and domestic problems would receive top priority. Confrontation with Malaysia promptly ceased, and cordial relations were quickly established. Given their deep antagonism to the Communists, moreover, it was not surprising that Jakarta had no further interest in an alliance with Peking, P'yŏngyang, and Hanoi. Indonesia reentered the United Nations and made it abundantly clear that its commitments had changed. Nonalignment was reasserted as the guiding principle of Indonesian foreign policy, but in both economic and political policies the tilt toward the West was pronounced.

It took a considerable period of time to sweep away the old debris and make preparations for the new and different policies. During this period, a number of "advanced" nations led by the United States were most helpful. Debt-rescheduling agreements were worked out with a group of thirteen states, collectively known as the Inter-Governmental Group on Indonesia, most of them Western nations—plus Japan. Huge sums were advanced in aid and credit. In exchange, very liberal terms were arranged for foreign investors. The new leaders signaled that they were prepared to see the economy operate with minimal restrictions.

The result was development—and new problems. Less than a decade after the onset of the new era, a number of grievances were being voiced, and the leadership showed signs of concern, even fear. What are the issues? On the economic front, the primary problem lies in the imbalanced nature of development, hence, the persistent problems of social and economic justice. With a heavy reliance on foreign investment, growth has been taking place in very select areas. The rural-urban gap continues to grow. Jakarta becomes ever more resplendent (in special areas) with its new skyscrapers and superhighways, but with the projected urban growth rate for the next fifteen years put at 4.6 percent per annum, the problems of economic maldistribution in the cities are bound to grow. Meanwhile, rural Indonesia continues to exist in poverty and with very limited mobility. The government has undertaken modest rural aid, offering each village a lump sum of money with which to improve itself—but the programs thus far scarcely begin to match the needs. Some problems, such as population, have barely been touched, and growth is running at about 2.7 percent per annum, one of the higher rates in Asia.

Corruption represents another serious problem. Even when one makes allowances for Indonesian patterns, and seeks to avoid the application of utopian standards, the evidence suggests declining political morals within the upper levels of the new elite. The system itself, particularly the encouragement of enterprises run by military administrators to generate funds for their own units, strongly abets this development. So does the high degree of autonomy, financial as well as political, that continues to characterize operations.

The problem of corruption is certainly not a new one, but it appears to have expanded in scale, possibly because of the accelerated developments in the economic field. Some foreign observers argue that it is still considerably below the Asian norm, and they may be correct. There can be no question, however, that with certain segments of the population, especially the student-intellectual community, it has become a matter of deep concern and rising anger. Although Suharto himself is generally exempt from charges of personal involvement, many other key figures, including his wife, are not.

The issue is made more explosive because it is tied to the influx of foreign funds, especially Japanese monies. With incontrovertible evidence, critics ascribe to the Japanese a series of unsavory practices involving large-scale corruption of the political elite. This was the immediate issue, indeed, which lay behind the Jakarta riots of 1974 at the time of Prime Minister Tanaka's visit.

Thus, it has been possible for disillusioned individuals to assert that the revolution has been betrayed, with a need existing to rekindle the spirit of 1965 via basic changes in policies and personnel. Needless to say, the government does not take kindly to such charges—and it has responded with increased severity, ostracizing or detaining some of its more prominent critics, and cracking down hard on signs of dissidence in student circles and in the press. Temporarily at least, these responses have had the desired effect. One can discern an increased reluctance to express political grievances and a rising atmosphere of fear.

Behind the economic and social issues exist some broader political problems that stem from the cultural variations of this society, its particular distribution of peoples, and the institutions that were fashioned to serve it in the postindependence era. Perhaps because it had been proposed by the Dutch, the Indonesian Founding Fathers rejected a federal system and established instead a unitary state. Due to multiple weaknesses, it has not been possible to operate such a state effectively, and a considerable amount of warlordism has prevailed, as suggested earlier. Nevertheless, Javanese domination of Indonesian politics is implicit in this system. More than one-half of all Indonesians live on the island of Java. From here came most of the central figures of the nationalist movement. Thus, political developments on Java have always been critical to the evolution of Indonesian politics, although the Javanese themselves have represented a highly diverse, complex political mosaic.

Peoples of the outer islands have naturally resented Javanese control, be it in the form of military governors or central directives. Their protests—and revolts—have been unavailing, however, largely because the balance of military and political power is against them. Yet there remains a very limited prospect for unity among such peoples, given the wide diversities among them. The economic wealth of the outer islands makes it certain that the central government will insist on greater rather than less control. This would not necessarily militate against allowing greater indigenous representation in the ranks of political leadership. Some outer island representatives, it should be noted, do hold important positions in the national government and armed forces. Yet localist ties and suspicions continue to run high. These will be moderated only as the general course of economic and social modernization unfolds, a task of decades even under optimal conditions.

Domestic Prospects

Given the problems of nation-building and economic development, can Indonesia maintain a sufficient degree of political stability in the decade ahead to pursue coordinated policies at home and possibly extend its influence abroad? On balance, the answer is probably in the affirmative. If the difficulties are formidable and, in some cases, not susceptible to "solution," Indonesia's resources—using that term in its broadest sense—are also formidable. Further, in playing up the problems of the government, one must not ignore or minimize the disadvantages of those that might seek to challenge it via revolution.

As has already been indicated, Indonesia possesses large oil deposits, with new discoveries in off-shore fields being reported periodically. In 1974, oil revenues amounted to nearly $4 billion U.S., and this will continue to grow. Nor is there any reason to believe that Indonesian minerals—tin, copper, nickel, and aluminum, among others—will not command rising prices, together with her commercial agricultural products. Only the collapse of the economies of the Western nations and Japan could alter this picture significantly. In sum, Indonesia—unlike many developing societies—has the means with which to undertake a modernization program, even one with sizable elements of error and waste.

Beyond this, the Indonesian military are powerful, and their key leaders have no intention of relinquishing authority in the near future. In terms of modern weapons, training, and organization, the armed forces are growing steadily more powerful, indeed, making an "outside" revolution seem most improbable. It is true, of course, that the military are no more monolithic than other parts of Indonesian society. Factionalism bred of many causes exists, and the political shifts at the top in recent times are reflective of this fact. There has been a certain tendency, moreover, for Suharto to assume greater individual power as his tenure in office has lengthened, drawing people toward him when he needs them, sending them out when their usefulness declines, and allowing no one to remain next to him permanently.

Suharto's death, substantial pressures from within the military that produced new figures, or—*in extremis*—a military coup could conceivably produce some important changes of policy as well as of personnel. The likelihood of an upheaval having the significance of the epic events of 1965–1966, however, seems small. It should be understood, of course, that this is not a pure military regime. Its civilian components are of critical importance, especially in the bureaucracy and the foreign service. Nor has the evolution of the political system ceased. Despite delays and setbacks, experimentation with greater functional representation in government will continue, its pace determined by the general climate.

To appreciate fully the strength of the military, however, one has to examine the opposition. Despite periodic alarms from official quarters, the Communist Party of Indonesia, once the best organized, most dynamic political force in the country, remains a broken vehicle, a movement unable to find a route to recovery. The government, alert to even the smallest signs here, intends to keep it that way, whatever means must be used. Nor can the traditionally active Moslem forces be regarded as political competitors at this point. The Moslems have demonstrated the capacity to influence governmental policies, but they do not truly share in power nor are they likely to do so. They too are deeply divided, and like the old Nationalist (PNI) figures, their senior statesmen are now passing from the scene—without nationally recognized leaders to replace them.

As in the case of India, therefore, there is not a close correlation at present between socioeconomic crises and the probability of political upheaval. In this type of society, political stability is underwritten by the absence of any linkage between "national" elites and "local" masses. An organizational challenge to the prevailing authority is thereby missing. In part, this situation is related to the low level of socioeconomic development, hence, the persistence of traditional patterns of political behavior. But at an earlier point in Indonesia, national parties, including the Communists, illustrated that they could use traditional behavioral patterns effectively to augment their strength. Thus, the government must control dissident elites, but if it does this effectively, while at the same time presiding over a slow process of socioeconomic development, especially in the rural areas, it will find the nature of the threat to it reduced. Under such circumstances, a government may confront riots, but not revolutions.

At a later stage, when basic socioeconomic changes have begun to alter the structure of village life fundamentally and the self-contained character of the village has largely disappeared, these techniques—at least as they are now employed—will probably not suffice. At some point, more social and economic goods will have to be delivered. Greater mobility will have to be afforded. These possibilities will depend on the capacity of the system to produce more and the degree to which considerations of social justice have been incorporated into the fabric of attitudes and policy. In these regards, the urban centers will present the earliest and most insistent demands. Later also, the flexibility of political institutions will be more thoroughly tested, with the need for constant adaptation to an ever more rapidly changing society. But all of this lies ahead—and probably a considerable distance ahead. For the next decade at least, political stability involves more elemental considerations, such as keeping the price of rice for the city-dweller low.

Meanwhile, the government has not been entirely oblivious to the issues set forth earlier. It has shown itself particularly sensitive to the charges made against it in the name of nationalism, namely, allowing the Indonesian economy to be controlled by foreign interests and threatening the survival of an Indonesian identity by permitting a flood of foreign influences. Terms for foreign investment have been tightened, and in many other respects a new nationalist surge has gotten underway with implications for the foreign policy arena.

Domestically oriented reforms directed at corruption or agrarian problems are still negligible, but the pressures .on behalf of these will undoubtedly continue. At some point, the government may well discover that an encouragement of low-capitalized small and medium industries in rural areas, coupled with a multipronged approach to agricultural modernization, represents the meaningful course for Indonesia. Such programs would not inhibit resource exploitation and selective urban industrialization.

Indonesian Foreign Policy: Regionalism

In the context set forth here, let us explore trends and alternatives in Indonesian foreign policy. The central issues pertain to Jakarta's future relations with the region of which she is a part. Will Indonesia seek the type of dominance in Southeast Asia now represented by India in South Asia? Or will regional cooperation be achieved on a more equal, multilateral basis via ASEAN (the Association of Southeast Asian Nations) or some similar group? Is a third alternative worthy of consideration, namely, a strong, coherent regionalism failing to develop here, product of the numerous diversities with which Southeast Asia is plagued and the Indonesian need to give full priority to its domestic programs?

As was indicated earlier, Sukarno's policies carried strong overtones of hegemony, particularly toward the Malay world. In the early 1960s, Indonesia was seen as a major threat, not merely by the governments of Singapore and Malaysia, but by other neighboring governments as well, partly because of the Jakarta-Peking alliance. At one point, it looked very much as if every government in the region might collapse under these pressures.

Today, the situation is radically different. Indonesian-Malaysian ties are cordial, yet they do not unduly disturb Singapore—although Chinese life in a Malay sea has its moments of tension and its long-range uncertainties. The effort to apply joint Malaysian-Indonesian control over the Malacca Straits, denying it the status of international waters, is one example of cooperation (albeit not one pleasing to the major powers).

In recent years, the Indonesians have evidenced their concern over the prospect of Communist victories in Indochina in a variety of ways. Some training was given to Republic of Cambodia armed forces, making very clear the Indonesian position here. Jakarta also accepted a position on the International Control Commission in Vietnam and served as a non-Communist representative, with all of the frustration which that entailed. There can be little doubt that although relations with Hanoi and P'yŏngyang were retained from the Sukarno era, Jakarta very much hoped that Communist control of Indochina could be prevented, and its reaction to Communist successes in 1975 was one of anxiety tinged with bitterness—the United States serving as a clear target.

However, there had never been any indication that Indonesia would actively intervene in an effort to halt such a development. On the contrary, the Indonesian leaders have signaled that they do not intend to become involved in overseas military operations, unless the security of Indonesia is directly threatened.

It is conceivable that under some circumstances, Indonesia might extend its power beyond present boundaries, either in the form of playing the role of dominant state or reshaping those boundaries. Any breakdown of order in Malaysia, particularly one involving an enhanced Chinese power, would be powerfully disturbing to the leaders in Jakarta. Even a sharp swing to the left in Singapore would create strong reverberations, as the Indonesians continue to worry—rightly or wrongly—about their own overseas Chinese. By extension, some of this concern might apply if Thailand were to enter into prolonged political weakness with its attendant uncertainties, although the ties here are less intimate.

Thus, one cannot rule out the first alternative, even though it does not seem probable under present circumstances. As recent history has shown, much depends on developments both in Indonesia itself and in the rest of Southeast Asia. One of the great weaknesses of the island cordon-sanitaire thesis advanced by some Americans is that in this region, as in others, developments on the Asian mainland matter very much to the island nations offshore. Any attempt to base policy on the assumption that they can remain unaffected is unrealistic and doomed to failure.

In recent years, however, Indonesia has placed its emphasis on mutual responsibility and interaction among non-Communist Southeast Asian states rather than on the dominance (or prime responsibility) of Indonesia. Using such themes as "Regional Resilience" and "Make Southeast Asia a Peaceful and Neutral Zone," it has sought to build up the status and role of ASEAN, hoping that this body can gradually evolve toward meaningful economic, political, and security functions.

On occasion, Jakarta has made concrete suggestions. It has proposed joint economic action to protect member states against the pressures of the large consumer nations. It has also advocated political actions directed at preempting the intervention of outside major powers in the region. And it has supported the idea of cooperation among security agencies to reduce the dangers of internal subversion.

One must assume, however, that regionalism in Southeast

Asia will grow very slowly, and with serious restraints on its effectiveness in any of the fields just mentioned. First, this is a region torn by deep political, ethnic, and socioeconomic divisions, one that will not achieve any substantial unity easily. The northern tier of states comprising the Southeast Asian region are now either Communist or under considerable Communist influence. Given Hanoi's determination to exercise ultimate hegemony over Indochina and the nature of political trends in these states, the basis for cooperation between them and other states of the region is currently doubtful. Visions of such projects as the Mekong River Development notwithstanding, Communist systems are closed, highly exclusivist systems, at least during the initial purification and mobilization stages, preaching and practicing self-reliance. Internationalism is a strictly subordinate consideration.

Apart from ideological-political and systemic differences, there can be some question as to whether Indochina in general, or North Vietnam in particular, can have the same international orientation as the other Southeast Asian states, especially Indonesia. China must be of special importance to small countries on its peripheries, irrespective of their politics. Hanoi's task, along with that of P'yŏngyang, has been to balance off Soviet and Chinese influence. That type of "neutralism" is not precisely the same as the nonalignment sought by the non-Communist states, even if it may reflect similar broad nationalist goals and lend itself to some common tactics.

In the economic realm also, interests held in common must vie with diversities and competitive instincts. In the aftermath of the energy crisis and the growing realization that stocks of natural resources are rapidly diminishing in the light of exploding world demand, analysts have had to create new categories of nations. The old technique of dividing states into "advanced" and "emerging" ones no longer suffices, the critical question being which are rich in resources, which are poor.

Within Southeast Asia, the differences would appear to be significant, although future discoveries may alter the present picture. Taking the region as a whole, Laos and North Vietnam would appear to fall at the lowest end of the scale, Indonesia and Malaysia at the top, with the other countries in the intermediate range. In general, Southeast Asia has good growth potential, requiring only peace and political stability, together with sound policies. In this, it differs greatly from South Asia. But this is a general picture. Portions are poor and, unless external aid can be obtained (or the region of control expanded), likely to remain so.

Thus, the cooperation of equals is not made easy. An indigenous program of aid, sponsored by the wealthy and directed toward the poor, could be meaningful, at least in theory. In addition to current political difficulties, however, there also exist the strong priorities within even the "wealthy" states to use internal resources to accelerate their own development and alleviate the living conditions of their poverty-ridden people. Meanwhile, any successful cartel-type price-fixing for minerals and commercial crops will necessitate cooperation outside the region, for Southeast Asia does not hold a monopoly or near-monopoly on the production of any single item. Despite OPEC achievements in this regard, it remains an enormously difficult task.

A final problem lies in the incomplete stage in which the nation-building process is to be found at this point, hence, the limited, inward-looking tendencies that dominate the region, and the high priorities that must be given to domestic problems. If the achievement of nationhood lies in the emergence of a people integrated around common political values and allegiances, there are few if any Southeast Asian nations. Most states here are composed of a mosaic of peoples, product of successive migrations from the north, the infusion of Chinese and Indian laborers during the colonial era, and of boundaries drawn by European rulers. Ethnic animosities are omnipresent, and little progress is being made in resolving them—far less, for example, than in the United States. This problem is particularly explosive in Malaysia and Indonesia, where the powerful role of the Chinese in commerce and finance is deeply resented, and easily exploited, with periodic outbursts of racial violence.

The "backward" minorites, however, fare even worse than the affluent ones. Throughout Southeast Asia, discrimination against the hill peoples, and those living in more remote regions not a part of the dominant cultural group, is extensive. Frequently, these people are also members of a religious minority—Christian or Moslem. Their resentment against the treatment accorded them periodically breaks out in open rebellion or collaboration with a foreign party, as has happened in Burma, Thailand, Laos, South Vietnam, the Philippines, and Indonesia.

Under these conditions, it is not surprising that the political horizons of most of the people are exceedingly limited, and even the national leaders view events through narrow prisms. Such regional or international ties as are forged, indeed, may challenge "national interest," such as the Philippine Islamic rebels' identification with Libya's Khadaffi, the affinity of certain Thai Meo with their brethren in the Pathet Lao, the proclivity of some tribals in north Burma toward the Chinese-sponsored White Flag Communists, or the Maoist commitments of Chinese-led Communist movements in Malaysia and Singapore. Fragmented states do not make good material for regional solidarity.

To recite these obstacles is not to write off Southeast Asian regionalism completely. Bilateral and multilateral interaction within the region will grow. The widely shared support for an eventual neutralization of this region and the general movement toward equidistance in relations with the major external powers, even though these goals cannot be fully realized under present conditions, will abet the trend. And Indonesia will play a considerable role, as befits its size and strength.

Southeast Asia, however, can be neither self-sufficient nor unified. Some involvement of the major outside societies is both inevitable and essential, either economically or politically. As we have noted, moreover, the various states of this region must respond to very different pressures and opportunities, and this fact will be reflected in their domestic and foreign policies.

Thus, Indonesia will not play the same role in Southeast Asia that India is now playing in South Asia. It will be the paramount but not the dominant state in the region, and its regional commitments will be considerably more limited than those of New Delhi. Correspondingly, it will devote greater attention to domestic concerns, as directed by the shift from Sukarnoism to Suhartoism. In sum, in all probability, the future lies in a combination of the second and third alternatives set forth here.

Despite Indonesia's decided tilt toward the advanced democratic nations after 1965, certain values and tendencies derivative from the past have remained. Thus, Foreign Minister Adam Malik could assert on more than one occasion that his nation remained committed to *Panjasila*, the harmonization of nationalism, religion, and socialism, even though recent policies have moved in a different direction. Throughout the post-Sukarno period, moreover, Indonesian spokesmen have insisted that nonalignment remains a goal, with the acceptance of peaceful coexistence as a cardinal principle of Indonesian foreign policy. And as we have noted, by the mid-1970s, the shift was toward a more strongly Indonesia-centered nationalist stance. Quite possibly, events in Indochina and trends in American foreign policy will accelerate that shift.

Relations with the Communist States

Indonesia's position in the international arena has thus been a relatively complex one. Repeatedly, Jakarta officials have insisted that their domestic anti-Communist policies need not constitute a barrier against friendly international relations with Communist states. To a limited extent, this thesis has been translated into positive policy. Strengthened relations with Eastern Europe have been actively sought—reflective of Indonesia's old associations with the "nonaligned world." The ties earlier established with North Vietnam and North Korea have been retained, although at a very subdued level. Toward the large Communist states, however, Jakarta has shown a considerable caution, especially toward the People's Republic of China.

Indonesia has clearly been in no hurry to reestablish normal relations with China, despite its assurances that this will come "at the proper time." The reasons relate primarily to recent history and to certain domestic concerns. Although the precise facts remain controversial, Peking's involvement in the abortive leftist coup of 1965 is regarded as proved by Indonesia's current leaders. Some facts do appear to have been established: Chinese arms shipments so that the Sukarno government could establish a people's militia in contradistinction to the regular armed forces; the important role of Chinese doctors in diagnosing Sukarno's health as deteriorating, thus setting the stage for accelerated political maneuvering; and the close relation that had been established between the CCP and the PKI (Communist Party of Indonesia) during this period, as Aidit, the PKI leader, veered from Khrushchev to Mao.

Thus, Jakarta sees Peking as quite capable of intervening in its internal affairs, and prepared to do so. This feeling is strengthened by the continued residence in Peking of a few high-ranking Indonesian Communists, stranded there after the 1965 failure. These individuals, pursuing an orthodox Maoist line, attack the Indonesian government regularly and seek to rally the Indonesian people around PKI banners. There is no indication that they have made any serious inroads or, indeed, that they can even reach Indonesia with their propaganda at this point. Under conditions of normal Sino-Indonesian relations, however, access might become easier.

Of at least equal importance is the fact that Indonesian

leaders have a strong fear—justified or otherwise—that their own Chinese community might be powerfully affected by the reestablishment of official ties with Peking. They know that the Chinese community has many legitimate grievances and that it still constitutes a very significant element within Indonesian society, given its role in commerce and finance. The recent anti-Chinese riots in Bandung and Jakarta, while illustrative of the degree to which the Chinese can serve as scapegoats in the presence of other ills, also signals the unbridged gap that continues to separate Indonesians and Chinese in this nation. The government is not prepared at present to cope with the possibility that an official PRC presence in Indonesia might lend itself to the increased politicization of its Chinese community.

No such problem complicates Indonesian-Soviet relations. Here too, however, the watchword is caution. Relations are "normal" but circumspect. As a part of its general efforts to strengthen its presence in Southeast Asia, the USSR has shown an interest in improving its position in Indonesia despite the vigorously anti-Communist character of Jakarta's government. Following the successful debt-rescheduling agreement reached with Western and Japanese creditors, the Suharto regime achieved a similar agreement with the Soviet Union. The Russians also offered to increase trade and cultural relations, and to supply badly needed spare parts for the Soviet-derived Indonesian navy and air force.

A comprehensive trade agreement, however, has been delayed, and Indonesia has chosen to turn mainly to non-Communist states, primarily the United States, in seeking the modernization of its armed forces. Meanwhile, Soviet projects commenced earlier remain generally suspended despite Russian offers of renewed help. Cultural relations also have been minimal.

What are the problems? In the purely economic realm, Indonesian leaders have never been happy with the quality of

Soviet products, compared with those of the West and Japan. Political considerations also loom large. Like China, the Soviet Union is regarded as a state consorting with Indonesian Communists and basically hostile to the current leadership. A few Indonesian Communists live in Moscow as exiles, issuing polemical attacks against the Jakarta government periodically. Official Soviet organs echo their criticisms on occasion, albeit at a somewhat lower decibel count. And another issue has presented itself. The powerful Indonesian Moslem community has not been happy with the treatment of Islamic adherents in the Soviet Union, and this constitutes an additional brake on cultural-political relations.

There are more general considerations. Jakarta senses that the Soviet Union has been gearing up for political battle with Peking throughout Southeast Asia, hence, seeking everywhere to increase its presence in this region. The Indonesians naturally want to avoid any involvement in the Sino-Soviet confrontation, and this makes them leery of an expanded Indonesian-Soviet relationship at this point. They are also concerned, it might be noted, with the possibilities of a heightened Soviet-American rivalry in the Indian Ocean, and they have not been pleased with the insistence by both of the superpowers that the Malacca Straits must be considered international waters.

Initially, the Indonesians flatly rejected Brezhnev's proposal for a new collective security system for Asia, calling it vague and without substance. Later, the proposal was treated more cautiously, indicating an Indonesian desire to avoid taking an abrasive position that might antagonize Moscow. The concept was now interpreted as support for neutralization, a laudable goal.

The inhibitions on close Indonesian-Soviet relations are substantial, and they will remain so. Under present conditions, Jakarta has little need for Soviet aid, or even trade. The Indonesians do not want to pursue policies that might produce complications with Peking beyond those already existing, and they also remain suspicious of long-range Soviet motives. At the same time, however, some Soviet presence is regarded as desirable, a symbol of nonalignment and counterpoint to the closer ties that have been forged with certain other major societies.

Relations with the Industrial Societies

In the past decade, Indonesia's relations with the advanced industrial states, and notably with the United States and Japan, have been far more intimate than those with the leading Communist nations. Will this continue? Problems have emerged, particularly with Japan. In the initial stages of the new era, when Jakarta was soliciting aid and investment from any quarter, private Japanese investors flooded the country. Many represented medium-scale concerns without long established roots, anxious to make quick profits. Sometimes, the Indonesians got bad bargains. Bribery became commonplace in connection with these deals, large and small. The Japanese in residence, moreover, exhibited an exclusiveness that brought the war years back to many an Indonesian mind.

Thus, an anti-Japanese sentiment that had its counterpart in various other Southeast Asian states quickly emerged. As in the case of anti-Chinese sentiment, the resentment against the Japanese masked other grievances, many of them actually directed against the Indonesian government. There can be no doubt, however, of the intensity of the feelings. Prominent critics were even to assert that the Japanese were the major contributors to the corruption affecting the upper echelons of Indonesian officialdom. Unfair or not, this accusation found ready acceptance among the articulate elements of the public.

The Japanese government is well aware of the problems that have been generated. Recently, it has sought to provide additional "guidance" to Japanese firms doing business in the region and to pursue complaints lodged against its nationals. The new Japan Foundation, a government-supported body, is directing sizable funds toward an expansion of education and cultural relations between Japan and Southeast Asia, with Indonesia receiving considerable attention.

These actions will not remove all of the problems. There is good reason to believe, however, that Japan will continue to represent a vital factor in the Indonesian modernization program. Japan will remain a prime market for Indonesian exports. Japanese technology will also be of critical importance, given the plans for the future. The Japanese may not be loved, at least for the near future, but they represent no military or political threat, and they have a utility for the Indonesians which few societies can currently match.

Indonesian relations with the United States have been closer than with any other major power since the events of 1965. This is understandable, given the politics and policies of the new Jakarta government. The United States could and did take the lead in helping Indonesia begin its climb out of the economic morass bequeathed by the Sukarno years. It also rendered early support in the modernization of the armed forces, after the abrupt turn away from the Communist states. Yet the American profile was kept reasonably low, with Washington anxious to avoid the appearance—and responsibilities—of extensive involvement.

The issues that have developed in connection with Jakarta-Washington relations fall into two categories which on closer examination turn out to be opposite sides of the same coin. As noted earlier, Indonesia requires a low-risk, low-cost foreign policy if present goals are to be achieved. It therefore wants to avoid finding itself in the path of any major power confrontation. Thus, the possibility of a growing U.S.-Soviet presence in neighboring waters concerns a number of Indonesians, as does the attitude of these powers regarding the Malacca Straits. Jakarta is sincere in hoping that eventually Southeast Asia can be neutralized in such a fashion as to preclude the involvement of any big power in the region.

On the other hand, the most immediate concern is not an

overweaning American presence but, on the contrary, an inability or unwillingness on the part of the United States to maintain its Asian commitments and, consequently, a substantial change in the Pacific-Asian power balance. In sum, it is the credibility, not the threat of the United States that is at stake with the men who influence Indonesian foreign policy. Can American commitments be trusted? Or will accommodation to a substantially altered political-military situation in the area as a whole be required?

Specific issues exist on which the Indonesians take positions different from those of the United States, notably on the question of the Arab-Israeli dispute and the related energy crisis. Under certain circumstances, these could become more serious problems. On the whole, however, the political differences between Jakarta and Washington are not great, and the broad interests of both countries coincide at this point. The general course of American foreign policy in the Pacific-Asian area, however, will be watched carefully in Indonesia for signs indicating the extent of the swing toward isolationism.

Meanwhile, Indonesia has shown an interest in keeping its relations with one neighboring state, Australia, moving in a positive fashion. Potentially, this can be a more meaningful relation than it has been in the past, although neither in security nor economic terms can Australia play the role of a major society. For this reason among others, the Jakarta government has shown a limited interest in the proposal of Prime Minister Gough Whitlam for a more intimate relationship.

In Summary

Indonesian foreign policy is the product of a number of factors, historical and contemporary. It is influenced by geopolitical considerations and by legacies of the colonial and Sukarno periods. Today, however, it stems centrally from the priorities which the Suharto government has set for itself and from Jakarta's perceptions of international trends. The Indonesians see, or hope they see, in this era a growing detente among the major powers and the continued trend toward multipolarism. Ideology will play an increasingly limited role in foreign affairs, they believe, and the threat of a war between major powers will also steadily decline.

Events dictate an ultimate equilibrium involving the United States, USSR, PRC, and Japan in Indonesian eyes—with their chief concern the fear that the United States may not play its full part in securing this development. Hopefully, equilibrium will lead to that prime objective: the neutralization of Southeast Asia, namely, the emergence of conditions guaranteeing that no single external force will seek to establish its hegemony or overweening influence in this region. In the long run, the Indonesians clearly fear China most, although the possibility of an economic hegemony by Japan has been a matter of considerable recent concern.

Indonesia does not see alliance as a method of meeting these challenges, nor is it likely to do so except in the direst extremity. It recognizes that alliances of the type initiated shortly after World War II are no longer feasible. Nor has it ever been attuned to such relations. Nonalignment will continue to be the slogan; equidistance, the ultimate goal.

In Southeast Asia, "neutralized" or otherwise, Indonesia can be expected to play a steadily more important role. Its natural wealth and substantial power underwrite such a course. For reasons already outlined, however, this is not likely to be the same role as that played by India in South Asia, at least not over the region as a whole. Nonetheless, by the 1980s if not before, Indonesia will have become a highly significant regional power. Its influence on the global scene will remain quite limited—by choice. For some decades, the priorities must be on domestic issues—this lesson from the past is not likely to be lost on the next several generations of Indonesian leaders.

Chapter 6

The USSR:
A Rising Asian Power

A few years ago, one of the hotly debated issues at Afro-Asian-Latin American conferences was "Is the Soviet Union an Asian State?" The question was never resolved, at least to the satisfaction of all concerned.

The Soviet Union is not an Asian state in the conventional sense. The Asian components of its population, although spread out over a very considerable land area, are a decided minority in total numbers and play a limited political role. Like other Soviet citizens, they have benefited from increased educational opportunities in recent decades, and a number of Asian technicians, scientists, and professionals have emerged. To date, however, the political and economic gravitation of the USSR has been strongly to the west, to the region known as European Russia.

Almost certainly, this will be less true within a few decades. This is not to suggest a resurgence of Asian power in Central Asia. The days of Genghis Khan and his successors are over. Soviet citizens of Asian origin will show an increase in proportionate numbers, as their birth rate is considerably higher than that of European Russians. Possibly, a few will emerge into nationally prominent political roles, although that is far from certain. Soviet politics will continue to be dominated by European Russians, and Moscow will remain very much the political heartland. We can expect a great eastward movement, however, one progressively affecting the character of both politics and economics in this complex society.

Central Asia and Siberia constitute one of the largest underdeveloped regions of the world. Siberia in particular is an area rich in natural resources and industrial potential. The severity of climate and vastness of distances have inhibited migrations from the west, and they will continue to pose obstacles. At this point, nevertheless, nothing can stop Siberian development from receiving a very high priority, despite the major difficulties posed in achieving goals.

The acute Soviet interest in this project is not related to economics alone. Security considerations now assume equal importance. As noted earlier, like all of the major powers of this era, the Russians created their empire from within, expanding outward at various stages to form a contiguous whole and in the process encompassing diverse peoples and lands. Over some of this territory, the Russian hold was still precarious at the time of the Bolshevik Revolution. To guarantee the right of secession from the Soviet Union, as was done, might have been hazardous if full freedom to exercise that right had been allowed.

Ethnic relations throughout the Soviet Union remain complex, and clearly Central Asia is no exception. As was mentioned earlier, the problems are made vastly more sensitive as a result of the Sino-Soviet cleavage. On both sides of the border, campaigns have been periodically waged against the rival government with allegations of discrimination and suppression of minorities. For many decades, European Russian immigrants have been arriving in such regions as Uzbekistan and Kazakhistan as settlers in "frontier" regions. More recently, the Chinese have actively cultivated a similar program, as was noted earlier, partly to people their side of the border with a much stronger Han population.

In Siberia, the ethnic issue is generally less prominent. Here, an ethnic group that represented potential problems, the Koreans, was moved to the Central Asian region much earlier, and most others are small in numbers. All along their 4,800-mile frontier with the Chinese, however, the Russians are extremely conscious of facing a huge population, and one more nationalist than at any point in China's past. Historic fears are thus reinforced. The current Asian policies of the Soviet Union stem in very considerable measure from "the China problem," although a number of other factors are involved. Prior to examining these policies, let us touch briefly on those trends in the Soviet domestic scene that bear directly on foreign policy considerations.

Internal Politics

On the surface at least, the Soviet Union appears to be more stable politically than most if not all of the societies with which we have dealt. Its authoritarian system has been modified but not fundamentally altered by post-Stalin developments. The citizen still has very limited political rights, and the state is still omnipresent. Political institutions, however, have acquired a strength lacking at this point in China, and the role of personalities seems less prominent. There was no Cultural Revolution in Moscow, nor can the Soviet Union at this stage of its evolution have a Mao Tse-tung.

Some would assert, indeed, that constitutionalism of a type is emerging in this, the oldest Communist state, in the form of a regularization of procedures, including that of succession. This thesis may soon receive its test, at the time of Brezhnev's retirement or removal. Clearly, the secretary general of the Communist Party remains the most important single official by a considerable measure, even if he is by no means absolute in his authority. It would also appear that the Communist Party enjoys a degree of power not duplicated by the governing forces in open or quasi-open societies. Nor is the Party subject at this point to the same external and internal challenges facing the Communist Party of China. Factionalism unquestionably exists, as do policy differences. Under some circumstances, these—especially the latter—might become serious. But the uncertainties that surround the late Maoist era in China seem less pronounced in the USSR today.

Perhaps this is an erroneous conclusion. At a more fundamental level, one can argue that the Soviet Union is becoming increasingly susceptible to new pressures and problems, many of them potentially divisive. Compared with the past, the USSR is a relatively porous society at present, receiving external stimuli at an accelerating rate. Tens of thousands of visitors are pouring into the country, coming from many parts of the world, but especially from the more advanced, industrial West. In European Russia, a variety of information and entertainment via radio is available from Western sources, with most jamming having ceased. On a much more modest scale, officially endorsed cultural exchanges have expanded.

Alongside these developments, Soviet living standards have been rising. The average Russian is far from having attained the level of his counterpart in Western Europe (or in many parts of Eastern Europe), but improvements have taken place in the past decade. As might be expected, his appetite has been whetted for greater and faster improvements. The government now feels consumer pressures gradually intensifying and taking many forms. They are particularly acute at "middle"- and "upper"-class levels within the bureaucratic and professional segments of the society. Undoubtedly, the Party can resist these pressures when it decides that this is necessary from the standpoint of national interest. There are other, more powerful interest groups such as the military. Here, an equilibrium seems to have been achieved, with the military forces receiving approximately what they desire in exchange for rendering full loyalty to the Party. Nevertheless, a consciousness of public opinion is growing within the Soviet official community, and it is not ignored in decision-making.

Détente and Its Challenges

The future may well hold the prospect of an increase in countervailing pressures because of the very nature of Soviet society. To an extraordinary extent, Russia exhibits a dual character: one part superpower, one part backward society. If this gap is long continued, it could endanger internal cohesion. But it can be closed rapidly only if external technology and economic assistance are obtained. One of the principal motives behind détente has lain here. The Soviet Union needs at least two decades of peace and rapid development if it is to catch up with the advanced nations, a pledge long made to the Russian people.

Détente policies, however, have produced various reservations and doubts. Two powerful currents run in this society. One is the desire to turn outward once again, a sentiment that has periodically manifested itself throughout modern Russian history. The other is the urge toward isolation, a mood that betokens a xenophobic, traditionalist element of Russian culture, one easily combined with a new nationalism to produce hostility and suspicion toward the external world. These two forces remain in powerful conflict, in individuals, groups, and the society as a whole.

The practical question thus turns on what Soviet leaders are willing to give in the détente process, and what they expect to receive. At this point, they have signaled clearly that they will not accept what they regard as interference in their internal affairs. The debate over accepting the Jackson amendment must have been serious, and may have hurt certain leaders, including Brezhnev. Its rejection appears to set one type of limit. What of others? Critical questions relating to SALT II and a host of other issues, including the limits that might be put on external military aid in global trouble spots, remain to be resolved.

Détente in any case is a process, not a single act. In its

origins, it related primarily to Europe and the broadest trends with respect to American-Soviet relations. The initial concessions were made primarily by the United States, although they had been en route for a long time. Two were crucial: an acceptance of the status quo in Europe as established by World War II, and acceptance also of the principle of military parity between the United States and the USSR. From the beginning, it has been clear that significant concessions from the Soviet Union would be necessary if the détente process were to be kept dynamic and progressive. Soviet attitudes in turn were certain to be connected with a host of interrelated considerations: the decisions reached concerning domestic policies; trends in Sino-Soviet relations; developments in various global crisis zones in which the USSR had a stake; and an appraisal of the situation in Western Europe and in the United States.

In the recent past, the signs have been mixed, but on balance not overly encouraging—at least for the short run. As important as any single factor has been the Soviet perception of the United States, specifically, its problems and its capacities. The American economic crisis, the trend toward isolationism following Vietnam, and the malaise in American politics after Watergate combine to raise grave questions in Moscow as elsewhere about American credibility as a world force. Individual leaders like Brezhnev may well be strongly committed to détente, but what if, in the midst of declining American credibility and the emergence of new crises, targets of opportunity—perhaps sources *demanding* assistance—are presented? Might such developments affect the Soviet internal political balance and decision-making process? Herein lie the gravest issues.

Many of the same factors may influence Soviet appraisals of the European scene. Understandably, Western Europe is seen as currently in deep trouble economically and politically. Increasingly separated from the United States on a series of issues, the Western European states also seem incapable of finding political unity within their own community. On the contrary, nationalism is everywhere manifesting itself on the European continent. Thus, there is a good chance that the USSR can deal with these states individually, avoiding the problem of a solid Western European bloc. Finally, NATO has never seemed less capable of playing the role assigned it, that of upholding the military equilibrium in this region. In this setting, portions of southern Europe now seem promising new arenas for Soviet influence.

Meanwhile, Moscow can afford to be more relaxed with respect to the China problem, at least for the time being. Although there are as yet no signs that Peking is prepared to reach a comprehensive settlement with the Soviet Union, Chinese internal conditions seem sufficiently fragile at this point to minimize threats from this quarter. And perhaps they augur prospects for future improvements in Sino-Soviet relations.

None of these factors is conducive to promoting Soviet flexibility at this stage in the détente process, despite indications that current Russian policy remains firmly wedded to pursuit of an understanding with the United States. The international situation could change once again. And as we have indicated earlier, there are some impressive factors constituting pressures in an opposite direction, not the least of which is the evolution of Soviet society itself. Uncertainty, however, is the hallmark of the present.

Basic Goals

In this complex, transitional setting, what are the broad trends and prospects with respect to the Pacific-Asian policies of this major Communist state? Let us commence with the most basic considerations influencing these policies. Now and for the foreseeable future, Russian leaders will regard their nation as a Eurasian state, inextricably involved in the affairs of both of the great continents across which the USSR serves as bridge. The only parallel is with the United States, which during the twentieth century came to recognize itself as both an Atlantic and Pacific power. In modern times, Russia's preoccupation has normally been with its western flank, and for good reason. Power lay to the west, and twice in this century Russia found itself under savage attack from German invaders. Security on this front became an obsession, and it formed almost the sole basis for the post-1945 policies of the USSR in Europe. In turn, these policies, so distasteful—and so dangerous—to the West, provided the basis for Western unity in the era after the war.

Today, Russia's security on its western flank is more effectively guaranteed than at any time in its history. An extensive and reasonably stable buffer-state system has been created, composed primarily of small Communist nations that are, in one sense or another, client states despite nationalist aspirations. Certain of these states have caused the Russians much trouble, and in general terms the trends are toward increased diversity and some relaxation of Soviet controls, voluntarily or involuntarily. In considerable measure, however, these trends are made possible by the development, through trial and error, of a commonly understood, clearly defined perimeter of political action on the part of the buffer states, both in domestic and foreign affairs.

Beyond its buffer states, the Soviet Union looks at present to a Western Europe in the throes of the most severe crisis since the 1930s, as just noted. It is by no means inconceivable that Communism might score a victory in such a state as Italy via legal, parliamentary means. Portugal and Spain also represent major political question marks for the future. In any case, Europe has neither the will nor the way to challenge the Soviet Union. In its multiple weaknesses, it might eventually become the source of renewed problems, as in the Fascist period.

Indeed, leftist regimes, even Communist ones, might ultimately pose complex new difficulties for Moscow. But such a challenge is not on the horizon at present. Meanwhile, the United States has accepted the status quo and signaled the possibility of its retreat from the European theatre. Even the Soviet proposal for a Europewide collective security program, ridiculed when it was first introduced nearly two decades ago, has been given a formal hearing.

From a Russian perspective, the situation on its eastern flank is not as satisfactory. Here, no buffer-state system exists, or can exist, to separate the USSR from China, that massive and unpredictable giant now emerging. At every level of Soviet society, an uneasiness if not outright fear persists that whatever the gains of the moment, the problems of coexistence with China will represent the gravest single problem to be faced over the next century. In confronting this problem, moreover, few ready allies are at hand, at least in Asia. The small Communist states of the region, excepting Mongolia, have opted officially for neutralism, although in the case of North Korea the proclivities are toward Peking. Little more can be expected from the small non-Communist Asian states. Ties with Japan remain strained and incomplete. The alliance with India may be of greater cost on balance than of benefit.

In sum, the general situation in Asia at present is at once more fluid and less susceptible to Soviet manipulation than has been the case in recent decades in Europe. Moreover, in Asia, despite its physical presence, the Soviet Union remains half-foreign and forcibly reminded of its still incomplete struggles to create of itself a multiethnic nation. Not surprisingly, confrontations in Asia evoke strong racial feelings and the clash of strikingly different cultures.

All of these circumstances argue powerfully that in the coming decades the USSR will find itself increasingly drawn to the development of its Asian sector, and placing a much higher priority on Pacific-Asian policies than during the decades immediately after 1945. This will not be accomplished easily. Many factors, including the emphasis to be given already developed industrial regions, thrust in a contrary direction. Nonetheless, the broad trend just described will prevail.

Despite the apparent differences, the Soviets are approaching Asia in a manner similar to that used in Europe. First, they are displaying their general commitment to the status quo rather than to change, although they would presumably not be adverse to alterations advancing Russian interests. It is interesting to note that the Soviet Union has truly intimate relations with no revolutionary movement or Communist Party in Asia today, with the exception of the Communist Party of India, itself a member of the Indian establishment. Even with North Vietnam, Russian relations are correct and "friendly" but not those of bosom allies, despite the extensive Soviet assistance being given. Meanwhile, the Russians have increasingly sought to advance their position by establishing normal relations with most non-Communist states of the area, including some pursuing vigorous anti-Communist domestic policies. Now that the Vietnam War has ended favorably for them, there is no indication that the Russians of their own volition would change a single boundary in Asia, including those of the two Koreas and China/Taiwan.

Russia's broad formula for Asia, moreover, that of an areawide collective security program, bears a marked resemblance to the prosposal forwarded with respect to Europe. Since Brezhnev first advanced this idea in 1969, it has been kept vague and undefined, deliberately so, say the Russians, to avoid the charge that they are seeking to impose their own plan on other peoples. As in the case of Europe, the Soviets have merely asked for an endorsement in principle, and then the hammering out of the specifics at an all-Asian conference. Asian support for this idea has been slow and begrudging, although a number of countries have now made polite remarks artfully phrased so as to avoid the appearance of being totally negative. The general fear is that the real Soviet purpose is to enlist allies in the containment of China, and that by supporting this Moscow-sponsored scheme a state will have taken sides overtly in the Sino-Soviet dispute. Peking's vigorous attacks on the proposal underwrite this fear. Nor is the concept regarded as realistic, given the present conditions prevailing in the Pacific-Asian region. Nevertheless, as in the case of the European effort—which produced some results only after a fifteen-year campaign—the Russians can be expected to persevere in this effort.

Meanwhile, there can be little doubt that the USSR will steadily augment its military power in the Asian theatre. Increases will take a number of forms: expanded installations and facilities in Siberia, including the Pacific coastal regions; increases in naval units assigned to both the Pacific and Indian oceans; and the movement of new, sophisticated equipment to Russia's eastern flank—especially that portion fronting China—as it becomes available. Despite China's extensive military efforts of recent years, the gap between the military capacities of the PRC and the USSR may still be widening, as the Russians intend the case to be. Moscow sees only one hope of bringing Peking to reason: the Chinese must be presented with overwhelming force as the alternative to a "reasonable settlement" of the dispute.

As the Soviet Union has a fairly extensive involvement in every part of Asia, let us examine Russian policies as they apply to each region, with special attention given their implications for major power relations. It is appropriate to commence with the Continental Center, as a discussion of general military policies has naturally brought us to that point and in any case Sino-Soviet relations lie at the heart of Moscow's general Asian policies.

Sino-Soviet Relations—A Soviet Perspective

In our earlier analysis of Sino-Soviet relations, it will be recalled, we set forth the future alternatives and advanced the reasons why neither a major war nor a reestablishment of the old alliance seems likely. Let us now examine the problem from a Soviet perspective. The Russian view is that the Soviet Union is the victim of gross ingratitude, having made a major contribution to Chinese Communist victory via policies pursued in Manchuria after World War II and having given massive assistance to the fledgling PRC after 1949 despite the grievous war damage suffered by the USSR.

Soviet spokesmen insist that the critical problems did not emerge until 1958, and came in connection with the second Taiwan Straits crisis. Mao, according to their account, was prepared to risk nuclear war with the United States at this point, and actually appeared to relish the prospect of a Soviet-American conflict. From the Russian refusal to abandon the hope for détente, assert Soviet authorities, all subsequent Sino-Soviet difficulties ensued.

It may not have been that simple, nor on the basis of data presently available can we attest to the accuracy of this account. It does signal, however, the irrefutable fact that differences over how to handle the United States constituted one of the key issues that precipitated the Sino-Soviet conflict. Also implicit in the Russian version of recent history is the thesis that Mao Tse-tung himself is primarily responsible for the quarrel with Moscow, and that it is he who has led China down a false path both with respect to domestic and foreign policy. Mao is viewed as a peasant and a poet, but not a philosopher and certainly not a Marxist-Leninist—as a man who out of a Sinocentric nationalism betrayed the cause of international socialism for the greater glory of China. (As we have indicated, the attacks on the "Khrushchev-Brezhnev clique" emanating from Chinese quarters have not been less severe.)

In this fashion, each side has been drawn inextricably into the internal politics of the other. Here, there can be no real parallel with Soviet-American or Sino-American relations. The geographic proximity of the two contending parties, moreover, exacerbates the problem. The repercussions in Soviet politics would seem to have been limited thus far, with the greater strains on the Chinese scene. At any rate, Mao has thunderously accused his leading opponents of following the Soviet revisionist line, and even of being traitors prepared to sell out Chinese sovereignty in exchange for vassalage under the new Russian czars. The Russians, however, insist that individuals like Liu Shao-ch'i and Lin Piao were not "pro-Russian" as the Maoists assert, but merely men courageous enough to oppose Mao's foolish and erroneous policies.

Officially, like the Chinese, the Russians proclaim that when the people have gotten rid of the current regime, true socialism can be reestablished and then Sino-Soviet relations can be put on its proper course. Is the Soviet Union prepared, under certain conditions, to "aid" the Chinese people in reestablishing "true socialism"? As noted earlier, in recent years, this has been the primary concern of the present Peking leaders. A host of circumstances can be envisaged in which the Soviet Union might lend one form of support or another to some dissident group or rival faction in the course of a post-Mao struggle for power, either at a regional or at a central level. Certainly, such a course of action promises more and at vastly less cost than a general Soviet military strike.

Naturally, the Russians deny any intention of interfering in the internal affairs of their neighbor. Do they think that Mao will be "dethroned" ideologically and politically from within China after his death? Some Soviet analysts assert that in the initial post-Mao period, the thrust will be toward the "leftists" and not propitious for an improvement in Sino-Soviet relations, but that this period will be quickly followed by a restoration of "correct Marxist-Leninists" to authority, permitting a shift to occur. Even when the latter conditions prevail, however, these analysts insist that there will be no return to 1950. Sino-Soviet relations will resemble instead those currently prevailing between Russia and Yugoslavia. Moreover, China will not be allowed to play off the Soviet Union and the United States against each other, assert these authorities.

In truth, deep uncertainty would appear to characterize Russian attitudes about the future of China at this point, a position shared by most other observers, probably including the Chinese. Consequently, until the outlines of the post-Mao era become clearer, the Soviet Union is not likely to deviate greatly from the policies already in effect. At root, as we have seen, those policies revolve around a very big stick and a substantial carrot. Hundreds of thousands of Soviet troops remain on the border, together with the most sophisticated equipment available. Although some alterations in troop disposition have been made—possibly as signals or tests—the Russians have given no indication that they are prepared for any general withdrawals, at least until a satisfactory settlement of the present boundary issues is achieved. On the contrary, Moscow gives every indication that it regards Soviet power as critical in this situation, and it has not slackened in the slightest its efforts to keep far ahead of the Chinese with respect to military capacity. There are even some indications that by improving the accuracy of their missiles, the Russians represent a graver threat to the Chinese today than when Peking commenced its drive for a meaningful nuclear deterrent.

On the international front, meanwhile, the Soviet effort is directed squarely at the containment and isolation of China. This effort takes various forms. For some years, the Russians have sought to get other Communist parties to join in the condemnation and ostracism of the CCP. Although this drive has not been completely successful, and indeed it is no longer possi-

ble to convene a full-fledged convocation of Communist parties
or discuss the Chinese issue officially, a number of the parties
most closely allied with Moscow have roundly and regularly
criticized Peking.

Coupled with activities at the party level have been those involving state relations. Here, the USSR has endeavored to surround Peking with an arc of alliances, special understandings,
and political-economic ties aimed at severely limiting the
PRC's influence and reach. As will presently be made clear,
Soviet policies toward every nation in Asia have been colored
by this objective. Once again, success has not been complete,
yet the Chinese have been made powerfully cognizant of a rising Soviet presence in Asia, and not merely on the Sino-Soviet
frontiers.

At the same time, the Russians hold open the door to a
possible alleviation of tension and shift in policies. Periodically,
Brezhnev and other high-ranking Soviet officials have
reasserted their interest in reaching an understanding, commencing with state-to-state relations. As the Russians view it,
the initiative here lies wholly with the Chinese. When Peking is
ready, for example, it can easily drop the unacceptable proviso
that the Russians admit that in centuries past they un-
justifiably seized Chinese territories, and then serious negotiations on the very minor adjustments possible can get underway.
Because the Chinese themselves have asserted that the admission itself would suffice, with no demand for restitution to
follow, the Russians understandably regard this position as a
deliberate effort to create a stalemate, one that can and will ultimately be removed.

As can be seen, there is a striking parallel between the
current position of the Soviet Union vis-à-vis the People's
Republic of China and that which the United States occupied a
decade and more ago. Then, it was the United States that
sought to get its allies to condemn Peking, and ostracize it, both
economically and politically. Washington's policies were those

of containment by isolation, coupled with a close-in American military presence that confronted Peking with overwhelming force. But beginning in early 1961, the United States also held out the prospect for an alleviation of tension and a shift in policies, offering Peking a step-by-step movement toward improved relations. The stick-and-carrot approach has rarely been more graphically displayed.

In the case of the dramatic change in Sino-American relations, the prime motive force was Peking's legitimate fear of Soviet power and intentions. If a major change comes about in Sino-Soviet relations in the near future, it will have been produced by Peking's reevaluation of America and the decision that the United States is weak and unreliable. This, far more than any fundamental trust in or respect for the Soviet Union, could induce Peking to reach an accommodation with its powerful near-neighbor.

If some accommodation were reached, what would be the consequences? If the détente were a limited one, improvements in state-to-state relations would be reflected in the economic as well as the political realm. Trade would increase, and some Soviet technical assistance might be resumed—although in these respects, as the case of India shows clearly, there are sizable limits to Soviet capacities at this point. Nor are the Chinese likely to opt for extensive dependence on the Russians, with recent history so vividly in mind. Presumably, public attacks on each other would cease, or be heavily muted, but party conclaves might still be impossible. One area of likely progress would be the reduction of military forces on the border, followed by a possible willingness to enter into multilateral arms control discussions.

Relations might indeed resemble contemporary Soviet-Yugoslav relations in many respects, although the radically different scale (and, hence, concern) marking Sino-Soviet interaction makes any precise parallel dangerous. Even if the détente were limited, it could liberate a great deal of power (and anxiety) for possible application elsewhere. The policies of the small states, Communist as well as non-Communist, on the peripheries of these two massive nations would be made more complex, the opportunities to play off Russia against China less easily exploited. As the intensity of the Sino-Soviet conflict declined, the pressures imposed on certain parties and states to identify themselves with one side might be reduced. On the other hand, at some point, détente might lend itself to the reestablishment of the implicit spheres of influence that characterized Party affairs in the early 1950s, with Europe being essentially the Soviet bailiwick, Asia that of China. Conditions, to be sure, have changed mightily since that period, and hegemony would not be easily imposed.

Even under conditions of limited détente, it is difficult to see how a certain element of "interference" in the internal affairs of each other could be avoided. Granting the decline of ideology, it remains important for Communists to have an official version of truth, a set of cosmic principles serving as a benchmark against which to justify specific policies. Even when one has accepted the right of each party to adjust Marxism-Leninism to suit the special requirements of its society, the issue of heresy still lurks in the background. In this particular case, moreover, that issue becomes more acute because the timing and character of the modernization process differ significantly, and these two parties have already established themselves as rival claimants to the role of ideological leadership. When to this is added the factor of geographic proximity, and the likelihood that for neither nation will the road ahead be smooth, the potentialities for a difficult relation would seem considerable. How could such a relation ever become truly stable? How could a sense of intense competition ever be absent?

State-to-state relations, however, can sometimes bridge great social fault-lines, at least for short periods of time, when national interests appear to dictate such a course. One must never forget that political elites can make decisions based on a sense of immediate interest or need that may be considered tactical and that bear only a limited relation to fundamental sociopolitical proclivities. Once, the Sino-Soviet alliance was regarded as both natural and immutable. Now, it is seen as inconceivable by some observers, with war being declared the inevitable wave of the future. It would be wiser to assume that there is *no* inevitability about the Sino-Soviet relationship except that it will be complex.

Irrespective of precise developments in its relations with China, however, the Soviet Union can be expected to make its part of the Asian Continental Center an area of steadily increased Russian economic, political, and military power. The task of developing and strengthening the Russian empire centers on this region, and it represents the most formidable as well as the most pressing task confronting Moscow at this point in time. The immensely powerful practical arguments favoring détente with the West stem from this fact.

Soviet Interest in Northeast Asia

The thrust of Soviet policies in Northeast Asia is closely related to the same considerations. Moscow intends to make the eastern Siberian region into a source of major economic and military strength. It expects to duplicate the famed trans-Siberian railway, expand the region's seaport and naval yard facilities manyfold, modernize airfields and develop new ones, and exploit Siberia's natural resources on a much more comprehensive basis. Most of Siberia is truly a frontier region at present, with only a few modern industrial enclaves. The future lies here. Considerably before the end of the twentieth century, Russia will have made major strides in becoming the *Asian* power she claims to be.

In this, there is both promise and problem for the Japanese. On the surface, it would appear that Soviet plans implicitly place a very high premium on Japanese assistance. No nation in the world is better equipped to render effective aid to this audacious modernization venture. As has been indicated, however, Soviet-Japanese relations continue to be plagued by a series of unresolved issues. The Soviet economic system itself poses certain basic limits on cooperative ventures with the private sector of a foreign state. Time and experience may reduce those limits, but it will not be easy. An extensive and truly dynamic interaction might threaten a subversion of the Communist system. At this point, in any case, the Russians are convinced that the Japanese will need them in the years ahead far more than they will need the Japanese, given the crises in which the advanced industrial world finds itself. Hence, they have not been disposed to offer more generous economic terms recently, or take the promotional initiative.

On their side, as we have seen, the Japanese must remain sensitive to the implications of technical or economic assistance in Siberia for their relations with the United States and the People's Republic of China, and for their own security. Already the Russians use their considerable power in this region to enforce their position on such issues as the northern territories and fisheries. The Soviets occupy the four small islands off the coast of Hokkaido claimed by the Japanese as historically theirs, and show no signs of relinquishing them. Scores of Japanese fishermen remain Soviet prisoners, accused of poaching in Russian waters. Conflicts over a great many additional ocean-bed resources may lie ahead. In point of fact, the Russians and Japanese must live together as closely as the Russians and Chinese, for the bodies of water that once separated them now constitute a common meeting-ground.

Powerful though it is, the Soviet Union should logically find hostile or minimal relations with *both* China and Japan very much contrary to its own best interests and, hence, work to avoid such a situation. There can be little doubt that the idea of Pan-Asianism, particularly the suggestion of a close Sino-Japanese relationship, does disturb Moscow. The Russians were quick to indicate their unhappiness with the swiftness and thoroughness of Japan's normalization of relations with China in the early Tanaka regime. To date, however, the prospect of a Sino-Japanese alliance has not seemed sufficiently great to warrant resolute counteraction. Fundamentally, the Soviet Union believes that Japan's closest ties will continue to be with the United States, and for the time being at least it regards this as desirable. The Russians have no objection to the U.S.-Japan Mutual Security Treaty, primarily because they view it as insurance against Japanese Gaullism.

If the initiatives in Soviet-Chinese relations lie largely with the Chinese, those in Soviet-Japanese relations lie largely with the Russians. If it chose, Moscow could dramatically change the climate—and the course—of its relations with Tokyo. This is not to minimize the deep antagonisms and suspicions with which the history of those relations are beclouded. Throughout this century, Russian-Japanese contacts have been marked by conflict and betrayal, toughness and an absence of understanding. By certain acts and gestures, the Russians could open the curtain on a new, more harmonious era, made all the more spectacular because it would be unexpected. A return of the northern islands, a generous fisheries settlement, the proffering of truly attractive economic terms for Siberian investment, and an expanded cultural relations program all lie within the Soviet capacity, at least theoretically.

There is little prospect that all of these events will come to pass for, as indicated earlier, the Russians see neither the necessity nor the desirability of making so many concessions. In the coming years, nevertheless, the network of Russian-Japanese ties will grow. Recently, for the first time in memory, informal discussions took place between a group of Soviet and Japanese social scientists regarding the future of Asia and their mutual relations. More sessions are contemplated. Japanese enterprises have committed themselves to Siberian ventures, and more will follow. Trade fairs are being held in such cities as

Khabarovsk, and Japanese tourists are going to Siberia in increasing numbers.

The growth of these ties is more likely to be steady than to be spectacular, but a decade hence the cumulative effect could be a major one. The Soviet-Japanese relation will not be that of alliance, but one of mutual convenience, the interaction of opposites, each with an interest in seeing some equilibrium achieved in this strategically vital region without sacrificing progress, each extremely mindful of its relations with the other major societies of the region.

Historically, one of the bones of contention between Russia and Japan has been the Korean peninsula. Korea was the immediate cause of the Russo-Japanese War of 1904–1905, as of the Sino-Japanese War a decade earlier, and it remains a serious problem for all of the major societies of Northeast Asia. A unified non-Communist Korea is acceptable neither to the Soviet Union nor China. A unified Communist Korea would pose a grave threat to Japan and represent a major defeat for the United States. But there is also a very real question as to whether the Russians want a unified Communist Korea—especially one dominated by Kim Il-sŏng.

Since the early 1960s, Soviet-North Korean relations have been generally cool, and on occasion frigid. At one point, in the period around 1964–1965, almost all trade and aid were terminated, and the North Koreans found themselves in difficult straits. Trade, including the supply of military requirements, has resumed, but Kim's relations with the Russians are now those of necessity, not of love. Like the leaders of most small countries, Kim seeks to avoid total dependence on any single external source today. His tactics include those of playing off the Russians and Chinese when this is feasible. In recent years, however, with the exception of a brief interlude during the Chinese Cultural Revolution, the North Korean government has tilted toward Peking. A host of factors explain this—past experiences, cultural affinities, policy requirements, and ideological predelictions. Nor can one omit geography. The North Koreans share common borders with both Communist giants, but they are especially conscious of being very close to China's great industrial cities of the northeast.

As indicated earlier, the Russians have sought to improve their relations with P'yŏngyang recently, taking advantage of some slippage in Chinese credibility in 1973. These efforts do not appear to have succeeded. Most Russians appear reconciled to the probability that on balance, a Communist Korea—whether representing the whole of the peninsula or only one-half of it—is likely to be more closely affiliated with the Chinese than with them, a probability reinforced by Kim Il-sŏng's visit to Peking in the spring of 1975. For this reason, a unified Communist Korea is not necessarily in the Soviet interest; indeed, it might be quite adverse to that interest. Consequently, the USSR has given some indications of being satisfied with the status quo, despite the verbal support given the DPRK in the United Nations and elsewhere. At an earlier point, it signaled quite clearly an interest in establishing cultural relations with South Korea. North Korea's vigorous protests and Peking's promptness in seizing on this issue produced a retreat, but privately a number of Russians admit that "in due time" the logic of events may well dictate an acceptance of two Koreas, de jure as well as de facto.

It may also be doubted that Moscow really wants an American withdrawal from South Korea at this time. Once again, support for this DPRK demand is insistent enough at the U.N. to appear convincing, but any other public stance would be impossible. Yet the Russians would have good reason for concern if a pull-out of all American military forces led to an escalation of military preparations by both Koreas, including the emergence of new weapons. Such a turn of events would not only greatly increase the threat of war on the peninsula, but could easily put additional strains on Soviet-American relations, and possibly on Soviet-Chinese relations as well.

Moscow certainly does not want another Korean War.

Is the Soviet attitude toward the Taiwan issue similar? Here, various complications must be added. On the one hand, the Russians have no desire to see a hostile China acquire a major new base that would enable Peking to dominate the Taiwan Straits and extend its power deeply into the western Pacific. The Soviet Union expects to play its own military role in these areas and is steadily augmenting its Far Eastern forces to that end. Furious at Chinese efforts to cultivate all Soviet opponents, moreover, Moscow spokesmen sometimes infer that Peking cannot take the Soviet position on Taiwan for granted. On the other hand, because the Russians want to play for the next generation of Chinese leaders, or the one after that, they do not want to jeopardize whatever prospects may exist by speaking or acting on this subject prematurely. Taiwan might serve as a subtle bargaining point. Nor has Taipei solicited Soviet support to date. Thus, on this issue, the usual Russian position is a somewhat ambiguous one: "Let the passage of time take care of the matter." But Soviet leaders are definitely unenthusiastic about any change in the status of Taiwan now.

In examining Soviet policies and attitudes with respect to Northeast Asia, therefore, two trends predominate. The power of the Soviet Union, military and economic, is growing and will continue to grow in this region irrespective of other developments. If there is to be a counterbalance, it must be provided by the United States, for no state indigenous to the region, including China, can play that role in the foreseeable future. The second trend is the movement of the Soviet Union toward an acceptance, even an appreciation of the status quo in this region. Most changes that are possible or conceivable would not serve Soviet interests. A Sino-Japanese rapprochement, of course, would be anathema. A Korea unified on any terms would be a problem at a minimum, a threat if the new state were to find its interests best served via interaction with another major society in the region. Nor, as we have seen, could the USSR be currently well served by an amalgamation of Taiwan and China.

Although it does not relish a permanent American military presence in the region, Russia finds such a presence useful at this point in time. An American withdrawal from Japan in the form of the dissolution of the Mutual Security Treaty, for example, would raise uncertainties in Moscow about the future of Japan. The USSR hopes that its relations with the Japanese will improve, and as we have noted, it is directing some efforts toward that end—thus far, insufficient ones. The old suspicions are still alive on both sides, and it is not difficult for the Soviets to conjure up a series of potential horrors relating to Tokyo. On balance, they see the American role as a predictable and restraining one. Similarly, the Russians privately see no advantages in an American withdrawal from South Korea unless and until measures promising greater prospects for peace and stability are inaugurated. Private and public positions, to be sure, do not necessarily coincide on these matters.

Russia and the Pacific

As might be expected, there is a correlation between the Soviet position in Northeast Asia and that in the adjoining region, the Pacific Ocean. The Russians recognize that the Pacific has been essentially an American preserve, in military terms. They do not intend to challenge the United States here directly and immediately. A steady increase in Soviet power in this region, however, is implicit in Russian plans. The large conventional naval force now being developed by the Soviets will not make the Pacific off limits, especially as some of it will be stationed in the Far East.

Will the Russians seek bases from among the newly independent island communities of the Pacific region? This is not inconceivable, but it seems doubtful unless Soviet-American relations take a serious sustained downturn. Such a move

would definitely meet with American resistance, and the opposition also of most other states along the Pacific rim. Russia
can be expected to stake its claims as strongly as possible for its
share of Pacific resources. It must be assumed, moreover, that
in the event of any crisis in East Asia involving force or the
threat of force, whether relating to Russia's relations with
China, the United States, or Japan, the Pacific would become
an active military theatre. One weapon, pioneered by the
United States, could be the blockade, an especially lethal
weapon if applied against Japan.

Southeast Asia

In relative terms, the Soviet Union assigns
Southeast Asia a low priority. Its interest in the region stems
from four objectives. First, the Russians want to offset Chinese
influence in this region to the extent possible, competing for
support among the Communists and acceptance by the important non-Communist states. In this sense, the Russians, like
other major power-holders, have the problem of maintaining
their credibility. Second, the Russians would like to have some
facilities in this region, particularly in the form of coaling and
repair stations, that would lend themselves to a strengthened
Soviet military presence, and at a minimum, the Russians want
access to such strategically important areas as the Malacca
Straits. In these respects, the commitment is one of countering
the American presence in the region, not merely the containment of China. Third, Russia expects to be consulted and involved in any international settlements pertaining to the region,
and its commitments will continue to be sufficient to guarantee
this. Finally, although the economic resources of the region are
not of the same vital importance to the USSR as they are to certain other major societies, the Russians can be expected to pursue an open-door policy with respect to trade and access to raw
materials.

Of these objectives, the first remains the most important. In any policy of containing China, Southeast Asia cannot be omitted. Here, the Russians have certain advantages and disadvantages. Let us first explore their assets. Most of the states in Southeast Asia are concerned about the role of China, in the future if not now. Fear of Chinese hegemony prompts the desire for neutralization as the optimal goal and a political-military equilibrium among the major powers as an acceptable intermediate stage. In both cases, the Russians must be involved, especially in light of the uncertainties currently characterizing American policies.

Communists as well as non-Communists are affected by these considerations. The Vietnamese, for example, have had a history of close interaction with, and strenuous struggle against, the Chinese. At points in their history, they have come under Chinese suzerainty and in many aspects of their culture been deeply influenced by their important neighbors to the north. But at the same time, the quest for independence has been long and sometimes intense. Today, it must involve the existence of a balancing force. For Hanoi, the Sino-Soviet dispute has thus been a benefit as well as a handicap. Not only did the Russians demonstrate conclusively that they—and only they—could furnish the sophisticated equipment so essential after American involvement (and in doing so, changed profoundly the Communist strategy of warfare in this region). They have also made it possible for Hanoi to maintain a "neutrality" between the big Communists and, in some degree, even play off Moscow against Peking.

Hanoi's status remains precarious, and more dependent on Chinese policies than most North Vietnamese might like. The USSR, after all, is a long way from North Vietnam, as the Chinese went to some pains to prove at the height of the Vietnamese War, when they insisted that only Vietnamese could personally accompany Soviet military shipments across Chinese territory and refused to allow the Russians landing privileges for shipments by air. With China on the border, and a waning American presence in the region, North Vietnam is not in the same geopolitical position as Yugoslavia—or even North Korea. Moscow, moreover, made it clear some time ago that there were limits to Soviet aid, although the maintenance of Soviet credibility as an ally far exceeds that of the United States in this area as of 1975.

In addition to the perceived need to sustain their credibility in the face of Peking's challenges, the Russians have viewed the North Vietnamese as buffers to the extension of Chinese influence throughout continental Southeast Asia, and this has formed a part of the rationale for the massive support given them. Indeed, Moscow would be far less concerned than Peking were Hanoi to gain full control over the politics of Indochina, establishing in one form or another a coordinated political system. The only drawback from a Soviet perspective would be the possible repercussions of such a development on Soviet-American relations. As suggested earlier, the Chinese would probably prefer to deal with small, discreet political units in this region, units more easily manipulated or controlled in the event of recalcitrance. In its treatment of Sihanouk, moreover, the Russians have given a clear indication of their distaste for those who turn to the PRC in the effort to find a protector. This lesson has probably not been lost on others—including the Vietnamese and Laotian Communists.

Certainly, the non-Communists of Southeast Asia have no fewer apprehensions about future Chinese policies in this region than some of their Communist brethren. For the most part, therefore, they have not been adverse to a Soviet presence. At this point, the USSR has established normal relations with almost all of the Southeast Asian governments, and in some capitals it has sizable missions. On balance, however, the Russians have not expanded their aid programs (Vietnam excepted), and generally they keep a relatively low posture.

In part, this is because at earlier points the Russians had

their share of failures and embarrassments in connection with more ambitious programs. At one time, the Soviet presence in Burma and Indonesia was sizable, yet in neither case can Russian objectives be said to have been achieved. We have now turned to the debits. As noted earlier in connection with Indonesia, Soviet motives in Southeast Asia are scarcely less suspect than those of Peking as far as non-Communist governments are concerned. Russian behavior in the region, moreover, has not always been conducive to alleviating these suspicions. On occasion, the Russians have sent some of their most capable diplomats to the area, signaling its importance as a listening post or locus for major power discussions. Yet in their dealings with indigenous people, they have often been heavy-handed—and very foreign. Rarely have such relations been marked by understanding, warmth, and intimacy.

Within the Communist movements of Southeast Asia, the Russians face additional problems. In some cases, these movements are dominated or strongly influenced by ethnic Chinese, making the linkage with Peking a natural one. The Communist parties of Malaysia-Singapore and Thailand are outstanding examples. Even where this is not the case, geographic proximity to China and the appeal of Maoism as a tactic of revolution have combined to give the CCP a decided edge in this region, outside of Vietnam and Laos—two very special situations. In some instances, the movement is split, with a pro-Soviet faction continuing to exist, but generally in minority status and representative of the "older" elements. The more dynamic forces appear oriented toward Peking. This is particularly true where, as in the case of the Burmese CP, the Chinese are providing significant material support. In sum, the Russians are doing badly in holding or gaining support from the self-proclaimed Communist revolutionary movements of the region. This is an additional reason for placing primary emphasis on state-to-state relations with existing governments.

In pursuit of their second objective, that of acquiring

military facilities and augmenting their military presence in the region, the Russians have concentrated primarily on the critical area around the Malacca Straits. Overtures have been made to Singapore, a most logical coaling and repair facility. It is well known that Lee Kuan Yew not only regards Peking as a serious threat but that he has also been deeply disturbed by evidence of a general Western withdrawal from Southeast Asia. An identification with Singapore would have a mixed impact on the Malays of this area. On the one hand, it would serve to make them more cognizant of Soviet power, hence, of Soviet interests. On the other hand, antagonism on the part of Malaysia and Indonesia to any such move might well outweigh the caution induced. In any case, the Soviet Union will continue to regard the Malacca Straits as of vital importance in connection with its new drive for naval power in the Pacific-Asian area.

As a result of the events of the past decade, the Soviet Union has demonstrated that it cannot be ignored in any overall agreements—political or military—that may be reached concerning Southeast Asia. Thus, the question, "What does Russia want?" becomes germane. Regarding Indochina, we have already suggested the probabilities. Moscow wanted a Hanoi victory, albeit not at the cost of the détente with the United States. After the January 1973 truce, it may have counseled patience and caution—but it does not appear to have stinted in furnishing military supplies, including tanks, heavy artillery, and missiles. North Vietnam has become heavily dependent on the Soviet Union militarily, having adjusted its tactics and strategy to Russian equipment. Yet there is no evidence that the Russians exercised any restraining influence on Hanoi. Could it have done so? Undoubtedly there are limits on Soviet power here, including the eagerness of the Chinese to drive a wedge between Moscow and Hanoi whenever the opportunity presents itself. It is by no means clear, however, that American policies in Vietnam after the Ceasefire Agreement constituted any pressure on the Soviet Union to exercise influence or that Washington made the issue one of major importance.

When the complex balance-sheet is finally added up, the willingness of the Russians to promote a genuine peace in Vietnam, and one that gave the non-Communists a real chance of survival, appears to have been minimal. After all, even the United States acquiesced in the continued presence of some 165,000 North Vietnamese troops in the South at the time of the 1973 Paris Agreement and in subsequent congressional acts signaled the end of its commitment. Under these circumstances, was it logical to expect Moscow to put serious obstacles in the path of Hanoi's renewed drive to seize the South by force?

In Cambodia, the Soviets may have a stake in the complex divisions that have sprouted up in Khmer Rouge and Sihanoukist ranks. Within the Khmer Communist movement, the dominant external influence is currently that of Peking, offsetting Hanoi's earlier dominance. Russian hopes naturally ride with the Vietnamese. Some of the old Cambodian Marxists, moreover, came to the movement while they were students in France, and their affiliations were at least initially to the USSR via the French Communist Party. The Russians, however, have no love for Sihanouk or for others whom they regard as protégés of Peking, and this fact dictated their refusal to break with the Lon Nol government until a late point, despite the opprobrium heaped upon them. With the Khmer Rouge victory, Moscow favors any solution for Cambodia over that of allowing the Chinese to enjoy predominant influence, but Soviet leverage is limited and may have to be exercised primarily through Vietnam.

In Laos also, the Russians seek to maintain a competition with the Chinese for influence on the Pathet Lao, cognizant of the fact that the leading role here is again being played by Hanoi, and that Soviet presence in the area cannot match that of the Chinese. The current coalition government is probably quite satisfactory to the Russians, as it does not augur undue Chinese influence.

When the knowns and the unknowns are put together, one may surmise that the Russians are playing very much their own game in Indochina, but that they may often be as puzzled as others as to what is in their own best interests. Although Moscow is not totally trusted by Hanoi, the Russians are probably more sympathetic to North Vietnamese objectives than other major powers. Thus, on balance, the situation currently unfolding probably pleases them. At the same time, Moscow must have pondered more than once the consequences of a full-fledged Communist victory in Indochina and a complete American withdrawal. What will be its impact on Soviet responsibilities and the prospect of greater Chinese involvement?

There is a broader question that must also have been considered. Is it in the Soviet interest to favor the neutralization of Southeast Asia? Should the major powers agree that regional security is to be handled wholly by internal arrangements, underwritten by multilateral understandings among the external powers? On balance, the Russians should look favorably on this concept, because, as noted earlier, they cannot afford to place a high priority on this region, given their other, more strategically vital commitments. Their primary concern is that of a rising Chinese influence, and if the strengthening of internal organization of a regional character, coupled with external guarantees, can prevent the hegemony of any single power, Russian interests should be satisfied.

In the years ahead, the Russians may find the markets of this region of increasing interest. A number of minerals and commercial crops are produced in Southeast Asia that could be of service in the next phases of the Soviet industrial revolution. Should the Soviet leaders elect to turn outward appreciably in their efforts to speed up the developmental process, the products of this area would be attractive. The problem, of course, is to find suitable exports, in quality and price. Past experiences are not encouraging, from the standpoint of the Southeast Asian countries. In theory at least, this could change—but the changes are likely to be slow and inadequate.

In sum, in Southeast Asia as in the regions to the north, the Soviet Union has become more interested in the status quo, but with its commitments to North Vietnam posing a basic contradiction to that general position. Now Hanoi's victory has removed that contradiction. This region is lower in Soviet priorities than either Northeast Asia or South Asia, and its most powerful interests are negative ones, namely, to prevent Chinese hegemonism while balancing as effectively as possible the influence of the United States. It has no overwhelming economic interests here at present, nor does it have any real hope of creating a sphere of influence for itself in this region as a whole, even if that were an objective. Hence, a set of practical measures that underwrote the neutralization of the region and permitted "equal access" might well secure Soviet support.

South Asia

In South Asia, the Soviet stake and Soviet commitments are considerably greater. Once again, history proves to be a valuable guide. In the days of the czars as well as those of the commissars, Russia's underbelly was a matter of periodic concern—and action—for the men in the Kremlin. Soviet leaders managed to hold on to czarist possessions here, but they have never been satisfied with the relations prevailing with most border states, at least until recently. Today, however, Soviet influence in the entire region from the Middle East through South Asia is greater than at any time in Russian history, although it still does not reach British influence at its height.

In this connection, a growing linkage should be noted between these two adjoining regions, with Iran as well as the USSR scheduled to play a vital role. Blessed with bountiful oil, the shah is determined simultaneously to modernize his nation and make it into a regional power of significance. The Iranian military forces are rapidly expanding, and soon Teheran will have one of the most effective forces in this area. Iranian influence now extends from Egypt in the west to India on its eastern flank, thanks to a combination of diplomacy, military power, and economic wealth. There is no absence of problems, as witness relations with Iraq. Iran, however, is rapidly emerging as a leading force in the area, one capable of influencing both the Arabs and the South Asians. Pakistan and India alike have vied for Iranian support, as noted previously, and the shah has shown himself anxious to play an expanded role in South Asia, one combining assistance with mediation.

Will the new Iran be interpreted as a challenge or threat by Moscow? Thus far, Teheran has been careful not to antagonize the Soviet Union. Through his oil policies and other activities, the shah has revealed himself quite capable of independence from the United States. From Iran, the Russians managed to extract a statement favorable to Moscow's quest for an Asian collective security program. At the same time, the shah sent his empress to Peking and signaled in a variety of ways his continued interest in the future of Pakistan. Thus, potentially at least, Iran does represent a force competitive with the Russians in this region, and problems might emerge, especially if the Soviet Union decided to make the Indian Ocean a place of naval concentration.

The Iranians, of course, are well aware that they can never match Soviet power, and they are also aware of the increasing reach of that power throughout their sphere of growing influence. The Russians equip Syria and Iraq, as they do most other Arab states. Especially noteworthy has been the expansion of Soviet influence in Afghanistan since the recent coup. This is a poor country, backward and sparsely populated, stretching over a large area. Once, the United States and the USSR balanced each other here in some measure, both providing assistance in the development of communications and other programs. Now, Soviet influence is paramount, and through Afghanistan additional pressure is exercised on Pakistan, directly or indirectly, with the border tribal issues providing a perennial problem.

Russia's South Asia policies, however, center on its relations with India. From a Soviet perspective, these relations serve several important purposes. First and foremost, they form a vital link in the containment of China. The Soviet-Indian alliance presents the Chinese with the problem of a second front, one that drains Chinese resources and manpower from the north even though its activation seems highly remote. Second, the special ties enable the Russians to have some leverage on Indian politics and policies. Here, to be sure, great caution must be exercised, lest a boomerang effect be induced. Generally, the Soviets have adopted a very low public posture and have given no indications of interference in India's internal affairs. Nevertheless, recent Soviet-Indian relations have influenced the placement of certain individuals around Mrs. Gandhi and serve to underwrite the Communist Party of India, an ally both of the Congress and the Russians.

Earlier, we indicated the elements of instability in Soviet-Indian relations. The Russians have now clearly signaled the limits of their capacity or willingness to provide economic and other forms of support, and these fall considerably below Indian needs. From the very beginning, it might be noted, a Soviet apprehension about involvement in the Indian "morass" has existed, as well as doubts about the Indian future. Depsite her tilt toward nationalization and authoritarianism, Mrs. Gandhi's way is not the Russian way, nor can the two be made compatible.

Like the United States, moreover, the USSR has been the frequent victim of what it regards as ingratitude from an ally. Hence, an uneasiness exists in Moscow over the reports that New Delhi would prefer a greater measure of equidistance in its relations with the major powers.

India's achievement of that goal, as we have seen, is strongly dependent on the policies of the People's Republic of China and the United States. In both instances, there may be some variation from recent norms, but major changes seem unlikely. Thus, whatever their ideal, the Indians cannot have a perfectly balanced set of relationships with other large societies. The special relation with the USSR will continue for a considerable period of time, although like other such relations of today, it will permit policy differences between the two countries, and it will not be without its problems. If there were a dramatic change for the better in Sino-Soviet relations, Moscow might rethink its extensive South Asian commitments. But such a development does not seem in the immediate offing.

The Soviet Union's relations with the other states of this region are essentially a reflection of its ties to India. Thus, Bangladesh was accorded early recognition and support. Unfortunately for the Russians, they are easily tarred with the Indian brush. The decline in Indian popularity in Dacca has influenced attitudes toward the USSR. Generally, the Soviets remain aloof from Himalayan politics, acknowledging the prior role of their ally. Toward Pakistan, the Russians exert some pressure, for example, urging support for the Asian collective security concept. Moscow would like to weaken the ties between Pakistan and China. Under certain circumstances, one can conceive of the Russians moving to adopt tactics like those of Iran—seeking to deal with both Pakistan and India.

Once again, the Russians are relatively satisfied with the status quo in this region. Extensive changes would not be likely to benefit them, and consequently they can be expected to make those commitments necessary to preserve the existing order. The new linkage between the Middle East and South Asia makes the Indian Ocean of greater importance to Russia, as to other major states. The Soviets may well increase their naval strength here, as suggested earlier. In any case, it seems improbable that they will accept South Asia as a "nuclear-free zone," even though they are not sympathetic to the emergence of India as a nuclear power. The Russians would prefer that *they* control nuclear weapons in this region, acknowledging, of course, that they cannot prevent Chinése nuclear development. Whether a "zone of peace" approach, neutralizing the Indian Ocean from external power encroachment, might be acceptable is less clear.

A Summing Up

Summarizing the probabilities with respect to Soviet policies in Asia, a number of trends appear reasonably certain. First, in the coming decades, the USSR will increasingly be an *Asian* power, both in terms of its internal developments and external commitments. Second, its Asian policies will be derived in major degree from its relations with China. Thus, the Continental Center will continue to be the truly vital region. Given the uncertainties surrounding China's future and that of Sino-Soviet relations, the Russians are not prepared to gamble on a "soft" China policy. On the contrary, they intend to increase the size of their stick while still offering a large carrot, hoping in this fashion to influence the future decision-makers in Peking. Neither war nor an intimate alliance can be regarded as probable under prevailing or likely circumstances. The Russian hope is for limited détente, under which influence and mutual benefits can gradually be rebuilt. But for the near future at least, the Russians will continue to apply their containment policies against China with all of the vigor which they possess.

In this connection, the most critical external areas are Northeast and South Asia. The Russians have exhibited a concern lest Sino-Japanese relations become too close, but they have not yet found it possible to offer truly attractive alternatives for Japan. Here, Russian policies are still fluid, with some innovations possible. Meanwhile, the Russians can be expected to increase their military power in this region substantially and to oppose any changes—territorial or otherwise—that might accrue to Chinese strength.

In South Asia, the Soviet Union also prefers the status quo to any likely alternative. Here, it has acquired a formidable presence—and equally formidable responsibilities. Given the multidimensional problems plaguing this region, it would not be logical to predict a smooth future. A great domestic upheaval in India could affect Soviet-Indian relations, and indeed all relations in the subcontinent. It is probable, however, that India, despite its travails, will remain intact and governed nationally by the Congress Party. Under those conditions, the special ties between the USSR and India will continue to have validity for both parties.

The increased power of the Soviet Union in Asia will in part take the form of augmented naval strength. This will project the Russians into Asian oceans, including the Pacific, in more substantial measure. It will mean added competition, and possibly confrontation with the United States. In the Pacific-Asian area as a whole, however, the United States and the Soviet Union are much less in conflict over issues than was true two decades ago. As has been indicated, the Soviet Union has increasingly become a status quo power in Asia in recent times, and one seeking to apply the principles that led to détente in Europe. Setting aside Indochina, American and Soviet policies in the Pacific-Asian area, although far from identical, may come to exhibit a considerable degree of harmony. Some of the tests lie just ahead.

Several final observations are in order. In analyzing Soviet policies, we have set forth those policies that appear to represent the consensus of the present. In the USSR as elsewhere, policies are in reality the products of an intricate decision-making process, with the interests of various party, bureaucratic, and military forces always in some measure of conflict. At various stages, compromises must be made, and in some cases the consensus may be precarious. That is likely to be especially true of certain policies pertaining to Asia, where the element of uncertainty is so great. Nothing in this work is intended to convey the suggestion that foreign policy is a product of some simple, monolithic process, whether the subject be Moscow, Washington, Peking, or Tokyo. Nevertheless, our concern is not with the process, but with the product—and its potentialities for continuity or change.

Second, although the evidence strongly supports the thesis that the basis of Soviet Asian policies currently relates to the China problem, other factors should not be completely ignored. Indeed, some observers hold to the thesis that more comprehensive motivations are at work. They see the Soviet Union in this period of its evolution genuinely committed to playing the role of global power and, hence, insistent on expanding its political and military authority to match this role. Moscow will progressively demand recognition in these terms, they argue, and insist that no international "solutions" be sought or reached without its full participation, in Asia as elsewhere. Thus, what was a Pax Americana in the years immediately after 1945, must now be a Pax Russo-Americana. There is some merit in such an analysis. Certainly, no major power has so expanded and extended its reach in recent years as has the Soviet Union.

Will this continue? One variable will undoubtedly be the degree to which the Russians find themselves satisfied with contemporary conditions and trends, especially the nature of American-Soviet relations. As our brief survey of internal conditions suggested, moreover, another variable may relate to the pressures surging up from within the Soviet Union itself. Russians as citizens are weary of postponing domestic advances on behalf of foreign commitments. The enormously burdensome military expenditures, together with those involving foreign aid, are becoming an issue—and they may become a truly critical issue before the end of another decade.

Soviet specialists caution us not to overestimate this

possibility. Correctly, they point to the fact that the USSR remains a strongly authoritarian state capable of imposing its will on its people in powerful fashion when the political elite regards this as necessary. Nevertheless, recent events indicate that the debate over priorities—domestic and foreign—has begun in Russia, and it affects elitist as well as nonelitist circles.

From all of the data, however, one conclusion emerges. Whatever one's assessment of the motives and the exigencies of Soviet internal politics, all projections of Soviet policies in Asia, if realistic, must be based on the assumption of increased Russian commitment and power.

Chapter 7

THE
UNITED STATES:
Shift of Course?

Among the major societies with which we have been concerned, the United States can be considered the most peripheral to Asia. Only a very small portion of its territory lies in the Western Pacific, within the Asian perimeter. The Asian part of its population remains tiny in comparison with Americans of European background and, with the exception of Hawaii, of limited political impact. Because the balance of economic, political, and intellectual-media power still inclines toward the eastern seaboard of the United States, moreover, these conditions are accentuated. In the most basic sense, American politics and the American people have always been Europocentric, and the ethnic groups strongly influencing American foreign policy, non-Asian.

Since the late nineteenth century, however, the United States has been inexorably drawn toward the Pacific-Asian area. The primary reasons have not been economic, but political and strategic. Until recently, the economic importance of Asia to the United States was rather negligible, although now it is increasing rapidly. With the acquisition of the Philippines and Guam as a result of the Spanish-American War in 1898, however, the United States became a part of the Asian order, subject to the reverberations of major developments there.

The Background

Certain basic American positions with respect to Asia had already been enunciated, even before a U.S. physical presence was established. Antagonism to European colonialism and the efforts of any single power to establish hegemony in Asia derived from a combination of self-interest and altruism. As a continental-mass society, blessed with abundant resources and with energies fully consumed in the development of its internal empire, the United States found it easy to condemn European colonialism as immoral despite its own lapses. Even in its colonial rule, the United States took pride in inaugurating programs of mass education and tutelage for self-government that underwrote democratic themes and made of Philippine nationalism a legal movement, one working within the system instead of pursuing revolutionary, guerrilla routes.

The central objections to European colonialism, however, probably lay in the fact that it denied the access of others, promoting its own form of closed society. As most of South and Southeast Asia had come under European rule at an earlier point, the focus came to be on China. At first the threat was from Europe; subsequently, from Japan. The American effort to uphold the territorial integrity of China took various forms, from the Open Door Notes at the very beginning of this century to the cumulative pressures on Japan that finally resulted in Pearl Harbor. In essence, however, American policy was built around the use of moral suasion.

Moral suasion represented an effort to obtain collective agreements pledging support for given principles and courses of action on the part of the concerned powers. What if the agreements were violated? Here lay the Achilles' heel. Consultation was provided, but no system of economic, political, or military sanctions was devised. In the final analysis, therefore, there was no enforcement mechanism if the order were challenged. Supreme symbol of this era was the Kellogg-Briand

Peace Pact of 1928, via which almost all nations of the world solemnly agreed to outlaw war as an instrument of foreign policy.

For the United States, moral suasion was an ideal policy in the short run, for it involved limited commitments and risks, yet accorded with the very considerable self-righteousness and sense of morality that accompanied American attitudes. In a sense, it was the opposite side of the isolationist coin. Sweeping aside the initial reluctance to become involved in World War I, the United States had finally made a full commitment, militarily and morally. A pendulumlike swing toward noninvolvement, including a rejection of the League of Nations, came quickly at war's end. The United States turned sharply inward, opting out of responsibility for any international order, and this was reflected in both its economic and political policies. Under these circumstances, moral suasion was an alternative, especially for Asia, eagerly grasped.

In the mid-1930s, it will be recalled, an effort to buttress American noninvolvement in world affairs came through the Neutrality Acts. Preceding these acts, congressional hearings established the causes of war: ammunition-makers' profits and the presence of Americans in belligerent zones. In retrospect, it seems incredible that this type of analysis could prevail even as the international order was crumbling and Hitlerism—in its varying forms—was mounting one assault after another.

Soon enough, however, the United States was to learn the difficulties of living in a world without order or any accepted system of handling grievances except that of force. Within a decade, America had once again made a total commitment at enormous cost. The lessons of this era, perceived or misperceived, have been very much with American policy-makers for the past three decades. Once again, however, the pendulum has swung in a familiar fashion—from "all in" toward "all out." Once again, the causes of conflict are being defined in such a fashion as to make past American policies seem foolish or criminal. And the supposed ingratitude of allies, combined with the rise of serious domestic problems, again generates a mood of withdrawal from the international scene. For these purposes, Vietnam has been turned into a crusade by many of its opponents, made synonymous with everything that is evil and misguided.

The Domestic Scene

Thus, as in the case of other Pacific-Asian societies, domestic trends in the United States are germane to the foreign policy alternatives available in Asia. Will the current trend toward isolationism sweep all before it? Is the United States any longer a credible ally—or opponent? Do internal economic and political developments augur a lengthy period of instability, one that will force attention to be focused almost solely on problems at home?

In certain respects, the United States has been the most revolutionary society in the world in the past three or four decades, claims emanating from other quarters notwithstanding. We use the term *revolutionary* here to mean basic changes in the social order affecting values, attitudes, living standards, mobility—and general way of life. Necessarily, these extend deeply into the political sphere, but they encompass all spheres. Has there been another people that has undergone such sweeping and continuous changes in these respects in a comparable period of time? In most nations proclaiming themselves revolutionary, the major changes have been largely confined to the elites, with the masses still living—and thinking—close to the old order. The advent of new political institutions, indeed, may merely camouflage the degree to which the past lives on, even in politics. Socioeconomic development has rarely reached the momentum necessary to transform the masses.

The ongoing American revolution is conducive to political instability at this point. Development has produced new problems, frontier problems of both an economic and political nature, for which no easy solutions are at hand. These problems, moreover, have had reverberations throughout that portion of the world closely connected with the United States economically. Thus, Peking and Moscow speak, not without reason, of the "crisis in the international capitalist world." In certain respects, however, the American problems are *sui generis,* not merely in the influence which they cast on the international community as a whole, but in their precise character.

The universal trend for many decades has been the aggrandizement of governmental power and authority. Almost all dynamic political movements of our times have advanced the position of the state, calling on it to handle the complex problems contingent to or concomitant with the modernization process. The United States has been no exception. Yet at the same time, America manages to preserve and advance freedom to an extraordinary extent. Thus, the unique phenomenon: a powerful state, and one casting an ever-longer shadow over the lives of its people, for good or otherwise; but also, the survival—indeed, the steady strengthening—of private interest groups, among them business, labor, and the media. Advances in personal freedoms have been equally spectacular in a number of spheres, freedoms relating to sex, speech, and political action.

After total freedom what? Actions defended in the name of private rights or moral judgments have been pitted against the authority and legitimacy of state actions. The state, itself heterogeneous and sometimes bitterly divided, has responded confusedly, sometimes making major concessions, sometimes standing firm, in the name of its own moral judgments. Morality on all fronts threatens law, as the late Professor Alexander Bickel so wisely observed.

No political system can remain viable if such conditions persist. In every circumstance, democracy is a fragile form of government. It is dependent on a relatively fine balance between authority and freedom, rights and responsibility. When in the midst of crises, government intrudes deeply into the arena properly private, democracy may collapse or, at a minimum, retreat. When government is rendered weak and ineffective by elements of the private sphere who presume to take on functions properly governmental in the name of morality or effectiveness, democracy is in equal peril. In some measure, the United States has recently been subjected to both of these threats in whiplash fashion. Fortunately, the first signs are now appearing that these twin dangers are appreciated. The demands for a reestablishment of an adequate balance are growing. Even within the all-powerful media, self-criticism of certain recent acts is beginning to be heard. The political climate in the United States, moreover, is not running in the direction of political upheaval. A deep disquietude does exist, and disillusionment has been extended rather evenly to many institutions of American society. Yet the current quest of the average American is not for struggle, but for a surcease from struggle, not for "Revolution" with a capital *R,* but for moderation. Only a serious, prolonged economic crisis could alter this mood. If it is conducive to a foreign policy of fewer risks and lower posture, it is also supportive of political stability.

But will economic factors intervene? Are the advanced nations in general, and the United States specifically, now entering a period when economic troubles will escalate, with no remedial measures sufficient? Dogmatism regarding this truly critical question is unwarranted. Experts disagree, and various apocalyptic predictions have been advanced. There would be wide agreement with the proposition that the time-honored policies and practices of the past will not necessarily suffice. It may well be a time for new initiatives, and a type of boldness not recently seen. But who is to say that the American genius for pragmatism and experimentation cannot rise to this callenge?

In our conclusions, we shall return to this question, probing its implications for new forms of regionalism and internationalism. Here, it suffices to note that the economic problems of recent years, including the energy crisis, have lent themselves to two strongly opposite trends. On the one hand, as was inevitable under the circumstances, a new interest in self-sufficiency has emerged, especially in such a critical field as energy sources. Beyond this, the forces of a more general economic nationalism have made their reappearance, as often happens in periods of recession or depression. Yet at the same time, the current crisis has evoked a renewed sense of interdependence, especially among certain nations and regions. There is also a feeling that the need for mutual cooperation and, in a broader sense, the need for an acceptable world order will grow, not diminish, as we move toward the end of the twentieth century. On balance, therefore, the momentum toward neoisolation, though still powerful, is being counteracted.

That this is a perilous age, no one should deny. Moreover, as noted at the outset, we have no blueprints for the future, or certain of the institutions that will be necessary to execute them after they are drawn. The failure of democracy on a global scale cannot be totally ruled out. The warning signals represented by population, resources, and the demands that will emerge from societies still struggling upward from the lower rungs of development are clear. Controls seem a more likely global prospect than freedom. In comparison with most if not all of the other major societies with which we have been concerned, however, the United States has a number of assets and strengths, some of which have been scarcely tapped. On balance, therefore, political instability can probably be contained within limits acceptable to the democratic system; similarly, economic problems, though not "solved" in any final fashion, will be alleviated in time to prevent a deeper crisis; and the United States will continue to play an important international role, particularly in Europe and Asia.

The U.S. in the Pacific Region

As in the case of the Soviet Union, the United States has been and will continue to be involved in all regions of the Pacific-Asian area. Consequently, we can again use a regional approach, coupled with an exploration of alternatives in bilateral relations with the key societies and some final observations about policies for the area as a whole.

The region of most immediate concern to the United States is the Pacific Ocean, for in this region are contained portions of American territory and basic security policies hinge on developments here. As noted earlier, American strategic domination of the Pacific heartland has been complete since World War II. In this connection, the United States acquired some 115,000 people as new wards, spread over a region of some three million square miles. In recent years, as various societies in the Pacific region have attained independence or autonomy, the issue of Micronesia's future has increasingly come to the fore, stimulated by diverse forces including the United Nations Trusteeship Committee and certain young American "progressives." Thus, a complex series of negotiations between Micronesian and American representatives have been underway for some time.

It now seems likely that the northern Mariana complex will acquire commonwealth status, making it an integral part of the United States in a fashion similar to Puerto Rico. This appears to accord with the indigenous people's wishes. They have always been affiliated culturally with Guam, a long-time American possession and key island within the Mariana group. Their differences from the people of the Marshalls and Carolines, on the other hand, are substantial.

With the latter groups, negotiations have been protracted and difficult. The trend is toward granting the Marshalls and Carolines full autonomy on domestic matters, but with defense and foreign affairs delegated to the United States. Some redelegation would be permitted, for example, the right to secure Japanese economic assistance. The agreement may be susceptible to termination unilaterally by either party after fifteen years, thereby providing the United States an opportunity to reevaluate the strategic situation at that point.

Numerous fissures have developed within the southern Micronesian groups, however, with much talk of separate arrangements. As long as the United States played the role of "opponent," a common rallying point was provided. As changes in that image occur, differences and hostilities emerge, with access to money—real or potential—being a primary source of division.

Irrespective of the final outcome, the United States can be expected to insist on the security arrangements deemed essential to its interests and commitments. In point of fact, however, the arrangements currently being requested are relatively minimal compared to initial projections. Essentially, they involve three installations: the possible development of a major air base complex on Tinian, augmenting the facilities in Guam; the retention of the Kwajalien missile complex; and a guarantee of base rights in the Palau Islands, four hundred miles due east of Mindanao.

These represent radically scaled-down military requests measured against an earlier era. Meanwhile, certain unanswered questions remain concerning security requirements. How important are these bases to the defense of the United States proper? Are they essential, and could they suffice alone in fulfilling American treaty commitments to Asian allies?

Any attack on the United States by the USSR, or another state that had acquired formidable nuclear capacities, would presumably involve this category of weapons. Given the nuclear strategies currently in vogue and the extreme vulnerability of bases of this nature, it is difficult to see how these installations could play more than a marginal role in such a conflict. From a variety of standpoints, however, it would be important to deny the bases to a potential foe. And it may be true that a significant American physical presence in the Pacific has a certain preemptive effect on other major powers, serving to forestall the type of "balancing" operations here that have taken place in the Mediterranean and threaten in the Indian Ocean. In operations involving any opponent except the Soviet Union at this point, moreover, these bases could be highly significant.

Whether they alone would suffice in the event that the United States were called on to fulfill current military commitments to Asian-Pacific allies is a debatable question. Most military experts argue that at a minimum naval bases in Japan and the Philippines are essential, for these facilities cannot be duplicated in Guam or elsewhere. Perhaps the issue turns partly on what a fulfillment of existing obligations would entail. If the terms of the Guam Doctrine are applied rigorously, the primary function of the United States is presumably to serve as a nuclear umbrella, restraining the actions of other nuclear powers. The assumption is that allies can handle nonnuclear opponents through their own capacities. If to this assumption is added the possibility of keeping important indigenous bases in a readiness condition, could not American credibility and commitments be maintained, at reduced political and economic costs?

Unfortunately, the fundamental problem is not this simple. As will be indicated shortly in discussing Korea, peace and security hinge on a complex set of factors, political and psychological as well as purely military. Timing is also of crucial importance. Thus, the question must be asked, would a complete American military withdrawal at this time to Pacific island bases trigger certain political and military developments on the part of both allies and erstwhile opponents destabilizing and highly detrimental to the prospects for eventual arms control and peaceful settlements in the Pacific-Asian area? To what extent are such developments dependent on a broad political-military equilibrium at this stage, one underwriting a lengthy, intricate negotiating process in which the major parties involved have roughly equal confidence and strength?

As indicated earlier, we must assume that the military element in the Pacific-Asian posture of both the Soviet Union and the People's Republic of China will rise in the short-and medium-range future. How that military element will be employed is less easily discerned. Already, Peking has successfully challenged a small state (the Republic of Vietnam) over disputed territory in the South China sea. To date, détente—in Asia as in Europe—has been less the product of convergence (a growing ideological and institutional identity) and more the product of balance-of-power politics in an era when there are no effective international institutions to keep the peace. The broadest options open to the United States in Asia are thus whether to take the risks and costs of continued strategic commitment in an effort to pursue stability through equilibrium or take the risks and costs of withdrawal, permitting other powers to assume the major initiatives. This is to express the options in their most simple, general form, to be sure. With each basic option, there exist various qualifying possibilities, as will subsequently be noted. Nonetheless, it is important to put the critical issue in bold relief.

Those who espouse the withdrawal position advance their cause from a number of perspectives. In terms of security, they assert, no threat is posed to the United States from Asia. China will probably attain a limited nuclear capacity to strike at the United States shortly, but the disparity in military power will continue to be so great that such an attack would be suicidal. The People's Republic, moreover, will not have the means for a long-range conventional attack for the foreseeable future. As for Japan, even if American-Japanese relations should deteriorate so badly as to produce a militant, hostile Japan, the extreme vulnerability of that nation to nuclear conflict and the equally formidable obstacles against its development of conventional capacities sufficient to threaten the United States make this threat highly improbable and easily foreseen. Finally, although the Soviet Union is a potential threat, given its near military parity with the United States, it represents a global, not an Asian problem—with the major points of United States-USSR friction elsewhere.

The thesis is also advanced that the United States can retain its involvement in Asian trade and investment without any military presence. Economic interaction is based on mutual benefit, it is asserted, not relative power. Sometimes, a different position is taken: our economic stake in Asia is not so substantial as to warrant extensive involvement. The ability of the United States to achieve relative economic self-sufficiency would minimize the impact even if a "worst-possible" scenario unfolded, with our access to Asian markets greatly restricted.

On the political front, it is argued, American policies of commitment have led to an underwriting of corrupt, dictatorial regimes—thereby confusing the image of the United States and flawing our moral as well as our political authority. In some quarters, indeed, it is felt that although communism is neither necessary nor desirable for the United States, it may be appropriate to peoples requiring a much firmer discipline and organizational effort if modernization is to occur. And in any case, it is asserted, are not the policies of the Cold War anachronistic?

As we have indicated, such arguments as these are bolstered by the present climate both in the United States and in the world. Beset with serious social and economic problems at home, the American people have recently displayed an increasingly isolationist mood. Foreign policies of recent years are now widely viewed with a jaundiced eye, both the policies of economic-technical assistance and those of military support. Korea and Vietnam revealed clearly how extremely difficult it is for a democratic nation like the United States to fight a prolonged, limited war—and the risks of a potentially shorter, more decisive total war, for most decision-makers, remain prohibitively high.

Foreign allies and "neutrals" have consciously or unconsciously added fuel to the isolationist fires. It has often been said that Americans would rather be loved than respected. The merciless criticism showered on the United States in recent decades, combined with the widespread reluctance of allies to accept burden-sharing, have cumulatively built up resentments among the American people and a progressive antipathy to international commitments. These sentiments have naturally been forwarded by the fact that such vital allies as the Western Europeans and the Japanese have achieved a greatly increased capacity to support constructive internationalism, partly as a result of early American aid, and yet seem prone to staunchly nationalist, even exclusivist policies—particularly in the case of Europe.

It is thus not surprising that the withdrawal mood not only has broad support at the grass-roots level in the United States, but also has a substantial number of adherents among such communities as those who work in the media and the universities.

What is the case for continued commitment, including a maintenance of basic defense treaty obligations? Turning first to the question of security, is not the assessment of threat on a nation-to-nation basis, as advanced here, an overly narrow, mechanical approach? In the final analysis, does not the security of a rich and powerful nation like the United States hinge on whether the international climate permits serious progress to be made on such questions as food, population, and weapons control, especially the control of nuclear weapons? In even broader terms, does not American security hinge in the final analysis on the achievement of a viable international order?

The political-military balance remains precarious in those two regions critical to any global order, namely, Europe and Asia. Would not a unilateral American withdrawal on a large scale at this point result in the type of disequilibrium that would foster simultaneously two interrelated and strongly destabilizing trends: sharply nationalist policies, in the defense realm as in economic and political matters; and under this aegis, efforts on the part of nations, large and small, to extend their influence through independent actions?

In the case of the major states, this situation would be conducive to drives for regional hegemony, justified as necessary defensive measures in a terribly insecure world. With respect to the small states, it could thus easily result in heightened external controls via such hegemonical tendencies or, alternately, in the eruption of "local wars" unrestrained by any form of international restraints.

The prevailing insecurity would almost certainly weigh heavily against the growth of politically open societies. Nor would the climate be generally supportive of a serious, sustained approach to the massive socioeconomic problems of this era. Finally, such a climate would scarcely be conducive to progress in the all-important field of weapons control.

Under these conditions, how long would it be before the United States was forced to choose between the "garrison state" approach, with all of its political and socioeconomic implications, and renewed intervention, now at extremely high cost?

From this scenario flow quite different conclusions regarding the economic and political consequences of withdrawal than those set forth by its advocates. In place of economic cooperation, economic warfare would be a logical concomitant of a heightened priority on nationalist and regional considerations accompanied by the seeming disintegration of any broader order. In such warfare, the United States would be in a relatively favorable position initially, but the thesis that we could live comfortably or securely in the midst of a combative, desperate world stretches credulity too far.

Finally, the extent to which the United States should be actively committed to the creation and development of democratic societies abroad is a debatable matter. Surely, our values lie with the democratic parliamentary system, but it can be argued that our primary concern in the realm of foreign policy must be with the international procedures that *all* states should follow, as these support peace or war, socioeconomic progress or stagnation, exchange based on rationality or irrationality. At times in pursuit of such basic goals, it is entirely legitimate to work closely with authoritarian states, even to give them various forms of support, direct or indirect.

A related point should now claim our urgent attention. Many Americans have unconsciously adopted radically differing standards in judging the domestic politics of other states. Toward states sufficiently open to allow some form of political opposition, they are quick to note and condemn at length various transgressions against civil liberties, especially if the state concerned is one dependent on or closely interrelated to the United States in some form. "Neutral" states receive far less scrutiny. And ironically, among states so closed that neither an indigenous opposition is allowed nor any but the most closely supervised access by outside observers, attention is most frequently focused on such issues as efficiency, the degree of discipline and order achieved, and trends in production. In this manner, not only are common standards avoided, but by implication the quasi-open society is rated below the closed one, and this by those calling for an adherence to democratic values.

The fact is that the path of political openness is a particularly thorny one in our times, for advanced as well as for "developing" societies. There is every reason to criticize the transgressions of all states proclaiming themselves democracies when their standard of conduct indicates otherwise. But one should never lose sight of the fact that it is vastly more easy to sustain or rekindle the democratic process in a quasi-open society—whatever the lapses of any given time—than it is to establish such a process in the closed societies of the twentieth century.

Certainly, a policy of precipitous withdrawal will not abet the cause of political openness in Asia. Already, the evidence on this score is impressive. The decline both in American presence and credibility in Asia of recent years has generally had the opposite effect. A strong American presence provided incentives—or constraints—on the one hand, and an atmosphere sufficiently protective to make experimentation in the democratization process feasible in such areas as South Korea. Now, certain leaders, feeling themselves in danger of abandonment, and with external threats scarcely diminished, reverse or retard this experimentation in the name of internal unity.

On a broader canvas, however, the political implications of withdrawal relate as much to erstwhile opponents as to allies. If relations between the United States and its allies deteriorate further, and if the United States signals that it no longer intends to be a major force in East Asia, will this not, at some point, have a profound effect on the foreign policies of the Soviet Union and the People's Republic of China, one almost certain to be sharply against our national interests and those of many other states of the Pacific-Asian region? In posing this central question, we have returned to an initial premise. We live in an era in which the most important international effort is to replace conflict with negotiations. These negotiations can currently rest on a perceived sense of national interests by the leadership of each state, interests defined in considerable measure by a sense of the risks and costs which go with various alternatives. This is true because there can be no ideological or policy commonality sufficient to govern the negotiatory process today, because of the radically different stages of development in which the major (and minor) states find themselves. Thus, if we forego presence and strength, the states critical to the future of the Pacific-Asian region will not find it in their interest to pursue the negotiatory process with us seriously. Such a basic decision, or even a tendency in that direction, will affect their relations with other states and their attitudes on various issues of vital concern to the United States.

In the final analysis, this is the critical risk which a policy of extensive withdrawal runs, although it is a risk largely un-recognized as yet, even among informed observers. On balance, therefore, the case against precipitous American military withdrawal from Asia is a powerful one, notwithstanding the domestic pressures currently supporting it. At a later point we shall explore ways of revitalizing an American commitment to a working internationalism. Suffice it to say here that they do not presume a continuance intact of the old practices—economic, political, or military.

As indicated at the outset, it has seemed desirable to pose the issue in its broadest, most simple dimensions, but one must be cognizant that the issues of gradation are critical ones. To oppose American military withdrawal from Asia at this point does not necessarily mean to argue for precisely the same disposition of forces as currently exists. The question is what American military forces are necessary both to sustain desirable treaty commitments *and*, in more general terms, to preserve American credibility in the area? This question will be addressed in more detail as it applies to specific regions and issues.

Our extended discussion of the central alternatives, however, is appropriately included here, because strategic considerations are the key to policy in the Pacific Ocean region. If the option is for rapid, complete American military withdrawal from eastern Asia, the case for additional military facilities in Micronesia is weak. The security of the United States proper, defined in narrow military terms, does not require such facilities, not now or in the foreseeable future, given trends in military technology and the capacities of potential opponents. If, however, the option is for a continued American military presence in eastern Asia of some dimensions, the facilities being contemplated at present are warranted, taking into account the full range of political and strategic factors.

Under the latter conditions, the island peoples of the Pacific Ocean will assume an importance, especially for the United

States, far greater than their numbers would suggest. In the future, they will be subject to more varied external influences than in the recent past. Moreover, they will continue to represent a tempting target in the international political arena, both for political and economic reasons. American-Micronesian relations thus represent a crucial variable in the region's future, and in this instance one must hope that the past is not the harbinger of the future.

Initial neglect in the years immediately after 1945 was followed by lavish expenditures. In neither case were the best interests of the indigenous people served. Typically, moreover, the Americans sent as administrators were of dubious quality and limited experience. Few if any mistakes were avoided, and the United States was saved from far greater difficulties only because it was dealing with such a small, scattered, and diverse population.

To move from the Pacific center to the region in its broader dimensions is to open another question of importance: should an attempt be made to create a Pacific Community? Already, an informal Pacific Basin group exists, but thus far there has been no effort to develop a full-scale regional organization either of the European Economic Community type or of a less ambitious character.

The arguments against such an effort are substantial ones. Most economic and social problems, it is asserted, do not submit themselves to such a grouping. They are better handled through existing, more comprehensive international organizations; different combinations of nations; or via bilateral ties. Already, a wide range of available instruments exists: the United Nations and its various agencies and subunits; the World Bank; the Asian Development Bank; the Trilateral Commission focusing on the United States, Western Europe, and Japan; and a number of bilateral bodies, official and unofficial. Any further proliferation, it is submitted, would be counterproductive.

Questions are also raised about both the membership and jurisdiction of such a community. Would it be exclusively composed of the more "advanced" Pacific nations, defined as the United States, Japan, Canada, Mexico, several Latin American states, Australia, and New Zealand? Or should it include certain "developing" nations as well? For political reasons, Taiwan in any case could not be included, for it is no longer recognized as a state by many of the states just mentioned. Would the concerns of such a community be exclusively economic, or would issues of a more strictly political nature be encompassed? In either case, would it be possible to accommodate the very diverse interests likely to be represented in any conceivable grouping, or would the attempt result in more friction than progress?

Set against these arguments are some equally important considerations. Of all of the oceans, the Pacific may well prove to be the richest in its natural resources, both of the type that are irreplaceable and those that may be periodically harvested. Although the issues of maritime jurisdiction must be resolved on a more universal basis, the utilization and conservation of Pacific resources vitally concerns all nations that lie on its rims, and particularly the more developed nations that are now requiring resources at an accelerating rate.

Trade relations, moreover, together with investment patterns indicate a strong affinity among certain nations of the Pacific region. Note, for example, the economic ties among the United States, Canada, and Japan—and one might add such nations as Mexico, Australia, and New Zealand to this group. Nor is there any reason to believe that the economic developments of the future will lessen the importance of these relations. On the contrary, there is a growing body of opinion that sees economic regionalism as the wave of the future.

No one can doubt, moreover, that economic relations between such "advanced" states as the United States and

Japan, on the one hand, and select "developing" nations like Indonesia and the Philippines is and in all probability will remain of vital significance to both sides. These relations, in a purely laissez-faire environment, risk continuous transgressions and misunderstandings, productive of mounting friction. Certain needs and problems in this connection can and are being handled through existing organizations. With each passing year, however, the desirability grows of establishing a regional institution making such relations a matter of central concern, seeking common policies in an effort to correct past mistakes and developing long-range, comprehensive programs for the future.

Nor can one ignore the political and psychological realities of today. The age of unilateral American aid is coming to a close. Some assistance will continue, primarily humanitarian in nature, but past aid policies can no longer garner sufficient support, either from the American people or their representatives, to make them politically viable. Nor do existing international bodies possess the requisite appeal. If American interest in international participation is to be rekindled, new ideas—and new institutions to accompany them—are urgently required. This is not to oppose such ongoing groups as the U.S.-Western Europe-Japan trilateral body, which has great potential utility for certain purposes. It is to suggest that the limitations of such a group are substantial, some of them stemming from the very regionalism now recognized for Europe but still absent in the Pacific.

The most critical challenge of the late twentieth century will be the fashioning of institutions that can operate effectively at the supranational level without seeking to overthrow the nation-state, on the one hand, or representing mere forums for discussion on the other. Our global capacity for problem-solving, possibly for survival, will be tested in these terms. And it will be essential for every nation, particularly the major societies, to operate at different levels simultaneously. Just as attention within a society cannot be devoted exclusively to any one level—be it local, regional, or national—so in the arena of foreign policy, circumstances require that the importance of bilateral, regional, and international relations each be acknowledged, with the respective commitments appropriate to the needs of the period and the issues at hand. Whatever the ultimate decision, the concept of a Pacific Community now warrants serious consideration, with these general principles kept firmly in mind.

Northeast Asia

Each of the broad issues thus far raised applies to regions of Asia in addition to the Pacific Ocean. Most particularly are they applicable to Northeast Asia. In the latter region, war/peace issues are of critical importance, as noted earlier, for all of the major powers regard Northeast Asia as of special significance to them and maintain some type of presence there. It is also in this region that complex political and economic problems abound, not the least of which are the issues surrounding the two Koreas and China-Taiwan.

Japan is the central nation within the region despite its relative political and military weakness. The American-Japanese relation since 1945, moreover, has been unique. Few if any bilateral ties have been of greater overall significance to the United States, be the measurement economic, political-strategic, or cultural. In broad terms, the movement has been from paternalism toward equality, from harmony toward conflict. Yet the intensity of this relationship and its mutual advantages have not changed appreciably; hence, its continuing importance.

In the initial postwar era, the United States served as tutor, supporter, and protector of Japan. It is easy to discern elements of arrogance and naiveté in the American performance, along with that pragmatism and essential humanity that are also hallmarks of American political behavior. What is important, however, is that American objectives, as they were ultimately defined, were successfully achieved. Much credit must naturally go to the Japanese themselves, and in impersonal terms to that stage of development which their society had previously attained. Yet it would be foolish to assume that American policies did not represent a critical variable.

It is tempting to discuss recent trends in American-Japanese relations in terms of the coming of age of one placed psychologically in the position of an adolescent. Japan, subordinated by total defeat and intense self-doubt, willingly accepted the inferior role, but with her rise to unparalleled economic power found the old attitudes and policies unacceptable. There is merit in that analysis, but it fails to capture some of the complexities that were always implicit in the scene.

In recent years, both sides have felt themselves to be the victims of inequities in the relationship. The United States sees Japan as having taken advantage of the economic benefits accruing to it in the years beginning with the Korean War, some of them products of American policy, without exhibiting a willingness to liberalize its own policies until forced to do so by unilateral acts from Washington. Even now, many spokesmen for the American business community complain that the Japanese system continues to inhibit mutual interaction, despite the truly major changes of policies that have taken place since 1971. The method of using "scientific research" often involving governmental support to detect promising foreign markets, followed by saturation or blitzkreig tactics in exploiting those markets, has inevitably created resentment. The highly competitive character of Japanese products has naturally provided an added dimension to the problem.

On security matters also, some Americans at least have felt that serious inequalities have existed. Since 1945, in their view, the United States has borne the great share of the military costs for the defense of Japan. No other major nation has expended so small a portion of its GNP for the military as Japan. Yet a high percentage of Japanese either oppose the Mutual Security Treaty or doubt the credibility of Washington. On this issue, however, the American position is made more confusing by virtue of the fact that officially the United States strongly opposes any movement on the part of Japan to develop nuclear weapons. Nor does there appear to be extensive American support for a Japanese effort to become a major military power.

Japan's grievances have been no less varied. With specific groups, Washington's tough economic measures of recent years created resentment, even though the rationale for such actions was often understood and sometimes accepted as justifiable. Less understood and never accepted have been certain political acts, specifically, the refusal to consult or even inform the Japanese government concerning the events leading up to the Nixon China visit. Many important Japanese, moreover, became convinced that both President Nixon and Secretary Kissinger were "anti-Japanese" because of various statements and acts ascribed to them.

At present, many of the substantive issues and personal antagonisms have been reduced or removed by events. In the economic realm, American-Japanese interaction is proceeding along a much smoother path than was the case a few years ago. This is due in part to Japanese liberalization measures and in part to the dramatic changes in the international economic scene. Problems still exist, but their immediate proportions are greatly reduced. In the political realm also, the atmosphere has generally improved. President Ford's visit to Japan—the first of an incumbent American president—serves as symbol of a more promising era. And in the field of security, despite the recent outcry over the possibility that some American warships coming into Japanese ports had nuclear weapons (undoubtedly true), the current defense arrangements are not a burning issue. The Mutual Security Treaty has not gained in popularity, nor have Americans shown a strong desire to defend Japan against all possible risks. Indeed, developments in Indochina and elsewhere have increased Japanese doubts about the American commitment in major degree. On both sides, a wariness exists. But the trends are not increasingly adverse. A status quo situation prevails.

The potentialities for future competition, even economic and political conflict, exist. As we noted earlier, Japan expects to export various heavy industries abroad in the period just ahead, in quest of more abundant labor and resources. At home, high-technology industries will be emphasized. This could mean increasing competition with the United States. We have also stressed the rising importance of Pacific Ocean resources—another area of likely competition. Already, Japan is moving back into the Pacific islands economically at an accelerated rate, as it is in most other parts of Asia. Americans overseas have often been unhappy about Japanese business practices in Southeast Asia, with or without reason.

Nor is Japan likely to follow precisely the same political policies as the United States. During the recent Middle East crisis, the Japanese government made it clear that in general it sided with the Arab states. In the future, policies relating to the various Communist states, including the People's Republic of China, could differ—as indeed, they do at present.

Beyond this, as we suggested in the earlier section on Japan, lie some basic psychological and political differences between these two societies. The attraction of opposites is real, but sometimes precarious. In the aggregate, Americans are extroverted, outgoing, and possessed of high quotients of individualism, open in personal relations. Generalizing, Japanese are introverted, a very private people, and still operating extensively through small, intensely structured groups. Japan is an open society composed of closed units. Given these differences, full communications are difficult to achieve, misperceptions not uncommon.

In truth, neither the United States nor Japan comes to alliance with ease. In the case of America, the historical attitudes have been those of self-sufficiency and superior achievement. If doubts have recently accumulated, foreign commitments are still regarded as acts of sacrifice, not necessity—to be gotten over within the shortest possible time, and with maximum efficiency. For Japan, exclusiveness and xenophobia have been proverbial, and relations with equals, whether at home or abroad, extremely difficult to establish.

Notwithstanding the impediments, however, American-Japanese relations are probably destined to be increasingly close in the years ahead. As we have seen, all current projections of the Japanese economy indicate that in the 1980s, as at present, trade and other forms of economic interaction with the United States will still be Japan's single most important foreign link by a wide margin, vital to that nation's prosperity. Indeed, some argue that Japan's dependence on the United States is destined to grow rather than decline in the years ahead. And economic intercourse will also be of substantial, though less importance to the United States. The elements of competition will be matched by those of cooperation. Patent sharing, together with joint ventures in research and development represent a potentially rich field for both societies.

Politics can also provide a meaningful linkage. Here are two democracies, sharing common political values and institutions in a world where political openness is an increasing rarity. Even in these societies, the tribulations of democracy recently have been considerable, the future unclear. Assuming that the system survives, however, there can be a sharing of experiences and ideas. Openness will make possible the expansion of an already sizable communications network informal in nature. Led by the business and academic communities, American and Japanese citizens are now organized into a series of discussion groups meeting regularly and considering a wide range of issues. Despite differences of language and culture, these exchanges have been increasingly frank and wide-ranging. The similarities in stage of development and political institutions lend themselves to the type of dialogue so difficult when the differences here are major ones.

The future of American-Japanese security ties is subject to a number of important variables. Conceivably, military relations could go through several stages. In the near future, little change is likely. Barring some major internal political upheaval, Japan will not exchange the present arrangements for the risks of either pacifism or Gaullism at this point. Nor is the United States likely to withdraw militarily from Asia in any total sense at the very time when the prospects are for a substantial increase in the regional military power of the Soviet Union and China. To contribute in this manner to a military disequilibrium and one certain to have immediate political repercussions would support neither stability nor peace. Ironically, perhaps, the big Communists themselves do not favor such a move.

In the middle and longer time framework, however, two types of developments might well occur. First, adjustments in the disposition of American military forces can and should be made in accordance with changes in military technology. Too often, a substantial lag exists in this respect, granting that political as well as purely military considerations must be kept in mind. The need for land bases, manned by Americans, in Japan or other populous areas of Asia should be regularly reexamined. At some point, the political and economic costs of such bases will strongly outweigh their psychological and military worth. The premium today is clearly on mobility, with the emphasis on sea and air forces. The political limitations on the use of American ground forces in Asia are so overwhelming now and for the foreseeable future that any military strategy failing to take this into account is short-sighted in the extreme. Burden-sharing in the defense arena, moreover, is as important as in other arenas. To cause bases to be kept at readiness level by indigenous forces is to foster a sense of responsibility, and to shift away from the psychology of dependence.

Changes here should have a logic and momentum borne out of political and military conditions. Thus, the appropriate timing could be related to the point at which new political and security arrangements pertaining to the region were consummated. Currently, there is some sentiment in favor of seeking nuclear-free status for Korea and Japan, but is this not to put the cart before the horse? The most immediate need is to move toward a multilateral guarantee of the territorial integrity of the various nations of Northeast Asia and a pledge to settle international disputes peacefully, including those between the remaining divided states. Guarantees regarding Japan alone are of questionable value, because profound changes brought about by violence could take place in the immediate environs (Korea, for example) that would have a long-term effect on Japanese security. Thus, the United States and Japan ought to take the joint initiative in seeking a meaningful new approach to the security of this region.

Our emphasis on the importance and probable strength of American-Japanese relations should not be interpreted as a plea for exclusivism. One school of thought argues, by implication at least, that Japan can constitute the sole interest of the United States in Asia. Such an argument has an instinctive appeal because it limits risks, relegating the rest of Asia to the "nonessential" category. It is related, moreover, to the views of those who would define Japan as a Western nation and move it politically out of Asia, assigning it to the U.S.-European column.

However popular, these positions do not accord with reality. One does not have to denigrate the significance of trilateral relations among the United States, Western Europe, and Japan to point out that Japan is and always will be an Asian nation in many respects, and one having a great stake in Asian affairs, economic, political, and strategic. To ignore the linkage that binds Japan to developments in the rest of Asia, to be oblivious to the need for some type of international order having applicability to the Pacific-Asian area as a whole or at a minimum to substantial parts, is to be blind to the most critical lessons of the twentieth century. American-Japanese relations cannot thrive in the midst of chaos or violence elsewhere, especially in those regions vital to Japan's economic and strategic interests.

In this context, let us turn to Korea, one of the several troubled parts of the Northeast Asian region. At the outset, it should be made clear that the Koreans strongly resent being treated by the United States as a problem contingent on and subordinate to American-Japanese relations. In microcosm, they reflect here a much broader issue. There were good reasons for a renewed American concentration on major power relations in the 1960s, and a reevaluation of basic national interests. Inevitably, however, this development has bred its own liabilities. The image of the United States with respect to political principles is no less blurred than that of other large states in an era defined as one of power politics. More importantly perhaps, it is widely assumed that in order to garner American attention, one has to be powerful—and also obstreperous. This is not merely a Korean view. It is widely held in Japan and in many other states, notably from the Third World. And it has had repercussions, both in the domestic policies of states like the Republic of Korea and in foreign policies. As we have noted, indeed, Peking has shrewdly played on the phenomenon of superpower "arrogance"—while not being immune from tendencies in that direction itself.

From an American standpoint, however, the issue of national interest will command central attention in an era where domestic concerns are demanding greater priority, and the swing away from the older forms of unilateral commitment internationally is pronounced. In major degree, of course, national interest as defined by leadership has always been the touchstone for foreign policy, in the United States as elsewhere, but at an earlier point the elements of altruism and ideology were more prominently displayed. Now, with respect to an area like Korea, policy critics are putting sharp questions. Does the United States have any stake in developments on the Korean peninsula? Even if the Communists take South Korea by force, would that unfortunate event adversely affect American national interests in any major sense?

These questions are naturally given greater force because of the recent deterioration of democratic practices and institutions in the Republic of Korea. Nor is the phenomenon an isolated one. In the Philippines, former pride of American tutors, democracy has also been set aside in an effort to tackle serious socioeconomic and political problems, with the promise of its eventual restoration. If the phenomenon is common, so are its causes. Democracy, as noted earlier, is a most fragile political system, and one requiring a delicate mix of authority and freedom. In societies where socioeconomic development is uneven and in a preliminary stage, and where nation-building also remains incomplete, the democratic system is rendered more precarious. In such a setting, it is only now being realized that the commanding presence of the United States in Asia at one point provided a countervailing pressure. As indicated earlier, much has been written about Washington's support for authoritarian regimes, but there is another, oft-neglected side of the coin. By underwriting the security of small nations in peril and clearly exhibiting its own value preferences through economic and political measures, Washington strongly encouraged political experimentation in openness in certain instances. In such cases, the declining presence of the United States has generally heightened insecurities and at the same time lessened the pressures for the use of the Western-style democratic route.

Observing recent trends, many Americans have argued that the moral imperatives for supporting such allies as the

Koreans and Filipinos are now gone. They contend that because there is no difference between one form of authoritarianism and another, the United States should not be put in the position of wasting its money and possibly the lives of its men on "corrupt, reactionary dictatorships."

This is a formidable argument, and it deserves close examination. Although it is convenient to argue that there is no difference today between, for example, Seoul and P'yŏngyang, it is not correct. Between the quasi-authoritarian and the wholly authoritarian state, there are major and important political differences, as suggested earlier. Whatever the adverse trends of a given period, as long as a political opposition exists, and as long as the stipulated goals of the government are those of parliamentarism and political openness, the evolutionary potentiality for movement in these directions is vastly greater than in the tightly closed one-party mass mobilization system. Anyone familiar with the situation in South Korea or South Vietnam under Thieu knows that a non-Communist political opposition has existed, and on occasion has been quite vocal. It may have been suppressed, but it was not obliterated. Thus, it continuously reemerged, in various forms. Moreover, as the private sector was a reasonably substantial one in the social and economic realms, competition with the state of a more basic nature continued. Such competition cannot be eliminated even in highly authoritarian systems, but it is infinitely weaker.

There is the further argument introduced earlier that most Asian societies are not ripe for political freedom, and that communism or some other form of authoritarian system of an extreme nature, particularly if it flies socialist banners, will benefit the common man more than an open political system. Whatever the validity of this thesis, embedded in it is a considerable cultural, even racial arrogance: only advanced Westerners can appreciate freedom and personal rights. The possibility that the Asian—farmer or urbanite—might not voluntarily choose a system that minimizes freedom on behalf of much greater collectivism and sacrifices for statist goals is dismissed. It is assumed that elites who proclaim themselves dedicated to the masses are in fact improving both the standards and quality of life.

The actual results would appear mixed, and difficult to assess or measure as against other systems. The greatest strength of modern authoritarianism—Communist or fascist—has been its capacity to put a platform or foundation under the lowest socioeconomic classes, raising them up from utter degradation. This is no small accomplishment, especially in a society like China. It is by no means clear, however, that in the subsequent stages of economic development such systems provide greater improvements and opportunities for the total development of the average citizen than systems based on mixed economies and a considerable arena of individual freedom and initiative.

These issues remain important to Americans, as indeed they should. The foreign policy of the United States can never be totally separated from ideological or moral considerations. At the same time, there is another range of issues, reflective of the real world in which we live, and in themselves requiring normative choices. Few Americans would argue that support must go only to Western-style democratic states. When is it appropriate or desirable to furnish a quasi-authoritarian or authoritarian state with economic, political, or military support?

American aid to Yugoslavia some decades ago enabled or at least abetted the survival of a state admittedly Communist but also seeking a stance independent from the Cominform, thus inaugurating a trend that was subsequently to grow. It could be argued from the perspective of American national interests that this was an act supportive of peace.

Seizing on this example, indeed, some have argued that Korea and Vietnam under Communist control would represent new Yugoslavias, and in their own way sustain the equilibrium important to international stability. There is some merit in this argument, but not as much as its proponents believe. The analogy between Yugoslavia and the divided states of Asia breaks down at several crucial points. First, Belgrade could emerge as an independent center because a political-military equilibrium between Western and Eastern Europe had already been achieved in very considerable measure. Yugoslavia, moreover, stood literally in the geographic center of this equilibrium, enabling it to be a part of the buffer zone, together with such non-Communist states as Austria.

Neither the geographic nor the political circumstances of Korea and Vietnam are conducive to a parallel development. A unified Communist Korea, sharing common borders with two massive states, China and Russia, might well seek to maintain its independence by playing off one against the other—as has historically been Korean policy. Under present or conceivable conditions, however, its dependence on these states in some combination would be overwhelming. It is difficult to see why the United States would give such a Korea significant support, since its potentialities for being a part of a separate, balancing order as is now the case with South Korea would be very limited. The best analogy in connection with Korea is not with Yugoslavia, but with the two Germanies, as the Russians at least have increasingly come to appreciate.

In the case of Vietnam, similar factors are present. The very existence of Communist Vietnam is closely related to the shift from Nationalist to Communist China, and Hanoi—greatly separated from either Moscow or Washington—must depend on an intricate political configuration in the region for its independence. With the Vietnamese Communists having seized power in the South and seeking to extend their influence throughout Indochina, will the United States be interested in supporting them against China? Political conditions are more likely to dictate either an effort to create countervailing strengths in the region, probably centering on Indonesia, or a full American withdrawal from the region. Vietnam's dependence on China under such conditions could easily grow rather than diminish, and its capacity to use the Soviet Union effectively in the event of any serious problem with China is questionable.

It should be remembered that Tito's Yugoslavia came into existence as an entity accepted by the Western allies, product of World War II. A unified Communist Korea or Vietnam can be produced at this point only through large-scale violence, as has now been made abundantly clear. To assume that in the aftermath of such violence and with earlier American commitments and sacrifices vividly remembered, public opinion and policy in the United States would swing toward a presence and program of support aiding these new states either in development or security is naive. American recognition and even aid has been or may be proffered, but on the principle that differences with their non-Communist counterparts will be resolved politically and peacefully.

A Communist seizure of South Korea would thus be adverse to American interests for a variety of reasons. It would further lower American credibility throughout the world and with respect to certain countries, such as Japan, create a major crisis in confidence as well as long-range problems. It would produce powerful new strains on détente with the major Communist powers, at least in the short run. It would signal, or appear to signal, a further trend toward disequilibrium, with other Asian states feeling forced to lean toward either China or Russia.

To accept these views, however, does not necessarily resolve some of the important questions concerning American policies toward Korea. First, should economic and military assistance be provided to South Korea now, and in what form? This question in turn can be divided into two parts. Is it desirable? Is it necessary? Recently, the view has been advanced that given the actions of the Pak government the United States should use its leverage on behalf of democracy by cutting aid and removing military forces unless remedial steps are taken. This is a thorny problem not infrequently encountered in American assistance programs. The basic arguments in favor of such action can be summarized as follows. Aid in any form is a privilege, not a right; it is a concession made by the donor. As such, the donor can and should insist on the fulfillment of certain responsibilities. If assistance serves the cause primarily of suppression or corruption, it is not in the interests of the nation concerned, nor in the American interests. To argue that the establishment of quid pro quo policies constitutes interference in the internal affairs of another state is to ignore the fact that aid itself is a form of interference. (We would define quid pro quo policies as taking the position, "If you do this, we will do that—otherwise, we cannot do it.")

It is difficult to fault the logic of these arguments. Almost invariably, however, the precise situation with which the policymaker is confronted is very complex. For example, the great majority of President Pak's opponents do not want the United States to withdraw militarily from South Korea at this time; nor do they desire substantial cuts in military assistance. The reason is simple: they fear the Communists even more than they dislike Pak and his policies. They do not want actions taken, therefore, that might be damaging to their long-range interests and possibly irreversible.

There are other complexities. As in the case of Greece, Korea represents a setting where a continuous American commitment—or an American withdrawal—has much broader implications, regional and international in scope. Moreover, as we have seen in Greece, the domestic political situation changed dramatically, and Greece now has a popularly elected government—one that decisively defeated the elements arguing for an anti-American policy. Had the United States taken drastic actions against the previous government, what hardships would have been worked on its political successors, what damages to the interests of the United States and other allies?

Retaliatory policies often boomerang, even when carefully used. They encourage an appeal to nationalism, and other emotional charges. Nor is their effectiveness invariably high. Some observers, indeed, doubt that American assistance at its current levels can be a decisive factor either in initiating or inhibiting domestic political changes. That may be true in many cases, not true in others.

None of this is to argue against flexibility for U.S. policy in this type of situation. What are the available options? First, it is the responsibility of American spokesmen repeatedly to make clear the middle- and long-range costs of authoritarian measures in terms of public and congressional opinion. This is merely to set forth a political fact of life, one having potentially serious repercussions on any aid program. The criticisms of responsible private groups and individuals, meanwhile, should not be discouraged.

Second, in a variety of ways the United States can signal the difference between its support for a nation and a people, and its commitment to any given leader. In this connection, incidentally, the democratic opposition to the Pak administration was generally satisfied with President Ford's 1974 visit to the Republic of Korea. Even though the government was able to use that visit in various ways, Ford was extremely careful in public not to confer support on Pak personally. Privately, he reiterated American concern over domestic political policies.

Finally, it is possible to take—or withhold—certain actions that will communicate American unhappiness, but actions that are subject to alteration as internal policies change. In general, the official signals given, both in words and actions, should be private ones, at least initially, permitting the negotiatory process to take place without either party losing face.

As can be discerned, there is a close connection between the issues which we have been discussing and the alternatives facing American policies toward far more rigidly authoritarian states. Earlier, we made a point which should be reiterated here. There is an unfortunate tendency on the part of many in the American academic and journalist communities either to apply a double standard when discussing quasi-authoritarian and strongly authoritarian regimes, or to blithely equate them with each other, making no distinctions. Granting the multiple differences within *each* category, neither of these tendencies is helpful.

The United States does not normally provide military assistance to rigidly authoritarian states, Communist or other (although on occasion it does), but it is certainly valid to assert that programs such as the most-favored nation treatment or credits constitute assistance. Almost everyone would agree that the United States is not going to remold either the Soviet Union or the People's Republic of China into a liberal society. (Or a great many states reflecting other authoritarian forms.) The attempt to impose liberal criteria is very likely to create a backlash, as indeed it did with respect to the emigration issue in the USSR. We would get no further in insisting on the right of the Chinese intellectuals to be allowed to express themselves freely.

To undertake such actions at an official level is a mistake. It can only result in failure. More importantly, it distracts attention from what must be the critical issues in state-to-state international relations. The criteria that ought to determine our official relations with states like Russia and China, including economic interaction, center on the international behavior of such societies, including the question of how they interact with America and others on war/peace issues. Here, the United States has both a right and a duty to measure its policies against their performance. They will undoubtedly pursue a similar course vis-à-vis Washington.

This most certainly should not inhibit private American groups and individuals from protesting transgressions against the civil liberties of individuals abroad, or the repressive policies of various states. Here, a wide range of policies can be pursued with some effectiveness, both at home and overseas.

Returning to the Korean issue, the current foreign policies

of the Republic of Korea, in distinction to its domestic political policies, are exceptionally enlightened and represent a major shift from an earlier period. Seoul has announced its willingness to enter into diplomatic relations with all nations prepared to accept it, including the major Communist states. It has set forth a concrete program of humanitarian, economic, and cultural exchanges that could enable a step-by-step evolution in South-North relations. Meanwhile, it has recognized the existence of the Democratic People's Republic of Korea, signaling its willingness to sit in the United Nations with that government as well as accepting recognition of both de facto states by other nations.

In contrast, the DPRK currently holds to strongly ideological, highly unrealistic policies that cannot contribute to a peaceful solution. It insists on dramatic military and political actions on the part of the two states, such as a reduction in the armed forces of each government to 100,000; establishing a "Confederal Republic of Koryo" via the convening of a "National Congress" representative of "all strata, parties, and social organizations," north and south; and entry into the United Nations as a single entity.

Parts of this proposal go back to the earliest Communist positions, taken prior to the Korean War. They bear no relation to the realities of the contemporary political-economic situation, and can only serve to obstruct developments in South-North relations that could be helpful, such as visits between divided families, an exchange of correspondence, barter trade, and a reduction of border tension. The two Koreas are now disparate in a host of ways: population, economic system, political structure, and international affiliations. There is a complete absence of trust between the two states, and understandably so. A program based on mechanical unity must be labeled propagandistic. To justify such a program on the grounds that "the Korean people want unity" is to obscure the critical issues, because the people of

South Korea do not want unity on Communist terms, and the people of North Korea presumably do not want unity on non-Communist terms.

Given this situation, the United States faces some important policy decisions regarding Korea. What attitudes and policies should it adopt with respect to the reunification issue, and the foreign policies of the two Koreas? What steps are appropriate to reduce the danger of conflict on this peninsula, and to move toward an international understanding here?

Broadly, the present foreign policies of the Republic of Korea are in line with American policies. The United States in recent years has been moving away from the use of nonrecognition as an instrument of foreign policy, with reason. That policy was rarely effective, and it confused two separate issues. One nation does not have to approve of another in order to recognize its existence. Only through recognition and an exchange of diplomatic representatives can differences be systematically discussed, misperceptions corrected, the risks of conflict reduced. It is in the American interest, therefore, to urge Communist recognition of South Korea, exhibiting a willingness, *reciprocally*, to recognize North Korea. As a preliminary measure, Washington should be prepared to match those informal gestures which Moscow (or Peking) are willing to display toward Seoul.

Both North and South Korea have asserted officially that the Korean problem should be resolved by the two parties themselves, without outside involvement. The North has made one of its principal demands the withdrawal of all American military forces from South Korea, a position vigorously opposed by the South. But the North is also heavily dependent on external support, for the bulk of its military equipment comes from the USSR, with China furnishing aid too.

Currently, the USSR and the PRC publicly support Kim Il-sŏng's position on troop withdrawal and U.N. recognition. Yet as suggested earlier, privately the major Communists have shown elements of flexibility from time to time. Indeed, it is not entirely clear that they—and particularly the Russians—want an immediate withdrawal of American military forces, or Korea unified on any basis.

At present, the United States has approximately 38,000 troops in South Korea. Although these forces perform certain important technical functions including, one may presume, control over the American nuclear weapons that are likely to be in this country, no one would regard this force as capable of withstanding a massive enemy assault, at least if the conflict involved conventional weapons only. Its purposes are at least as much psychological and political as military. It stands as symbol of the American commitment, in much the same fashion as the American forces in Japan and Europe, granting some differences, especially in the latter case.

What risks are involved in keeping military forces in Korea? Setting aside the fundamental argument explored earlier, namely, that the fate of Korea is not vital to American national interests, the principal risks would appear to be these: direct involvement in the North-South conflict, and one that under certain conditions might be initiated by the South rather than by the North; becoming entangled in hostilities with China or Russia as a result of another Korean War; and becoming trapped in South Korean domestic turmoil, with the possibility of rising anti-Americanism.

The risks involved in removing all American military forces at this time must also be enumerated. First, signifying another unilateral act of American withdrawal, this could have a profoundly destabilizing affect throughout Asia, and particularly in Northeast Asia. American credibility would be further damaged, and this could have repercussions in relations with China and Russia as well as with Japan and other allies.

Second, a full American withdrawal might be read by the North as a signal that it was free to undertake a much more adventurous set of policies, combining legal and illegal action on the Vietnam model. Almost certainly, it would lead to doubts and bitterness in the South, with the feeling that the United States was deserting an ally that had been staunch in its international support of American policies.

Finally, the withdrawal policy executed at this point could produce a dangerous escalation of military preparations by both North and South Korea, with the possibility of some lethal new weapons being introduced. The leverage of the major powers in this connection, and particularly the United States, would have been substantially reduced. Thus, war would be made more likely.

On balance, the risks of withdrawal outweigh those of retaining some American forces in Korea. This does not necessarily constitute an argument against further force reductions. Moreover, this is a time when broader, multilateral approaches should be carefully explored. In the past, off-the-record discussions on Korea with Russia and China have on occasion been helpful, and these should be continued. One proposal supported by some Americans is to make Northeast Asia a nuclear-free zone. Presumably, however, this would not apply to either China or the Soviet Union despite the fact that both are partly in this region. Its utility, therefore, is unclear—particularly if it were applicable only to Korea and Japan. By putting the premium on massive conventional forces, would the cause of peace be advanced in the region, especially in Korea?

The United States might advance a "zone of peace" concept based on the following points. First, each of the four major societies most vitally concerned (Japan, the PRC, the USSR, and the United States) would recognize the two de facto states and sponsor their admission into the United Nations with no barrier imposed or intended with respect to eventual unification. Second, it would be jointly agreed that unification should be pursued by peaceful means. In the event of armed aggression by either side, all parties would refrain from furnishing military assistance to the aggressor. Third, on conclusion of the preceding agreements, the United Nations Command would be dissolved. Eventual full American military withdrawal would be pledged, its timing dependent on the emergence of conditions conducive to peace in the region.

There is little chance that the preceding proposal would be accepted initially, given the current stance of Kim Il-sŏng and the complex Sino-Soviet-North Korean relationship. Peking's present position is particularly worrisome, as noted earlier. Has Kim Il-sŏng acquired additional Chinese pledges in connection with his quest for "liberation" of the South? Moreover, the General Assembly may remove the United Nations Command label independently. Nor could one guarantee any agreement on the identity of the aggressor in the event of war. The probabilities are otherwise. Although North Korean initiation of the first Korean War has now been admitted by no less an authority than Nikita Khrushchev, P'yŏngyang still clings to the line that Rhee began the war at American instigation. These problems notwithstanding, the proposals set forth here are logical ones, and over time they may well prevail. On some positions, in any event, the United States should be prepared to stand firm, awaiting the passage of time—as do the Soviets and the Chinese.

Meanwhile, Washington should continue to facilitate the settlement of problems between Seoul and Tokyo. Its services in connection with the Kim Tae-jun kidnapping and the assassination of Mrs. Pak have been considered very valuable by both sides. The South Korean-Japanese relation is at once vital to stability in Northeast Asia and bound to be thorny. The United States has good reasons from the standpoint of its own interests to play an intermediary role, being careful to treat both parties as equals.

One final issue of great importance connects Northeast Asia with the Continental Center, namely, Taiwan. Until 1969–1970, this issue served to block any improvement in relations between the United States and the People's Republic of China. As indicated earlier, American overtures early in the Kennedy administration were met with the adamant insistence that until the Taiwan issue was settled, no improvement was possible.

A decade later, Peking's leaders had shifted their position. Deeply concerned about China's security, Taiwan seemed of less immediate importance than the need to establish a more internationally oriented, complex foreign policy. In the Shanghai Communiqué which officially inaugurated the new era in American-Chinese relations, as we noted previously, the Taiwan issue was certainly not settled. The United States did make a concession, susceptible to different interpretations, when it acknowledged that "all of the Chinese people" on both sides of the straits regarded China as one, and Taiwan as a part of China. Had this passage read "both governments" instead of "all of the Chinese people" it would have been a mere statement of fact. But by acknowledging something untrue, the United States presumably paid the minimal price for initial normalization.

Yet Washington continued to have formal diplomatic relations with the Republic of China on Taiwan, and although it was agreed that the very small American military forces on the island would be withdrawn as conditions in Asia permitted, no agreement pledging changes in political and economic policies or in defense commitments was exacted. At a later point, moreover, Peking agreed to an exchange of liaison missions, with the same conditions prevailing.

Beginning in 1974, however, PRC officials signaled in various ways that the Taiwan issue was not being resolved in a manner satisfactory to them. China was prepared to be patient, it was asserted, but not to accept retrogression. This latter reference was to the appointment of a new, relatively senior diplomat, Leonard Unger, as a replacement to Ambassador Walter McConaughey and almost simultaneously granting the

Nationalists permission to open several new consulates in the United States. Behind these specific grievances, however, Peking now seems alarmed that Taiwan, despite its various diplomatic setbacks, is surviving so well, with foreign investments—particularly from the United States—continuing to flow into the island.

The invitation to President Ford to visit China in 1975 was seen by some observers as an effort to encourage new American steps regarding Taiwan, for a presidential trip, to be viewed as successful, should presumably be climaxed by an announcement of further advances in Sino-American relations.

What alternatives are available to the United States in this complex matter? At least five possibilities exist, each with several permutations. Washington might, in effect, accept Peking's position, breaking all formal political and military ties with the Nationalists, and using its influence to encourage the Taipei government to reach a settlement with Peking, one providing for the political and economic autonomy earlier promised.

A second alternative would be that of downgrading diplomatic relations with the Republic of China on Taiwan, and transferring full respresentation to Peking. Presumably, Taiwan would have a consul-general, or head of liaison mission—as now applies to Washington-Peking ties. Many of those advocating this alternative argue that it would not necessarily require a severance of current defense commitments to Taiwan.

A third alternative would be to seek from the Peking government a formal pledge that force would not be used to "liberate" Taiwan. With such a pledge, the Mutual Security Treaty could be caused to lapse, and the United States would retain merely economic and political ties, assuming that negotiations would eventually lead to some type of interrelationship between China and Taiwan.

A fourth alternative would be to take no action, allowing a

passage of time to take place which might enable clearer vision regarding the future both in the PRC and the ROC. The United States would not intervene, should negotiations at some point commence or forms of interaction begin. Indeed, it might actively encourage these developments. But it would also not change the nature of its present commitments.

Finally, the United States might take the position that the sixteen million people on Taiwan had the right to determine their own political future. Under this principle, it might urge a plebiscite or some other means of determining the popular will. In any case, its general policies would move in the direction of accepting and encouraging an independent Taiwan.

As noted, one can imagine some variants of these policies, but the basic alternatives would seem to be encompassed here. With each, there are advantages and disadvantages, opportunities and risks. To accept Peking's position has the advantage of "solving" the Taiwan problem, removing the central obstacle that currently affects Sino-American relations and thereby paving the way for interaction with, and possibly, influence on the largest nation in the world. Such a course of action would also adversely affect American credibility with most or all allies. It would be widely interpreted as a "sell-out" of the Taiwanese, not just of the government, but of the people as well. China has promised Taiwan autonomy in the fashion of Tibet. But the image of Tibet is not an appealing one outside of China.

In addition to its political and ethical consequences, could such a policy actually work in the manner intended? Would Taiwan capitulate under the combined pressures brought to bear on it, or would some act of desperation ensue—such as a Taiwanese rebellion? The possibilities for American embarrassment would seem considerable. In addition, would it be in the American interest to actively encourage the advent of the PRC as a Pacific power? Certainly, the Chinese would have to develop air and naval strength sufficient to maintain the defense of this major Pacific outpost. Over time, that would have profound strategic implications not merely for the United States but for every Asian nation.

The second alternative, that of switching political relations with the two states, may or may not be feasible. Would Peking accept this kind of substitution? In recent years, China has demanded a complete severance of formal political ties with Taipei as the price for full normalization or diplomatic relations. Assuming, however, that some arrangement were acceptable to the Communists and forced on the Nationalists, would the United States be able to maintain its defense agreement with Taiwan legally? If officially Taiwan ceased to be an independent, sovereign state, would not this agreement—and others—constitute unwarranted interference in the internal affairs of another state (China)? If the defense agreement were scrapped, would not the threat of force become much more meaningful, raising tension in the region and inducing both political and economic crises? In such a case, would not this come to represent the first alternative, on the installment plan?

The third alternative, that of exchanging the U.S.-ROC defense agreement for a PRC pledge to eschew force is not acceptable to Peking, and it is difficult to see how it might be made acceptable. The Chinese Communist leaders have taken the position that the treatment of Taiwan is an internal matter, hence, they will make no promises whatsoever. Indeed, in recent months, they have increasingly stressed the possibility that force may have to be used to "liberate" the island if other methods fail.

The fourth alternative, that of standing on present policy and awaiting developments, runs the risk of creating an impasse in Sino-American relations that at some point leads to deterioration. Some would assert that it could also make more likely Sino-Soviet rapprochement, or even a Sino-American conflict. The same objections can be raised concerning the final alternative, that of support for Taiwanese self-determination.

When these alternatives are carefully surveyed, however, the last two appear to accord in greatest measure both with the realities of the current situation and with the longer range interests of the United States. With the exception of a very brief and stormy period at the close of World War II, China and Taiwan have existed as two separate political entities throughout this century. In recent years, moreover, they have been moving away from, not toward each other—economically, politically, and culturally. The standard of living on Taiwan is infinitely higher than in China, and of equal importance, the way of life is vastly different. It is not surprising that Taiwanese commitments are overwhelmingly to this island, and the Taiwanese constitute some 80 percent of the population. Among the second-generation Nationalists, recipients of family as well as state indoctrination, the concept of "going home" has some appeal, but a considerable percentage of this group is currently migrating elsewhere, including to the United States. As long as political and economic conditions on the mainland remain unstable, moreover, campaigns to attract the people of Taiwan will have limited appeal.

In both China and Taiwan, it should be emphasized, the future is extremely difficult to predict. In the PRC, the issues and events of succession have barely begun to unfold. Whether the Fourth People's Congress of January 1975 is interpreted as a victory for the moderates or a holding operation, the advanced age of the key figures make it clear that China is in a transitional phase that could change rapidly. In Taiwan also, although the succession has taken place and Chiang Ching-kuo is pursuing certain new policies, bringing more Taiwanese into government and putting additional emphasis on self-reliance, he himself is *sui generis,* being the son of Chiang Kai-shek. From whence will come the leadership, and what will be the policies after Chiang Ching-kuo?

Given the multiple uncertainties, is it wise for the United States to embark on any new policies with respect to Taiwan at this time? In diplomacy, waiting also has great merit on occasion—as the Chinese themselves have tried to teach us.

There are those who argue that against human rights should be juxtaposed property rights—the historical claims of the Chinese to Taiwan and the likelihood that this island will become territory irredenta, spawning an increasingly more militant nationalist movement, if it does not revert to the PRC soon. Perhaps this is true, although as we have seen, the Taiwan issue has been raised and lowered, depending on other, broader issues such as those relating to the security of China proper. It would be equally logical for Outer Mongolia to be considered territory irredenta, as indeed it was for many years. It should be noted that the position of the Chinese Communists on the question of Taiwan has not been immutable. Mao Tse-tung himself, in the 1930s, asserted that China should support the struggle for Taiwanese as well as Korean independence, and even after the onset of the Sino-Japanese War, the Chinese Communists operated on this premise (see Edgar Snow's *Red Star Over China*, 1937 edition, p. 102).

The possibility that this issue will constitute a serious thorn in the side of Sino-American relations, and one productive of heightened Chinese militancy, should not be dodged. These factors represent the principal, perhaps the only reasons for considering a major policy shift. As long as the American defense commitment to Taiwan is maintained, however, no leadership in Peking would be so unwise as to commence military operations. At most, the route would be that of guerrilla warfare on Taiwan, and to date the socioeconomic and political foundations for such a course have not been effectively laid.

It is not necessary for the United States to pronounce on the ultimate—and possibly changing—views of the people on Taiwan in order to insist that their views should be taken into account, and that any political changes should be reached peacefully. To take any other position, for example, to connive with Peking in delivering Taiwan to the PRC without popular consent, would have the most serious adverse effects on the American image in Asia and on Washington's credibility as an ally.

To espouse the independence of Taiwan now has the disadvantage of seeming to freeze a situation which has a great many potentials for fluidity. There can be no doubt that the great bulk of the population on Taiwan would prefer independence—and a considerable rise in the quotient of Taiwanese political authority—to all other alternatives. Moreover, in de facto terms, Taiwan is independent, albeit under Kuomintang rule.

It is always possible, however, that at some point negotiations between Peking and Taipei will focus on realistic possibilities such as barter trade, exchanges between divided families, and similar matters. Thus far, negotiations have not seemed to be a promising route, because Peking has been interested primarily in discussing the terms of surrender for Taiwan. That could change. As we have also pointed out, the political evolution within both of these states is subject to unexpected developments. Alternative four in effect does recognize the independence of Taiwan—but it provides greater flexibility in dealing with the future. If alternative three could be so structured as not to preclude an option for Taiwanese independence, and not to interfere with current American commitments, it too might have a serious claim for support—but such conditions seem impossible of attainment at present.

In focusing on the important issue of Taiwan, we have, perforce, moved toward a discussion of U.S.-China relations, and hence begun to look at still another region of vital importance to the United States, the Continental Center. First, however, a few summary remarks concerning U.S. policies in Northeast Asia are in order. This region will continue to be one of the most sensitive in the world, and one of the most important. Any changes initiated here by force will be destabilizing in the extreme and create the risk of a major war. To prevent such a development, it is necessary to create a climate for negotiations, both among the states of the region itself and among the major powers having interests and commitments here. Past actions of the United States in facilitating this, both as mediator and participant, are praiseworthy and should be continued. Given the political configuration of Northeast Asia, neither the exclusive alliances of the past nor a new regional organization encompassing most states of this area is feasible. Thus, more informal, yet accessible, regularized communications become all the more essential.

The indications are strong that precipitous, unilateral American concessions at this point, whether in the form of full military withdrawal or the abandonment of treaty commitments, far from contributing to peace, would increase the likelihood of violence. None of the other major powers is in the mood to take similar actions. On the contrary, Russia and China intend to negotiate from such strength as they can muster—both with each other and with the United States. Indeed, for rather complex reasons, neither of the big Communist states wants America to engage in any full-fledged retreat at this point. Even they are well aware of the problems that would ensue.

Recent history has shown that wars are as likely to be caused by misperceptions as by incidents. The Korean War is a classic example. The Communists misread American intentions, and understandably so, for a top American spokesman had signaled the likelihood that the United States would not defend South Korea against attack. This should not be forgotten in contemplating policies in this region. Occasionally, an element of ambiguity is useful, even required. In general, however, it is important to make American intentions clear and credible—to potential opponents as well as to various allies.

The themes thus far set forth do not require policies and positions dedicated exclusively to the status quo. The United

States *does* have a very considerable stake in the present order (as do other major and minor states), and support for it should not be abandoned lightly. Yet American initiatives to induce change of certain types are needed. To advance the cause of peaceful coexistence, to extend the network of communications and interaction among states possessing different socioeconomic and political systems, and to search out multilateral approaches to such specific issues as Korea and regional arms control all challenge American ingenuity.

Finally, although Northeast Asia is a highly important region, it should not and cannot be treated wholly apart from other regions. This is also true of the most important bilateral relation held by the United States within this region, that with Japan. To argue, either explicitly or implicitly, that no other country or region within Asia has comparable importance to the United States, and that therefore American commitments and attention should be devoted exclusively here, is to move from a statement true in part to a faulty conclusion. In many respects, this is the most important single region and Japan is the most significant single country relating to the American future. But not in all respects, or for all purposes—obviously, for the Sino-Soviet-American triangle is of vital importance as it affects war/peace issues, and the rising problem of resources is making other parts of Asia increasingly important for economic reasons. In any case, it is totally unrealistic to believe that a single relationship can be developed in isolation, with no linkage to the regional and area context in which it must evolve.

The Continental Center

A portion of this context, as we have just indicated, relates to the Continental Center and Sino-Soviet-American relations. Sino-American relations have already been explored from the vantage point of China and via the central issue of

Taiwan. It remains to look at them more broadly from an American perspective.

In the most general terms, U.S. China policy has shifted in the course of twenty-five years from a policy of conflict and containment by isolation to one of peaceful coexistence via negotiations. A few observers have gone so far as to predict an American-Chinese alliance based on a common threat from the Soviet Union. Perhaps nothing should be declared impossible in international relations, but a Sino-American alliance defies logic on many counts. In all probability, as noted earlier, American-Chinese relations will continue to be important for certain purposes, but limited. The arena of cooperation will be significant but small; that of controversy and difference considerably larger. One American purpose will be to enlarge the former, reduce the latter.

Thus far, the elements bringing the United States and the People's Republic of China into a more meaningful relationship with each other have been largely negative: a shared concern over the USSR: the desire to avoid war with each other; the official rejection of policies that might lead to the hegemony by any given power over Asia. Differences between the two countries in foreign policies, both general and specific, remain wide-ranging. Communications continue to be sparse and irregular, although they have increased. Economic relations have also grown, but not without various obstacles that suggest substantial limitations.

Some positive factors exist. The American perception of China and the Chinese—politics apart—is generally favorable or, at a minimum, neutral—"Oriental inscrutibility" and similar images earlier implanted notwithstanding. Indeed, public support for the Nixon-Kissinger policies toward China and the extraordinary rise in interest in China are evidence of this fact. The United States, moreover, does not fear China, at least not in the same sense as does the USSR. It is not forced to live cheek-by-jowl with this massive, unpredictable society, and "yellow peril" themes currently have low appeal on the American market.

Cultural-political differences, however, and most especially the dramatically different stage of development in which the two societies currently find themselves, will continue to limit communications and the creation of common policies. In some respects, advantage can be taken of the latter difference, particularly in the economic realm, to encourage relations. Generally, however, evolution in American-Chinese relations is going to be cautious, slow, and uneven. And as indicated earlier, the event that could most easily affect that relationship adversely would be the retreat of the United States into isolationism, or a withdrawal from the Pacific-Asian area so extensive as to destroy American credibility. Then, a relation based on balance-of-power politics, not ideological or political convergence, would be truly imperiled.

American-Soviet relations are subject to somewhat similar constraints, and hence a similar analysis. There are some potentially significant differences, however. Russia, as we have noted, is a much more powerful nation than China, and hence of much greater potential danger to the United States in both security and political terms. On the other hand, the Soviet Union is a more porous, more rapidly evolving society than China. As such, it may be more accessible to the United States than China and at least equally desirous of American cooperation. The Chinese need for the United States today is primarily related to security, the use of the United States as a countervailing force against the Soviet Union. Secondarily, China found the United States useful in enabling the PRC to reenter the world, so to speak, and establish economic and political relations with a wide range of societies. To a considerable extent, these latter purposes have been served.

In the case of the Soviet Union, as we have indicated, the desire for American economic interaction is genuine, and based on substantial needs. Recent events have also made it clear that as two powers with global commitments and responsibilities, the USSR and the United States must cooperate in some degree if catastrophe is to be avoided. Here, the factor of sheer necessity looms much higher than with respect to China. Beyond this, however, in its policies toward Asia, the Soviet Union is more of a status-quo power at present than China, and that reduces, if it does not remove, the areas of potential conflict over specific policies with the United States.

Policy differences do remain, some of them—such as Indochina—of basic importance. As we have seen, moreover, new regions of competition and possible military confrontation such as the Indian Ocean are very possible. Using these as examples, indeed, Peking is once again predicting flatly that the coming war will not be between China and Russia, but between Russia and the United States. Yet here one suspects that the wish is father to the thought. American-Soviet relations are certain to be complex, on occasion crisis-ridden, and as in the case of China, uneven. The disaster of a Soviet-American war, however, is fortunately unlikely because each side knows that from such a war, there could be no victors—only victims.

There remains, however, an issue of unique importance pertaining to the Continental Center: American attitudes and policies toward Sino-Soviet relations. What development here would serve American interests best, and what, if anything, should the United States do in an effort to influence the course of events?

Presumably, there can be wide agreement that American interests would not be served well by either a Sino-Soviet war or the reestablishment of a Sino-Soviet Alliance, vintage 1950. Although both of these possibilities have been previously discussed, let us look at them briefly from an American policy perspective. A Sino-Soviet war would be devastating to both countries, and particularly to China. It would also have profound repercussions throughout Asia, and could easily thrust on the United States massive new responsibilities for which it was not psychologically, politically, or economically prepared. That the United States would be drawn into such a war seems unlikely. Nor is it probable that it would give military or economic assistance to either side. Yet it could not escape the consequences of the war as they showered down on the entire Pacific-Asian area.

The revival of a close Sino-Soviet alliance would also be highly injurious to American interests, as well as to those of all countries lying on the peripheries of the great Eurasian land mass. As indicated earlier, such an alliance would liberate enormous military power which could potentially be used elsewhere. It would be conducive to an effort to reestablish old spheres of influence. Even in regions beyond the Eurasian continent, new pressures would be felt, relating both to revolutionary movements and existing governments.

Fortunately, neither of these two "extremities" seems likely to occur. The more realistic issue, therefore, may well be whether some limited détente between Russia and China would be of benefit or at least not be injurious to American interests in comparison with the prevailing situation. Those who argue that limited détente could be helpful generally cite the following points. The present level of tension makes it difficult for a number of states, including several American allies, to maintain balanced relations with Russia and China. Pressures are exerted in an effort to tilt a nation to one side, and as a result, tension is transmitted to the Pacific-Asian area as a whole. Second, little or no progress can be expected in the field of arms limitation and nuclear weapons control under present conditions. Limited détente would offer much greater possibilities. Finally, as long as the cleavage between Russia and China is acute, small states, particularly small Communist states, can play one off against the other in such a fashion as to make the reasonable settlement of issues involving them difficult if not impossible.

To those skeptical of the advantages to the United States of limited Sino-Soviet détente, doubts persist concerning the validity of the preceding points, and counterarguments are advanced. Are balanced relations with the USSR and the PRC possible under any conditions, and are they necessarily desirable? Must not each non-Communist country follow the bent of its own perceived interests in extending or contracting such relations? With respect to disarmament and the settlement of other disputes, would limited détente facilitate agreements judged equitable and fair by non-Communist participants, or would it be conducive to a more coordinated, unified Communist position adding difficulties to any settlement?

It cannot be denied that the United States has benefited from the Sino-Soviet cleavage, along with many other countries, Communist as well as non-Communist. That cleavage, it should be quickly added, was not the result of any American policies consciously designed to produce it, although the issue of how to handle the United States was an important, possibly the central causative factor. Thus, Washington should be extremely cautious about rendering positive support to Sino-Soviet détente. When the balance sheet is calculated, it is by no means clear that such a development would benefit the U.S. or the world.

Commonly, it is said that Washington can do very little that will affect Sino-Soviet relations, and that any effort to intervene here is likely to be counterproductive. This is not quite true. At an earlier point, Peking itself believed that the United States could serve as a deterrent to any Soviet attack, both by making clear American opposition to such a move and by at least contemplating some military or quasi-military assistance—and it may still hold this view. There can be no doubt that the Russians become extremely upset when the subject of possible military assistance to China is broached, indicating that they have considered the possibility, however remote, to be worthy of concern. From the other side, Peking attacks American-Soviet agreements with a vigor indicating its continuous fear of a progressive rapprochement between Washington and Moscow. And from still another aspect of this complex picture, as we have reiterated several times, any major changes in American presence and credibility in Asia could easily have a direct impact on Peking's relations with Moscow. Thus, American policies *can* influence Sino-Soviet relations, and that fact should constantly be borne in mind.

In the Continental Center of Asia, a great drama affecting much of the globe will continue to unfold. Despite what has just been said, the chief actors will be Russians and Chinese. Decisions originating in Moscow and Peking will be the critical determinants. As we have indicated, the present situation serves American interests reasonably well, and it is not clear that any major change would be of benefit—although limited détente might offer certain advantages. Today, Washington has fuller access to both parties than has ever been possible. It is probably correct to say that there has been no conscious effort to play off one side against the other. Nevertheless, the situation itself has made possible certain types of agreements and understandings, both with Moscow and with Peking, that would otherwise have been improbable—at least at this point.

Looking ahead, what should be the American stance on its relationship with the USSR versus China? In general terms, equidistance is an appropriate goal. An alliance with either party or even a course of action that aimed deliberately at favoritism would be highly unsuitable. Selective, mutual tilts on the part of the United States are preferable to any sustained, uniform tilt. Yet it should be recognized at the outset that equidistance is not really possible, because the nature of American-Soviet and American-Chinese relations is bound to differ in great degree. The Soviet Union is moving toward military parity with the United States, if it has not already achieved this position. It has a massive presence in most of the regions of the world critical from a strategic, political, or economic standpoint.

Thus, like the United States, it bears a tremendous responsibility for peace or war, arms control or an arms race, and the settlement or festering of specific disputes. Neither Washington nor Moscow is omnipotent, and in some respects—as is well known—their power relative to that of others has declined. We term this trend multipolarism. But to a considerable extent, this is still a bipolar world in terms of the application or potential application of military power to a given crisis. China, at least, has not forgotten this. Consequently, American-Russian relations must be accorded a type of priority and a degree of importance not possible in other settings.

To make this point as forcefully as possible is not to denigrate American-Chinese relations, or other bilateral ties of significance to the United States. For certain purposes, and in certain contexts, Sino-American relations are very important. As we have noted, moreover, despite the uncertainties and clouds that hang over them, it seems improbable that they will revert back to minimal, hostile contacts following 1949. China is destined to be a major power in Asia—but not, one hopes, the sole power in Asia. The task of working out a political-military equilibrium and of accelerating socioeconomic development (the two, in some measure, go together) must involve China along with other Pacific-Asian states. In this, the United States has a very great stake.

Southeast Asia

Does that stake extend to Southeast Asia, and if so, in what form? No issue has been more hotly debated than this one, particularly in light of the Vietnam War. As we have seen, Southeast Asia is a heterogeneous region encompassing a population that is moving rapidly toward three hundred million, and with natural resources sufficient to make it one of the richer parts of the world. Yet much of its population remains poor, and it has been plagued with recurrent political instability, product of many factors including a recent (and diverse) colonial legacy.

This is not the place to attempt an extended analysis of Vietnam, a subject still intensely political in the United States and, hence, largely handled via polemics. Vietnam looms so large over this era, however, and may have such a pronounced influence over future policies in Southeast Asia and elsewhere, that it cannot be ignored. The effort here will be to present a succinct analysis of the major factors motivating past American policies, fully aware of the controversies that swirl around this matter, and then suggest the alternatives now available and probable courses of action.

Contrary to what some critics say, American involvement in the Vietnam War did not stem from economic considerations. Even now, the economic stake in Vietnam is tiny, that in Indochina scarcely larger. In recent years, most of the major industrial nations of the world, the United States included, have become much more interested in Southeast Asia's resources—particularly those of Indonesia and Malaysia. But this is a recent development—of extremely limited significance to the critical decisions of the 1950s and 1960s.

The primary considerations were always political and strategic, and they went far beyond Vietnam itself. In the first stage, a gradual shift took place after World War II, from a strong and almost exclusive commitment to anticolonialism to an ambivalence borne out of a rising concern over Communist expansion. The late 1940s produced a series of bitter confrontations with the Russians over issues ranging from Poland to Korea, quickly labeled "the Cold War." The victory of the Communists in China and the North Korean assault across the thirty-eighth parallel were additional blows. Growing American ambivalence made itself felt in Washington's policies toward Indochina, with increasing aid being given the French-Indochinese anti-Communist forces. But that aid stopped short of direct American involvement—a fact that the French have never forgotten or forgiven.

Then came the Geneva Agreements of 1954, agreements like those of 1973, too ambiguous and, in part, illogical to be enforced rigorously—even if the will to do so had been universally present. Two de facto states were now established and widely recognized. Vietnam had become another divided nation, albeit one that supposedly looked toward unification as did the Germanies, the Koreas, and the Chinas. Here, the instrument was to be elections—but as in the case of Korea, the most elemental prerequisites for meaningful elections never existed and never could exist, given the nature and commitments of Hanoi and Saigon.

The ultimate issue was inevitable, and not different in kind from that posed by other divided states: unification by force, or an acceptance of division? Because the Communist position had always been unification by any means necessary, as the prospects for "peaceful unification" receded, the commitment to forceful unification grew stronger, abetted by various internal developments in the South.

Meanwhile, each successive American administration had made certain decisions, by action or inaction, that constituted a legacy for the next group of policy-makers. The Truman administration eschewed putting firm pressure on the French to reach a generous agreement with Vietnamese nationalism at a point when the non-Communist nationalists were still powerful in the North and greatly superior in numbers and support throughout Vietnam. The Eisenhower administration, uneasy over its decision not to come directly to the aid of the French-Indochinese forces in the climactic weeks of early 1954, decided to give far-reaching support to the strongly nationalist Ngo Dinh Diem, new leader of the South. The Kennedy administration, feeling itself challenged by the Soviet Union on various fronts and with its overtures rejected by the People's Republic of China, decided to guarantee the survival of a non-

Communist government in South Vietnam as Communist attacks—now increasingly bearing the overt imprimatur of the
North—moved from wholesale assassinations of local officials
to extended guerrilla warfare.

By the 1960s, the issue viewed from Washington was essentially this: should Communist aggression in the pattern,
somewhat altered, of Korea be allowed to succeed here? The
issue was never seen as relating to Vietnam, or even Indochina
alone. The analogies were to Manchuria, Ethiopia, and
Czechoslovakia in the 1930s and to Korea in the 1950s. If Vietnam could be unified by force, would this not set a precedent
elsewhere, reversing the verdict of Korea? If the Communists
scored a major victory here, would they not be emboldened to
apply the same principles in other settings?

At the time these questions were being framed, the general
international situation looked gloomy to American policy-
makers, particularly in Asia. Southeast Asia was in great turmoil. Sukarno's alliance with Peking constituted a giant pincers
on the region. In the south, a hot war against Malaysia was underway. In the north, Chinese involvement throughout Indochina was on the increase, as was also the case in Burma. To
the west, China had launched the border attacks on India. To
the east, the second Taiwan Straits crisis still remained a recent
memory, amid rumors that Peking had urged a policy of
fearless confrontation with the United States on the USSR.

In retrospect, it can certainly be argued that the United
States paid far too little attention to the implications of the
Sino-Soviet cleavage which, despite the desperate efforts of
various parties, was steadily widening during this period. From
the vantage-point of 1961–1965, however, to the United States
and nations associated with it, the Soviet Union and China,
even when divided, appeared hostile—still capable of coor-
dinating their policies when their interests converged, or of
allowing the spheres-of-influence principle to operate.

Implicit in the American decisions of this period was a

domino theory, and subsequently the validity of that theory has been sharply challenged. As usual, the truth is complex and unsatisfying to the simple-minded folk of either side. Mechanically applied, the domino theory is false. The "fall" of country *A* will not automatically lead to the "fall" of countries *B, C,* and *D*—and on to Patagonia. There is little doubt, however, that events *can* set trends in international relations. They have done so throughout history, and they are doing so today. Moreover, a decisive turn of events in a given state or region can assuredly have a major influence on events in immediately adjacent states or regions. The implications of developments in one Indochinese state for the others and, second, for Thailand and Malaysia can scarcely be denied. The evolving policies as well as the statements that came forth in the aftermath of the debacle in Indochina in early 1975, moreover, are eloquent testimony that a wide range of states has been powerfully affected by the Communist victories. Nor are the repercussions limited to Asia.

It is another matter, of course, to ask whether the Vietnam failure, for all its trauma, truly affects the vital interests of the United States, and whether any countervailing trends can be set in motion to rectify the damage done. Both issues will be considered further at a later point. Suffice it to note here that countervailing trends in this instance remain dependent on a complex set of political involvements, including that of the United States.

By the time of the Johnson administration, in any event, the issue posed was simple yet painful. Should massive American aid, including air, sea, and ground forces, be committed to save South Vietnam from imminent collapse? At this point, it should be remembered, the United States was deeply involved in every aspect of Vietnam—militarily, politically and economically. Americans had trained South Vietnamese to fight a Korean War, adding problems to the non-Communist side. Washington had also allowed itself to be drawn in as a participant in the overthrow of Diem, adding greatly to its moral responsibility for the future. And American economic aid had become the bedrock of Vietnamese survival.

Currently, everyone is drawing "lessons" from Vietnam, many of them contradictory in nature, and nearly all of them designed to serve the broader, preconceived purposes of each individual author. The "lessons" presented here may not be exempt from this criticism, but in any case they should be subjected to such tests of data and logic as are possible.

The principal "lesson" of Vietnam is that the United States cannot fight protracted limited wars involving the use of American military forces without risking profound political divisions at home. This will be true, incidentally, no matter what nations or regions are involved. Rightly or wrongly, limited wars run contrary to the American culture, to the dominant feeling among most Americans that one should either make a full and firm commitment or none at all; either win, or get out. The nature of international relations being what they are, a strong case in logic can be made out for incremental commitments, including ones that involve the use of force. When the latter threshold is passed, however, the problems of sustaining public support for incrementalism—whatever the cause—have been shown to be tremendous, both in Korea and in Vietnam. In retrospect, moreover, military incrementalism in Vietnam has come under increased challenge. An argument can be advanced that had we posed an immediate, overwhelming military threat to North Vietnam in 1965, Hanoi would have had no option except to desist. It is possible to expand this argument to the thesis that American tactics should have been reversed: in place of military gradualism (and restraint), to which the Communists successfully adjusted, the response should have been swift and overwhelming; with respect to South Vietnam, however, in place of the massive American presence, and replacement of function, the thrust should have been restraint and the earliest emphasis on Vietnamization.

In any case, the problems of a prolonged, limited war are made more complex by virtue of media treatment of the conflict. Portrayed graphically, with emphasis upon its most sensationalist aspects, the public gets a view that is inevitably distorted—but also powerful. Divisions grow deeper, and the enemy begins to play on these divisions in a variety of ways. He would be foolish not to do so, and the Vietnamese Communists, it should be remembered, cut their teeth on French politics, many of them ascribing their victory over the French—not illogically—as attributable to their gains in the battle for French public opinion.

If this "lesson" is correctly perceived, it has profound and possibly disturbing implications for American foreign policy. Does it mean that if the United States is drawn directly into a military conflict in the future, it will either have to stop with noncombatant military advisers—or proceed to all-out war, using every weapon and means that is available? Whatever the answer to this last question, the Guam Doctrine was drawn up with this lesson in mind, as an effort to signal that indigenous forces would have to constitute first-line defenses, with the United States available primarily in the form of a nuclear shield. There is an intermediate position that has not yet truly been tested, namely, the use of air and sea forces but not ground forces. Even in this event, however, it seems likely that if the United States gambles again on limited war, it will have to gamble also on its being of short duration.

Perhaps this sustains the thesis of those who have long argued that American ground forces should not be used on the continent of Asia. This thesis has generally rested on several propositions: that Asians were prepared to expend manpower in a fashion unacceptable to Americans and that the strategic situation here did not augur well for an American victory, especially in a limited war. The latter premise would appear to be correct, at least if one concedes a critical variable—namely, that American staying power is relatively short in comparison with that of the enemy. One may doubt, however, that the thesis is applicable only to Asia. Ground forces abroad can still play a psychological-political role, as we have underlined earlier. Whether they can or should play a major military role is now questionable.

Connected with the first "lesson" is a second already signaled, namely, the importance of correctly perceiving the full dimensions of the conflict or crisis at hand, and working with the appropriate indigenous forces to bolster their capacities from the outset, rather than supplanting such forces. This lesson cuts in two different directions, those of overcommitment and a refusal to insist on accountability for aid rendered. Turning first to overcommitment, it accords with the deepest wellsprings of American culture to make a full commitment or none at all. Yet to make the struggle an American one, with U.S. troops dominating the scene and the tactics of massiveness operating at every level is to over-Americanize the conflict and in the course of doing so to lose sight of the critical internal dimensions which will be ultimate determinants. This is particularly true of the type of struggle that emerged in Vietnam.

At the same time, as was earlier indicated, aid in any substantial quantities brings with it responsibilities. Conniving in the overthrow of Diem, and particularly with no clear future course of action, was the height of irresponsibility. But so was the unwillingness at both earlier and later points to make emphatically clear the conditions under which assistance would be continued, and those under which it would be reduced or withdrawn. Here, as elsewhere, the United States on occasion appeared to be the slave of an ally. The concept of men like Diem being puppets was at the furthest end from the truth, and the critical issue was how to induce mutual responsibilities and rights—an issue that remained to the end.

In citing the implications of this second lesson, I draw different interpretations from some observers. For example, the theses that this was purely a civil war, that Americans ranged themselves against the force of Vietnamese nationalism, or that the U.S. supported "corrupt, incompetent dictatorships" have all been repeatedly advanced in connection with this lesson. Yet none of these positions does full justice to the facts.

The Vietnamese War was of course a civil war in the sense that it involved Vietnamese fighting Vietnamese, just as the Korean War commenced in this fashion and a war between the two Germanies would have been a civil war had it erupted. But as divided states, products of complex international developments, each contains a strong international quotient. Does anyone believe that if West Germany had sought to "liberate" East Germany, the Russians would have regarded that as merely a civil war? Or that the Korean War was viewed in this manner by any of the major societies?

The implication that only Ho Chi Minh and the Communists have been *bona fide* nationalists is naive. Almost all politically articulate Vietnamese are nationalists. It is scarcely necessary to subscribe to Marxism-Leninism to deserve that label. Nor, despite many writings to the contrary, did the Communists "capture" the entire Vietnamese nationalist movement. Throughout the years since World War II, there have been many ardent Vietnamese nationalists who were also strongly opposed to being dominated by the Communists. A number of them have played prominent political roles—both governmental and oppositionist—in the South.

Corruption and incompetence have indeed been serious problems in South Vietnam, as they are in much of the world (including North Vietnam, if we may believe the official Communist journals). The size of American funds that suddenly poured into the country, combined with the huge social problems that multiplied with the war, greatly aggravated these problems. Certainly Washington bore some responsibility here, and it is clear that it did not discharge its responsibilities adequately, as has already been noted. These are universal problems, however, connected with almost every aid program—bilateral or multilateral. South Vietnam is certainly not sui generis.

To call Saigon under Thieu a dictatorship, however, is to apply that term very loosely. In degree of authoritarianism, pre-Communist Saigon was in a very different category from Hanoi at all times. Transgressions on civil liberties were frequent. This was no Western-style democracy. But there was never an absence of opposition—nor of open criticism. In the atmosphere of Saigon, it was possible to have vigorous political discussions, with the government frequently brought under attack. In part, this was testimony to the weakness of the government, but in any case, can one imagine such a situation in Hanoi? Like other states of its type, North Vietnam has a totally controlled media, permits no political activity except that approved by the Communist Party (Vietnam Workers' Party), and keeps its intellectuals and religious leaders under a tight rein. South Vietnam offered evidence once again that the prospects for political evolution in a quasi-open society are considerably more promising than those to be expected from a totally closed system.

None of these criticisms, however, negates the second lesson. Based on its Korean experience, the United States initially trained the South Vietnamese to fight the wrong type of war, and one that was vastly more attuned to American than to Vietnamese proclivities. From this error, and certain unwise decisions that accompanied it in the political realm, Washington moved toward an ever greater Americanization of the conflict. By 1965, as noted earlier, the options were stark indeed. But long after the decisions for massive American troop involvement had been made, there was still a serious delay in commencing the Vietnamization process, with a meaningful program not getting underway until 1968–1969. By removing the Vietnamese from first-line responsibility, Washington cultivated irresponsibility and, at the same time, the myth of American omnipotence.

A wise Vietnamese observer once remarked that one of the greatest difficulties lay in the fact that American tempo was radically different from that of the Vietnamese. "You went up too fast for us, and then you came down with equal speed." Having first encouraged, even demanded that the Vietnamese fight a rich man's war *à la Américain,* as the political climate in the United States changed, Washington insisted with at least equal urgency that Saigon fight a poor man's war—and at the very time when the North Vietnamese, blessed with plentiful Russian military supplies, were moving in the opposite direction. Indeed, in the eyes of non-Communist Vietnamese of many political hues, the United States deceived, then abandoned a people to whom it had earlier committed itself in such a massive fashion. The Cambodian reaction was identical, as the final message of Ambassador Um Sim in Washington made so painfully clear.

A third "lesson" should be signaled, namely, once conflict is joined, defeat exacts a high price. This is not precisely the same as General Douglas MacArthur's famous dictum, "In war there is no substitute for victory." In limited war, a reasonable compromise that enables a live-and-let-live principle to apply, and prevents the enemy from achieving his objective, should suffice. Even this type of result produces a serious strain on a society acculturated to total victory, as the troubled American response to the Korean War illustrated so clearly. Thus, it constitutes another reason why limited war is not easily made compatible with the requirements of a democratic society. When the Communists finally succeeded in conquering South Vietnam militarily, however, the impact on both the world and America was substantial.

To a considerable extent, of course, the price of "defeat" had already been paid. The decline in American credibility throughout Asia has been the most pronounced and universal trend of recent times, a fact to which sources as diverse as Peking and Taipei, Tokyo and Bangkok, Hanoi and Jakarta are willing to testify. Some would argue that this is good, either because they are ideologically and politically committed against the United States, or because they regard the American role as having been too extensive in the past. But as we have noted, even among Washington's strongest ideological opponents, there is now apprehension lest the fragile order based on balance-of-power politics be upset by the precipitous withdrawal of the United States.

"Defeat" has also contributed mightily to confusion at home. On the one hand, the forces of isolationism have reemerged, representing a wide spectrum, and with strong grass-roots support. In addition to the more traditional form of isolationism, moreover, a new type has come to the fore. The thesis is advanced that the United States can isolate itself from the risks and costs of conflict by sharply downgrading military strength and commitments, eschewing balance-of-power politics, and concentrating instead on a global humanitarian role via active participation in international social and economic programs. The attractiveness of such a proposal can scarcely be overestimated, particularly at this point in time. But could a global imbalance of military power and highly unequal expectations with respect to the performance of the major societies as political actors lead at this point to a workable international order and true progress on the socioeconomic front?

Finally events have led to the substitution of polemics for serious studies, in as well as out of the intellectual community. A small but vocal group of "revisionists" has had a field-day depreciating American policies, past and present. In the more extreme cases, Vietnam has been used to "prove" that the United States is—and always has been—immoral, aggressive, evil. Inevitably, the pendulum will swing back at some point. Increasingly, it will occur to those interested to look more closely into Hanoi's record and the actions of the Communists in Indochina in recent decades. Even those who regard American policies in Southeast Asia as woefully misguided without attaching moral blame (and that is certainly one legitimate position) will find the facts considerably more complex and troublesome than many of them had realized. What a great distance backward has been traveled in these respects since the days of Bernard Fall and Robert Scigliano, when scholars sought to portray the situation with the complexity it deserved and would not rest satisfied with simplistic appeals to the emotions.

Will the sting of defeat be made more painful by feelings of American guilt in producing it? The Communist triumph in South Vietnam was achieved by force, not by any outpouring of popular support for the Communists. It was also achieved largely by North Vietnamese troops. The issue of American responsibility for this military defeat cannot be dismissed. It is now clear that in order to get the South Vietnamese leadership to accept a bitter pill, namely, the continued presence of large North Vietnamese forces in the South after the American troop pull-out, the American executive branch made certain specific promises. It pledged that the South Vietnamese would be given the necessary economic and military assistance to defend themselves and, further, that in the event of massive Communist violations of the 1973 Paris Accords the United States would not stand by idly. Yet massive violations commenced at a very early date, first in the form of supply and troop movements, later in the full-fledged Communist military offensive of 1975. Meanwhile, in the United States, a great many developments had occurred: Watergate and the resignation of a president; a serious economic recession; and widespread public opposition to further American involvement in Indochina, strongly reflected in the Congress.

Thus, the United States did stand by idly. Indeed, from the 1973 accords onward, Congress moved to place firm legal restrictions on the executive, making the fulfillment of vital earlier pledges impossible. Moreover, it slashed in half the economic and military assistance declared essential by

American advisers concerned with Vietnam. Similar policies were pursued with respect to Cambodia. By the summer of 1974, long before the Communist military offensive of the following spring, these developments had already had a serious affect on morale in South Vietnam, in both military and civilian circles.

Factors on the other side of this coin must not be ignored. The Communists—and many Americans—argue that by not reaching an agreement enabling the "Provisional Revolutionary Government" to participate in South Vietnamese politics, the Saigon government blocked a political settlement and was itself guilty of preventing the implementation of the Paris Peace Accords. Basically, the Communists wanted an enforced coalition government. They placed little trust in elections, and with good reason for their political appeal to the South Vietnamese population had been strictly limited—quite apart from the question of who would control such elections. The demand for coalition was rejected by a strong majority of non-Communist representatives and most formidably by President Thieu, thereby creating the impasse. Meanwhile, the South continued to be plagued by serious problems of inefficiency and corruption. But the most critical weakness was the continuing disunity among the non-Communist forces, even in the face of an increasingly dire threat.

In summary, history will record that the current phase of the Vietnam War ended in a fashion remarkably similar to the earlier phase involving the French. For Dienbienphu, one can substitute the Tet Offensive of 1968. To be sure, Tet was a military defeat for the Communists, not a victory—but it came to be a political victory of major proportions in the battle to influence American public opinion. Once the public mood in the United States had shifted (and in this, the American media played a major, possibly decisive role), the mood of Congress was certain to reflect this fact within a relatively brief period.

Those seeking to make out the case for a strong and continuing American commitment to Vietnam had lost the contest by the end of 1968. The outcome at Paris reflected this fact. Like Paris-1954, Paris-1973 produced an ambiguous, unenforceable agreement, permitting American withdrawal under conditions short of Communist victory. The United States officially proclaimed the results "peace with honor," but the honor presumably rested on a willingness of the U.S. to fulfill commitments to the Republic of Vietnam, an ability to negotiate with Russia and China a mutual control over external military aid, and success in inducing North Vietnam to place its priorities on its own economic rehabilitation rather than further large-scale military operations.

South Vietnamese non-Communist leaders were always deeply suspicious of the Paris Accord, seeing it as a camouflaged American surrender to Communist demands, but one designed to save American credibility. These suspicions were reinforced by well-founded reports that at a minimum the American hope was for a "decent interlude" prior to ultimate Communist victory to permit a deemphasis on Vietnam and the American stake in the outcome. Such a position, it could be argued, was not wholly incompatible with the hope that at a maximum, if the preceding conditions were met, a settlement might be reached which afforded some protection for the interests of the non-Communist majority in South Vietnam. However, conditions in the United States, in the Communist world, and in Indochina were not conducive to any such development, and grave doubts now exist that Washington made any serious efforts to achieve more than its minimal desires—with the result that these too fell short of achievement.

Thus, at this point, both defeat and the conditions of defeat have conspired to cast a long shadow on the credibility of the United States. A number of nations currently regard both the USSR and the People's Republic of China as more reliable allies, whatever they may think of Russian or Chinese policies. In their initial responses to American defeat, both the major

Communist states for the most part avoided rubbing salt in the wounds, signaling their continued commitment to on-going relations. The uncertainties relate not to immediate but to intermediate and longer range responses. Any sustained decline in American credibility would open up new issues potentially having a strong influence on both Soviet and Chinese foreign policies. If Moscow or Peking is presented with successive targets of opportunity, if international circumstances conspire to loosen restraints, can moderation prevail in the decisions pertaining to Soviet or Chinese foreign policy for long? No purpose is served in trying to cover up these dangers, although events are subject to rapid change. The price of defeat has been high, and it could grow higher.

Many observers would draw a final "lesson" from Vietnam, one to which we have earlier referred, namely, that the United States· should never commit itself overwhelmingly to a state entirely secondary to its national interests, and particularly in a situation where the odds against success are great. When the "lesson" is stated in this manner, it is difficult if not impossible to refute. Yet it can be argued that Vietnam presented no simple case in these respects. Was that nation ever capable of being isolated, or was and is it a political situation linked with the fate of a much larger region? In turn, is Southeast Asia of scant significance to the United States, or in its economic, political, and strategic trends will it affect the broader political-military equilibrium in the Pacific-Asian region, the attitudes and capacities of such diverse major societies as Japan and the People's Republic of China, and the central question of whether peaceful coexistence or force are to dominate international behavior?

These questions give rise to others. Can a Communist-controlled Vietnam or Indochina serve as a buffer against Chinese hegemony in the region, as many hope and expect? Or is the analogy with Yugoslavia faulty, given the geopolitical facts here? Even if rivalry ensues, will it benefit those nations and peoples who do not wish to live under Communist rule or in the shadow of nearby militant, highly mobilized societies?

In seeking to measure the American stake, moreover, does not time itself become a variable of importance? Was the stake of 1960, 1965, or 1975 the same as that of 1945 or 1954? The issue becomes impossible to resolve because we cannot play out the "what if" factors in history. For example, what if the old territories of Indochina had all come under Communist control in the decade of the 1950s without an American commitment? Would the United States have come to Thailand's defense in case of request, or that of Malaysia-Singapore—and with what results? Would events in Indonesia have been the same? What would have been the implications for China's role in Southeast Asia? For Sino-American détente? For Northeast Asia, especially Japan?

The bland statement that one should avoid situations where failure is likely—seemingly unexceptionable—is also no sure guide to the future. As noted earlier, a sizable and growing body of opinion both in the United States and abroad holds that military incrementalism was a critical error, and that if the United States at the outset had confronted Hanoi with the prospect of overwhelming force, the North Vietnamese would have had no choice except to desist. Right or wrong, the likelihood is that in the event of another conflict, that route will be chosen. In the meantime, a new doctrine with at least equally troublesome potentialities has emerged. Commencing from the sound principle that the costs of every effort should be carefully calculated in proportion to its possible gains, some reach the conclusion that in situations where one is confronted with formidable force on the other side, capitulation rather than resistance is the better course. In that fashion, one "stops the killing." But it does not take a great mind to realize that this is doctrine which if uniformly advanced, reestablishes the principle that "might makes right" as the law governing international conduct.

In sum, the implications of this final "lesson" as they apply to Vietnam are by no means clear, even in the hour of defeat. It has been our contention that Southeast Asia as a region is closely connected with the Pacific Ocean and Northeast Asia—although certainly one can conceive of a delicate balance within Southeast Asia not prejudicial to balance in the larger arena. Unfortunately, however, despite the tenacity with which the island cordon-sanitaire theory is held in certain quarters, and the degree to which it has influenced some strategic thinking, it is not truly viable either in Northeast Asia or here, as was stressed earlier. Malaysia, Singapore, and Indonesia must always interact closely—whether in friendship or hostility. These parts of Southeast Asia, moreover, are becoming progressively more important to the United States, both for economic and political-strategic reasons.

Whatever the future American role, Southeast Asia is one of the regions where the principles of peaceful coexistence and détente will both receive critical tests in the period immediately ahead. Can Communists and non-Communists work out a modus vivendi both *within* a common state and across international lines? Can the five principles that originally underwrote peaceful coexistence become more than mere propagandistic slogans? For example, will states in this region or elsewhere actually refrain from interference in the affairs of other states? Will societies possessing different socioeconomic and political systems be able to interact peacefully?

The non-Communists now seem likely to fare badly in the first tests, although the precise political configuration of Indochina as a whole and its separate parts even now cannot be fully ascertained. We cannot even be certain at this point of relations *within* the Communist fronts of Vietnam, Cambodia, and Laos, potentially a critical variable. Thus, the impact that Indochina will have on other relations within the area, including those involving the major powers, cannot now be foreseen. If the Communists not only gain a substantial hold in Indochina but establish de facto governance in portions of Burma and Thailand, will the non-Communist governments remaining be able to retain or acquire the necessary strength to survive? Will the Communists themselves find that their primary problems are with China, not their southern neighbors, or will they, in any case, have to accept a role not dissimilar from that of Eastern Europe via a China steadily increasing in influence in this region—despite Peking's pledge never to become a superpower?

If the struggle could be moved to the political arena, and particularly in the event of arrangements enabling a true coexistence of non-Communist and Communist forces in a single political structure, the prospects for rapid economic development throughout much of Southeast Asia are excellent, as we pointed out earlier. In that event, moreover, the United States could act in a variety of ways to facilitate the process. Let us assume, however, that a different scenario prevails, as now seems probable. Hanoi, victorious militarily, seeks to establish its power in Vietnam, Cambodia, and Laos—either directly or through its influence on the Communist forces of the area. Communist treatment of political opponents is conventional: the ruthless suppression of elements considered implacable opponents, but with accommodation to the new order allowed most non-Communists in exchange for positive allegiance—or at a minimum, silence. Concerned about rising Chinese power in its immediate region, Hanoi under these conditions turns to the United States for aid as well as retaining its ties with the USSR and Eastern Europe. To secure American aid would have the additional psychological-political advantage of constituting an admission of "war guilt" and would be internally exploited for these purposes.

This scenario appeals to some observers, but on balance it is unrealistic. Under any conditions, American economic and technical assistance in this region will be difficult to obtain in a period when the American people have grave reservations about the effectiveness and relative importance to them of such aid. That aid will be given in conjunction with military and political defeat—as a type of reparations—is highly unlikely. It would create a major domestic political crisis for any American administration. Far more probable is an American refusal to have more than minimal relations with Hanoi and its clients for a considerable period of time. Indeed, the American mood is one of withdrawal. Indochina, for many Americans, is best forgotten—although the refugees will serve as living memories of a lost war. Immediate economic interaction with the Communists of this region is probable only in the context of some variant of a political settlement enabling the survival of non-Communists as coherent political forces and mixed economies rather than totally statist ones, a situation dubious except possibly in Laos.

Actual developments in Southeast Asia over the next few years will be highly complex, representing various combinations of compromise political settlements and military "solutions," with correspondingly different impacts on American policies. In whatever event, this region will put American foreign policy capacities to the test in several respects. First, it will be important to avoid the extremities always tempting under the conditions that prevail here. Neither total withdrawal nor total involvement can serve American interests at this point.

Second, in few regions is there such a high premium on the ability to act, and coordinate action, at several levels simultaneously. Certain bilateral relations pertaining to Southeast Asia will continue to be important in the years ahead. Special bilateral relations with Indonesia, Thailand, Malaysia, and Singapore will probably have meaning for the foreseeable future. And in each case, some differentiation in treatment may be required. At the same time, every encouragement should be given to an indigenous regionalism that can be self-generating and begin to cope with political and security problems, granting the limits outlined earlier. Beyond this, it is now clear that truly international undertakings involving powers external to the region are essential if there is to be any comprehensive approach to current needs. Both informally and through existing institutions—or new ones, if required—the United States should seek to strengthen interaction with the PRC, the USSR, and Japan of the type lending itself to a shift from war to peaceful coexistence and mutual aid.

The United States should be able to support the so-called neutralization of Southeast Asia without qualms, for it has never sought hegemony in this region for itself, nor does it want others to do so. Moreover, its interests are not likely to be served by participation in new bilateral or bloc alliances here, especially ones formal in nature. Nor are its political proclivities in this direction. SEATO, (the Southeast Asia Treaty Organization) of which the United States is a member, has had recent meaning primarily for Thailand, and Bangkok is now actively exploring a more complex and more traditional method of protecting its security by seeking to move in the direction of equidistance in its foreign relations. Few regions in the world are so positioned and so structured internally as to provide a better test of the feasibility of "neutralization" supported by multipower guarantees and assistance. In this connection, there is no reason why the United States should not insist that the behavior of major powers here be a factor of consequence in determining relationships elsewhere, as the failure to do this more systematically in the past has been one of the serious defects in U.S. policy. To accomplish even minimal results, however, an American presence in Southeast Asia is required, despite the bitter defeat just sustained.

South Asia

In confronting South Asia, the United States is dealing with a region different in several vital respects from Southeast Asia. South Asia is resource-poor with limited exceptions and overflowing with population. Hence, with respect to economic and social development, it presents a tremendous challenge both to itself and to the world, as we have noted. Yet in these terms, it represents a massive problem, not an attractive opportunity. Few would see this region as one of economic advantage or need for the United States, especially given the economic game plans being currently pursued.

Politically, the region (like its neighboring region to the east) is characterized by a considerable diversity of systems and values. The gamut runs from traditional monarchies to modified parliamentary systems. As the rigidly authoritarian, mass-mobilization systems most often represented by communism today are not as yet present, however, it can be argued that South Asia has much more compatibility of systems than Southeast Asia. Equally important, this region now has a single dominant power, India, a situation most unlikely to be duplicated in Southeast Asia, as we have noted.

The considerations governing security in this region are affected not only by the singular role of India but also by the relatively self-contained nature of the subcontinent. Great land barriers separate it from other regions. In modern times, conquest has come from the sea, although the Chinese recently demonstrated that the Himalayan barriers can be breached by a modern army. Nevertheless, external dominance or even substantial penetration seems much more unlikely than in some of the more available—and attractive—sectors of the world.

This is not to dismiss the security issue. Repeatedly, South Asian states have called on outside assistance in connection with conflicts, internal and external. The Soviet-Indian alliance, moreover, presently underwrites both Indian dominance of the subcontinent and the rising self-confidence of New Delhi as it contemplates China. For this reason, despite increased Indian unhappiness over the angle of the tilt, this alliance is likely to endure, at least for the near future. The Sino-Pakistan entente is scarcely competitive, although the fact that China is a massive, neighboring state outdistancing other

Asian states in conventional as well as nuclear military power has its impact on every South Asian nation.

China and Russia, to be sure, do not represent the only concern. New Delhi openly worries that a greatly increased American presence in the Indian Ocean will lead to a new major power rivalry, with the Russians matching that presence. As we have seen, Iran also intends to play a more important role in the naval power configuration, a development which the Indians view with mixed emotions.

Given these various characteristics, how prominently should South Asia figure in American policy priorities, and what alternatives are available for U.S. policies? The case for making South Asia a fairly high priority rests mainly on considerations that go well beyond the region itself. Thus, it is argued that unless the tests of survival are met here through a concerted international effort in which the United States plays a major part, no meaningful world order will be possible while millions starve and disintegration progresses. It is further submitted that because this is a region representing real political alternatives to authoritarianism, any basic political equilibrium requires support for this region, and particularly for India.

Those taking a different view assert that, first, the United States is well served by the present situation. It takes a relatively low posture, politically and economically. On the political front, the Soviet Union assumes the basic external responsibilities for Indian security, and thus any undue Chinese pressure that might otherwise be applied is contained. Additional strains are placed on the Sino-Soviet relationship, but the United States is not forced to run serious risks vis-à-vis either major Communist state, nor further drains on its own treasury.

Soviet military and economic assistance to India has given the Russians a considerable influence in that nation, but it has also produced mutual uneasiness. Moscow appears increasingly concerned about both the costs and the results of its programs, and although these will continue as long as "the China problem" exists, true intimacy is not probable. In any case, far from constituting a revolutionary force, the Russians have thus far refrained from interference with the Indian political system. The threats currently posed to Indian democracy do not come from the Russians. In this case, the internal factors are the critical ones.

Soviet influence, together with that from other external sources, has helped to tilt India into a position of opposition to the United States on many issues—Vietnam and the Middle East among them. But as indicated earlier, given the anti-Americanism prevailing at the very top of the Indian government, the basis for political interaction based on mutual trust and understanding does not yet exist, and current developments widen the distance between our two peoples. This is true despite the presence in India of many who wish the situation were different.

In economic terms, the case against extensive American involvement rests primarily on two points. First, South Asia offers little that can benefit or be of importance to the United States. More importantly, the scope and depth of socioeconomic problems in this region are too vast and the combined capacity and will of the governments immediately concerned too limited to make massive American aid meaningful. Indeed, such aid under present conditions would simply enable the governments to procrastinate, postponing decisions until the problems had reached even more unmanageable proportions. Given the corruption and inefficiency that mark most of the economies of this region and the limited scope available to the private sector, indigenous or foreign, the system as presently constructed cannot possibly work. To prop it up with substantial sums is merely to make the inevitable worse.

In abbreviated form, these are the arguments that surround the broadest American policy alternatives regarding South Asia, and especially India. One fact seems clear. The former

American policy of seeking to support a political-military equilibrium within South Asia by giving substantial support to Pakistan is dead. This policy, it should be recalled, was not regarded by American policy-makers as anti-Indian, and in the years after independence India itself received massive aid from American coffers. Yet there can be no doubt that earlier policies greatly antagonized the Indians. They also made the United States subject to blackmail. But the essential reason for their demise is that they failed. The emergence of India as the dominant state of the subcontinent today is a fact that cannot go unrecognized.

Under present conditions, however, those who argue the case for an American low-posture position in South Asia have the balance of both data and logic on their side. Nor is it necessary to argue that South Asia is a region of purely secondary importance or no concern to the United States in order to make a strong case for this view. In some settings, an in-region high posture or a heavy emphasis on bilateralism cannot work, whatever importance may be assigned to the region. That is the case with South Asia today.

The current situation there is not disadvantageous to the United States. Any substantially increased involvement on a sustained basis would run grave risks, as recent history has shown, even if permitted by the American Congress, which is doubtful. It would complicate relations with either Russia or China, possibly both. Its effect on the politics of the region itself could easily be negative. The capacities of the United States or any single nation external to the region to affect conditions positively must be regarded as slim.

Certainly, some unilateral or bilateral activities can be justified. American humanitarian aid to the victims of man-made and natural disasters lies deeply in the tradition of the nation, and serves to signal the continuing concerns with human misery that should be an attribute of any civilized society of the late twentieth century. Even here, however, care must be taken to see that such aid is effectively distributed and used.

There could be a broad arena for the expansion of cultural relations and for the construction of a network of private communications of the type now emerging in American-Japanese relations, depending upon future political developments in India. A sizeable number of Indians now look to the United States, hoping that somehow democracy can recapture the political initiative at home and abroad. It should not be forgotten that by virtue of their political origins and training, the elites of South Asia have a rare capacity to communicate with Americans and many have a deep interest in synthesizing values and systems. This is probably declining as the era of British colonialism recedes and new generations emerge—as was suggested earlier—but it is still a powerful force, notwithstanding the anti-Americanism and repression currently in vogue at the very top of the Indian political structure.

There are also some unilateral actions that the United States would be ill-advised to undertake. The need for an extensive naval presence in the Indian Ocean is dubious. Certainly, in terms of the testimony thus far advanced, the case for such policies has not been made. Nor does it seem advisable for the United States to return to the position of major arms supplier for Pakistan, or any other state in this region, at least under present conditions. The United States does have an interest in seeing the territorial integrity of Pakistan in its present form maintained. Indeed, any significant change in the present boundary lines in the subcontinent or in the independence of existing states would have no advantage for Washington, and could easily present problems. It is doubtful, however, whether American military assistance can be of help here.

On occasion in the past, Washington has responded to the appeal of governments threatened by attack, external or internal. Emergency military aid was given to India at the time of the Sino-Indian border conflict. At various points, Pakistan was given major assistance. Sri Lanka got American support as well as aid from India and others in putting down a serious internal rebellion. There is every reason to believe that similar appeals will come in the future from this region, given the adverse socioeconomic and political trends now prevalent.

Each situation must be judged on its merits, and in some cases, aid may be justified. The danger, nevertheless, is clear. Military and economic aid can represent deep involvement in an internal conflict, even without direct participation. That conflict may or may not have justification from the standpoint of the values and interests broadly shared by Americans. It is clear, in any case, that the principles of peaceful coexistence cannot be contravened by one party without the grave risks that they will be contravened by others, and no grey area pertaining to interference in the internal affairs of another state is in greater need of discussion and mutual agreement among the major societies than that of military assistance. Indeed, the issue of military exchanges via sales and aid should be placed near the top of the agenda for multilateral discussion. This problem urgently requires some solution, difficult as that may be.

As noted at the outset, however, the truly grave challenges posed by South Asia to a world of progress and order demand international approaches involving the maximum cooperation from a wide range of states and individuals. A substantial number of innovative proposals have already been advanced, and others will soon come forth. They include ideas for a world food bank, coordinated support for family planning, a concentrated drive to advance scientific agriculture, and cooperation in the development and exploitation of resources, including the search for substitutes. If they are to reach fruition, some of these proposals will require new or revised institutions, both international and regional. We have now learned that it is neither necessary nor possible to wait for political integration of a more comprehensive type in order to move toward a wide range of supranational institutions that can deal with problems along the entire spectrum of mankind's current requirements.

To the reservoir of manpower and resources necessary for these tasks, the United States can and should make a major contribution. That contribution, however, demands both sensitivity and toughness. There is no room in the present scene for the naive sentimentalist of whom, unfortunately, we still have a plethora. Commitment to these programs must be wide-ranging and reciprocal, cutting across ideological-political lines. The United States should be prepared to keep the pressure on in this respect. Nothing is more important, moreover, than that the governments of the regions most centrally concerned—and South Asia is one—assume their full measure of responsibility. Unless this is done, no amount of American aid will suffice. And if a trend toward lethargy shows in a pronounced fashion, Washington should be prepared to take drastic steps, including the withdrawal of its participation. Nor should the United States sit by silently while certain states seek to make political capital out of the current socioeconomic problems in which the world finds itself. The time has come to challenge both the polemicists and the procrastinators, inviting them to share in solutions instead of abuse.

The Broad Alternatives

In summary, what principles should govern American policies toward the Pacific-Asian area as a whole? At this point, three broad alternatives present themselves. The United States can undertake a calculated withdrawal from Asia in political-strategic terms, regarding itself as no longer sufficiently affected by the developments in this region to warrant commitments other than those that relate to social and economic activities. If this course were to be fully pursued, it would probably be paralleled by similar policies regarding Europe. The United States would consider itself primarily a regional power in political-military terms, with emphasis on the North American continent and immediately adjacent waters, extending to American possessions in the Pacific. But it would seek to maintain a global presence in socioeconomic terms. We can consider such a policy isolationism in its late-twentieth-century form.

An alternative now widely promoted we may call the enclave policy. Under it, the United States would limit its political-strategic commitments essentially to Japan and Western Europe, with the possibility of Israel being included. In this manner, it would see its vital interests in strategic terms as being coterminous with the advanced, industrial world. Once again, such a policy would not preclude a broader reach with respect to social and economic policies.

Finally, the United States can pursue a policy of selective internationalism, retaining a significant political-military presence in East Asia and Western Europe, and basing its policies on the theory that some political-strategic equilibrium must be maintained in the critical regions of the world if détente is to work and socioeconomic problems are to be seriously tackled.

The strengths of the first alternative stem from the degree to which it accords with the current mood of the American people. There can be no doubt that a war-weary, crisis-ridden America yearns for relief from international burdens. Unless and until economic problems can be alleviated, moreover, and confidence in political leadership and institutions restored, the first concerns of the people will be with the domestic not the international order. It can also be argued, of course, that the United States—more than most nations—can survive in an atmosphere of international uncertainty or even disorder, placing the premium on self-reliance and America First. Such a trend, it has been submitted, might also induce a stronger measure of responsibility abroad once its full implications were realized. The thesis is also advanced that the combination of internal problems confronting both major Communist states and the complexity characterizing the contemporary world preclude the type of aggression that marked the 1930s.

Yet the arguments against isolation, even in its new forms, continue to be formidable, as we have earlier indicated. Are we to assume that in the absence of any restraints in the form of risks posed by a balance of power, nations, minor and major, will operate at the international level in such a fashion as to forward peace? Can regionalism suffice in an era when almost all critical problems, including those relating to nuclear weapons and arms control, demand international treatment? Could an atmosphere conducive to a garrison-state complex in the United States be prevented for long? If the answers to these and similar questions is in the negative, as seems likely, isolationism might well be short-lived and lead to a truly disastrous end.

The enclave policy is popular in certain circles because it seems to mesh well with both the capacities and the cultural-political propensities of America. The United States remains strongly Europocentric, and the chief disappointment of some commentators seems to be that Japan cannot be moved physically into the Atlantic. The thesis advanced is that Americans can understand the advanced world and interact with it—but have no business making commitments, particularly security commitments, to the emerging societies with which it has so little in common.

On close examination, however, the enclave policy has major defects. It ignores or minimizes the critical linkages that make up the essence of international politics in this era. Japan cannot and will not be isolated from the rest of Asia, even granted its vital ties with the West. Events in Asia and particularly in Eastern Asia will have the most vital consequences for it, and any policies seeking to deny this can only produce frustrations and failures. Similarly, Western Europe will be deeply influenced by development in peripheral regions, including the Middle East. Both psychologically and politically, moreover, a union of the advanced world—even if it were feasible—would have strongly negative effects, given the mutual interdependence that is now developing on such issues as resources, maritime jurisdiction, and population-food problems.

A policy of selective internationalism and one that treats East Asia as a region critical to America's national interests and in some measure interconnected remains the only realistic policy, notwithstanding recent setbacks. The task of political leadership—and in no lesser measure that of the intellectual community—is to rebuild an American consensus that will sustain such a policy. It is by no means clear that this will be done, at least in the near future. Thus, further erosion of American influence in Asia, and the development of a more serious unbalance cannot be ruled out. But the overriding issues just outlined are likely to come into clearer focus soon.

Even if one accepts the principles of internationalism, to be sure, both priorities and different types of relations are demanded in an area as vast and heterogeneous as Asia. From a strategic standpoint, the most critical regions are the Pacific Ocean and Northeast Asia, and these are also vitally important from an economic and political perspective. Southeast Asia is closely linked to these regions, although the precise needs of Southeast Asia—and the power configurations possible—differ.

The Continental Center represents an area of vital concern to the United States because of the spill-over effect of developments here to all other parts of Asia—and to the world. It is not a region calling for or permitting an extensive American presence, however, and intensive involvement would almost surely be counterproductive.

For different reasons, unilateral or bilateral policies in

South Asia reflective of older American policies are no longer desirable or feasible. In this region, American interests are secondary except as they can be expressed through international programs designed to come to grips with the global problems so accentuated in their severity and magnitude here.

Chapter 8

In Conclusion

In looking back on the late twentieth century, future historians are likely to say that man's political, economic, and social institutions in this era failed to keep pace with a process of change so rapid as to spawn a vast array of new problems and needs. Nowhere is this more evident than in the international sphere. At the close of World War II, with the number of independent political units (states) relatively small, a widespread consensus on the importance of a coordinated international discussion/policy-making body seemed to have been achieved. When the United Nations was launched, the costs stemming from the breakdown of such an international order as existed in the 1920s were still clearly in mind. Thus, despite the fact that a Communist/non-Communist fault line had already begun to appear, the U.N. founding was attended by both hope and expectation. Some, particularly in the United States and Western Europe, wanted to go further, faster. "One World" was an appealing theme, as was "Union Now."

In retrospect, one is wont to regard the early postwar years as a time when utopian theories commanded attention even from serious-minded individuals. Idealism *was* in vogue, product of the war itself, and it led down contradictory paths. Against One World was soon to be posed the Cold War, also a monument to idealism in certain vital respects. To save democracy from Communism took on the attributes of a crusade, and given the events that were unfolding in Europe, not without reason from a liberal perspective. For their part, of course, the Russians were speaking to more than ideology in their actions. They were voicing their suspicions of an emerging international order in which they were cast in the minority role.

Other crusaders began to unfold their banners in this period. The quest of colonial peoples for national independence was to dominate the decades immediately after 1945. Having fought two civil wars within the space of thirty years, Europe was exhausted, psychologically as well as militarily. Decolonization was thus as much a product of the lapse in European will as of the decline in European power.

Perhaps it is yet too early to seek a balanced analysis of the impact of Western Europe's domination of the world, a domination that lasted for several centuries, reaching its climax on the eve of World War I and coming to an end shortly after World War II. The advent of the small Western European countries to global power was essentially a product of their having come first to the industrial revolution. This gave them both the power and the need to turn outward.

Did European rule constitute a world order? It would be more accurate to assert that the European era laid the foundations for a world order by universalizing certain values and institutions that had previously been parochial manifestations of European political-economic culture. Anything remotely resembling a world order was unthinkable prior to the twentieth century. It was not merely the sparseness of communications and linkages, but the whole range of diversity that marked men and cultures. Europe provided a set of common values. Progress, democracy, nationalism, industrialization—to which political elite today are these terms unacceptable? Disputes over their means—and even their meaning—may be rife, but these are as close to universal values as the world has ever come.

The differences over the means to and the meaning of these values, however, continues to be profound, reflecting the diverse political cultures, timings of emergence, and natural/human resources characterizing each society. The rapid pace of developments in recent decades, moreover, has produced a series of new problems, some of them posing challenges to the fundamental values that have so recently been universalized.

What are the institutional means of handling this situation? In the political realm, a continuum exists, reaching from the hamlet, village, or town to the international arena, with each level having some organizational structure. No one would deny, however, that within this continuum, the nation-state now represents the unit transcending in power and authority all others. Both political values and institutions are primarily defined via this unit. It lays prior claims on the citizenry for allegiance, establishes the perimeters of permissible political behavior, and assumes the primary decision-making responsibilities in domestic and foreign affairs. No supranational political order of this era can exist without paying homage to these facts. In essence, therefore, when we have spoken of an international order in recent times, our reference, intended or not, has been in very considerable measure to the prevailing configuration of nation-states—their groupings, power, values, and policies.

At the close of World War II, there was only one nation that had the combination of power and will to operate in a truly international fashion, namely, the United States. For a crucial period of time, the United States stood in lieu of an international order, dispensing its resources and manpower in an effort to bring about the type of economic development and political evolution that would make such an order possible. Its power and responsibilities forced Washington to think in global terms, seeking linkages. Yet there was always a sense of priorities, with Western Europe and East Asia regarded as most vital. In these areas, American policies—albeit not without ambiguities and paradoxes—were directed toward stabilization through change, the precise emphasis varying with time and place.

In comparative terms, the Soviet Union during this period was operating as a regional force, at least initially. Its effort was the classic one of reconstructing a buffer-state system that would give it maximum security, the devastating effects of two wars being so deeply etched into Russian consciousness. Thus, on both its western and eastern frontiers, the Soviet Union sought to extend its power as a means of giving further protection to its continental heartland. In the first instance, therefore, one can say that the unfolding cleavage between the United States and the USSR was a product of differing perceptions of national need. The United States placed its primary emphasis on internationalism, with a stress on global interdependence, and interpreting its security as related to nothing less than an international order. The Soviet Union stressed regionalism and the construction of a security structure commensurate with its immediate capacities.

This distinction should not be made absolute, to be sure. Washington was not without its regional concerns, as its preoccupation with Western Europe and East Asia testify. Nor was the Soviet Union without its international interests, many of them stemming from its Marxist commitments. Yet the basic distinction is a valid one. And naturally, sharp differences of ideology and institutions exacerbated the cleavage.

The unfolding of these events and the nature of the new order can be seen in the Pacific-Asian context from an early point. At the close of World War II, Asia was largely a power vacuum except for the presence of American and Soviet forces, this notwithstanding the existence of large quantities of arms and ample numbers of soldiers. It was scarcely possible to talk of a nation-state system in the area. Authority and legitimacy were everywhere in doubt, and all political units were in disarray. Japan had been humbled and occupied. For China, exhausted and fragmented by war, more war lay ahead. Throughout southern Asia, there was a single independent state, Thailand (itself recently occupied), and various tired European nations were gathering themselves in an effort to reestablish a system whose time had passed. The nationalist forces that opposed these moves were rarely united or powerful, but in the next several years a combination of political and military factors intervened on their behalf.

The new Soviet presence mirrored Moscow's preoccupation with border security. Via the Yalta Agreements, the Soviet Union was able to regain with international consent all of the concessions once held by czarist Russia, including a substantial stake in the Manchurian railway system and Port Arthur. Quickly, the Russians occupied major portions of Northeast Asia, including Manchuria and northern Korea. The treaty of 1945 signed with China, moreover, was designed to inaugurate a new era of Sino-Soviet relations, one based on an acceptance of the postwar Soviet gains; Stalin, like most Americans, anticipated a long period of Nationalist control. In this fashion, the Soviet Union sought to protect its eastern territories.

American operations were less integrated, more extensive. The United States commenced to fashion its postwar Asian policies on the basis of three central premises: the wartime entente with the Soviet Union would continue, making possible the settlement of disputes peacefully and through mutual concessions; China, moving toward democracy under Kuomintang rule, would interact with the United States to become the backbone of the new Asia; and finally, the decolonization process would be relatively swift and painless, with a host of new nations emerging, all of them pursuing Western economic and political models. As each of these premises proved to be in error, American policies were rapidly altered.

On one count, initial American calculations were partly correct. If not painless, decolonization was relatively swift. In scarcely a decade, the political authority of Europe was replaced almost everywhere in Asia by that of indigenous elites. Certain of the new Asian governments, moreover, sought immediately to assume a prominent international role, serving as spokesmen for the emerging world. Another form of idealism had been born. Cutting across cultural and ideological barriers, a third force would be cultivated, one standing between the United States and the USSR, capable of articulating the interests of a majority of the world's people.

As this was a movement largely divorced from power, it was also easily divested of responsibility. Its primary weapon was moral suasion, and that gave it an aura of righteousness just as distasteful to the power-holders of the 1950s who had to make hard decisions as American righteousness had earlier been to Europeans. Perhaps, indeed, a competitive self-righteousness took form, with the United States still clinging strongly to its moral values, and the Russians no less insistently to theirs.

The nonaligned bloc was not without influence, but the influence was usually peripheral, and the bloc was not a solid one. It was here that the myth of a Third Force sprang up, whereas in reality a huge range of differences separated the emerging societies. A myth of equally dubious nature was that nonalignment emerged in the context of a bipolar world. Not only was there a great imbalance between American and Russian power during this period, but both of these nations regarded certain regions as vastly more important than others, and arranged their priorities accordingly. Over time, however, these myths became widely accepted, even in American and Soviet circles, and in truth bipolarism did come closer to being a realistic description of the trend as time passed.

Nowhere did the curious nature of the Third Force reveal itself more graphically than in Asia, and particularly with respect to China. The People's Republic of China, established in 1949, made clear its firm alignment with the Soviet Union from the outset. Indeed, Mao and his colleagues gave every indication of regarding nonalignment as morally reprehensible and politically impossible. Foreign relations were focused almost entirely on the Communist bloc, reflective of the fact that in this period alliances, Communist and non-Communist, tended to be all-encompassing, exclusive, and binding. Yet by the mid-1950s, China was showing an extensive interest in the nonaligned world, particularly that of Asia. In part, of course, this stemmed from the desire to build a united front against "American imperialism," and also to play a larger role in the international liberation and revolutionary movements. But it was also reflective of China's emergence as a new nation-state, with its own unique regional interests.

This complexity served as a harbinger of things to come. By the mid-1960s, a number of developments had occurred to disrupt the initial postwar order in Asia dramatically. Most important, of course, was the Sino-Soviet cleavage, which in its broadest outlines represented the triumph of nationalism over internationalism in the contemporary Communist movement (and in the political world at large). This event in turn initiated changes in the character of most alliances, including those centering on the United States. A reduced perception of threat coincided with an increased capacity for independent action on the part of many subordinate allies. Simultaneously, the major societies, seeking liberation themselves from the burdens of alliance and the perils of nuclear conflict, began to focus on their relationships with each other, and the era of détente was born.

If the old alliances have generally been weakened, international relations are not currently undergirded by strong political institutions of a regional or transregional character. On the contrary, nationalism has become stronger, both among the so-called advanced, industrial states and select "emerging" societies. At the same time, however, for some of the latter group, serious problems have emerged, slowing if not halting the nation-building process. In much of southern Asia, for example, ethnic and provincial conflicts remain unresolved. Thus, despite the growth of its military power, the state remains fragile, susceptible to various internal assaults. When socioeconomic conditions worsen, the pressures for change become more acute. As we have noted, there is no necessary correlation between economic crisis and political instability, but in most states subject to multiple divisions and problems, the external environment can play an important, even a decisive role in abetting stability or inducing instability. Is aid to the state available, and in what form? Can indigenous forces desirous of radical change acquire outside support, and in what amount?

Cognizant of the importance of such matters, the Asian states themselves formulated certain principles of peaceful coexistence some two decades ago, principles based on the acceptance of different political systems and noninterference in the internal affairs of others. Yet principles do not constitute institutions, and these particular principles have been violated repeatedly, in some cases by the very states that aided in their formulation.

When weak states can neither find firm allies nor count on an international order that holds governments accountable for their foreign policies through some collective sanctions system, they take the only route available, an accommodation to the prevailing balance of power, especially as it impinges most closely on them. Thus, most small Asian states, talking wishfully about the possible advantages of "equidistance," move in fact toward a complex set of varied bilateral relations, with the effort to shape each in accordance with perceived economic, political, and security needs. No set is fully balanced, nor precisely the same. In this era of uncertainty, some contemplate nuclear weapons while others advance low-cost, low-risk foreign policies in the hope that external threats can be kept minimal because of the preoccupation of major powers with their own domestic problems and their relations with each other.

Meanwhile, to meet internal issues or with the possible depredations of small neighbors in mind, the governments of these states almost invariably have been tightening their control over the political system at home, reducing the arena of political openness. The degree to which this is connected with the unstable international situation can be debated, but it seems clear that the current environment is not conducive to freedom at the national level.

An additional problem for these small states implicit in the contemporary world is the mounting confusion over what power is, and who holds it. It is easy enough to measure military power quantitatively, and to categorize major, medium, and small powers in this fashion. But power has never been more closely connected with economic and political capacities, including the will to use it. To what extent, for example, does public opinion and the Congress impose limits on the use of American power far more important than any measurement of capacities would indicate? Can open, democratic institutions cope with an age of intensive negotiations, when power is still an indispensable, if not a singular bargaining instrument? Are there comparable limits with respect to the Soviet Union, and other major societies?

There are no certain answers to these questions, either for the small states of Asia, or for Americans. On balance, the major (and minor) democratic states would seem to have signal disadvantages in this period. Leaders in open societies now have limited control over such vital aspects of the negotiatory scenario as timing and secrecy. Even their general capacity to direct foreign policy without being hobbled by congressional or special interest group interference is being increasingly brought into question.

Countervailing factors do exist. The slightest risk of nuclear war is sufficient to give pause to any government. Wars between major powers have been rendered unthinkable for rational men, for no victory is possible. Of all the major powers, moreover, the United States, despite its multiple problems, betrays fewer signs of backwardness, shows greater overall strength. Further, the mutual fear existent between Russia and China is both real and pervasive, deeply affecting every aspect of their foreign policies.

Indeed, it is upon the considerations just outlined that détente came into existence and continues. Détente, it must be reiterated, is not the product of the convergence of our respective political or socioeconomic systems. Rather, it is the result of the search for an alternative to war and the decision that a political-military equilibrium is essential if peace is to be maintained at this point. From a Communist perspective, Russian or Chinese, it rests on the premise that the United States will remain both strong and present, in Asia as well as in Europe.

Ironically, even in this era of rising isolationism and when its political capacities are cast into increasing doubt, the United States remains the only power with a truly universal reach. As we have noted at length, the Soviet Union is unable to communicate effectively today with China, and with a considerable number of other nations as well. China faces similar problems in addition to its very real military, economic, and political limitations. Japan and Western Europe fit into entirely different categories. The former is a universal power in economic terms, albeit one with sizable vulnerabilities. In the political and military sense, however, it is not even a regional power of substantial influence. Western Europe, currently as divided as united, is at most a regional force, and one in considerable difficulties.

When one surveys this scene, the reason for the present anxiety over the United States becomes apparent. At a time when the American will appears to be faltering and attention is directed inward, American strength and resolve are still desperately needed—even by those major powers having different ideological commitments and institutional structures.

Bilateral Relations among the Major Powers

Against this background, what is the nature of the major power relations in the Pacific-Asian area? If we look first at bilateral relations, only the extremities of ongoing war and exclusive alliance are missing. Otherwise, hostility, nonalignment, and the special ties representing the functional equivalent of alliance are all to be found.

Japan aims at a combination of nonalignment and special ties. In its relations with the USSR and the PRC, it hopes to achieve a balanced normalization, difficult though this has proved to be. Thus, the current tilt toward China may continue, but it will never reach the point of alliance, and the tilt could easily be reduced, depending on Soviet policies. In its relations with its giant Communist neighbors, Tokyo is served best by nonalignment.

Ties with the United States, on the other hand, continue to be vital ones, both in the economic and in the political-security spheres, and although the movement toward more independent policies will continue, it is difficult to see these ties being dramatically changed in the near future.

Toward India and Indonesia, Japanese policies will be confined largely to the economic and cultural realms, with the possibility of a gradual growth of consultation in the political field. The main thrust of Japanese foreign policy is and will continue to be an effort to eschew the risks of a high political-military posture, while striving to extend still further the Japanese economic reach.

China is still seeking to combine various foreign policy roles, ideological leader and pragmatic political practitioner, rising major power and spokesman for the emerging Third World. Thus, elements of ambiguity and paradox are reflected in its foreign policies, including its bilateral relations with the major societies of the Pacific-Asian area. Toward the "superpowers," hostility is combined with limited détente. Relations with the Soviet Union remain minimal and frigid despite Peking's recurrent assertion that state-to-state ties should and could be improved. The United States continues to serve as a counterforce to the USSR in Chinese eyes. Hence, limited détente prevails with Washington, combined with attacks on

"U.S. imperialism" in the international arena. The uncertainties of Chinese domestic politics, however, spill over into the field of foreign policy. Together with the uncertain impact of future American policies on Peking, they make predictions difficult. In the long run, China would be best served by a policy of equidistance between the two superpowers, and that may be the long-range trend—but in Sino-Soviet relations, the range of alternatives is wide indeed.

China's policies toward Japan are reflective of its current campaign to establish special ties with the Second World. No Sino-Japanese alliance is in the offing, however, and relations here will be measured primarily in economic terms. For the near future, at least, China's relations with India and Indonesia will be minimal and hostile. India is neither feared nor trusted, and currently regarded as a part of the Soviet containment bloc. Indonesia, though seen as under a "reactionary, anti-Chinese government," might be recognized if its leaders wanted such an action, but relations would not be cordial.

China is thus fashioning its bilateral relations with its first considerations defensive and security-oriented, but with an interest also in being a major Asian power, and one that keeps some ideological component in a foreign policy that is essentially based on balance-of-power considerations.

India's bilateral relations are a product of its successful drive to become the dominant power of the subcontinent. Thus, relations with the USSR are and will continue to be those of modified alliance. India would like to see those ties balanced in greater degree by American commitments, but factors involving both U.S. and Indian interests make that unlikely. Indian-American relations—at least for the duration of Mrs. Gandhi's tenure—will be correct but limited, hewing to nonalignment on both sides.

As noted, Sino-Indian relations, despite New Delhi's hope for some improvements, are likely to take their measure from the state of Soviet-Indian ties, but Peking could, if it wanted, tempt the Indians via generous overtures. In the long run, India too might be best served by the policies of equidistance—even though these are not currently feasible.

India sees Japan as a very foreign country; its relations will be economic, and tied to trends in the Indian economy—but never close. Indonesia, similarly, no longer represents the ideological comrade of the 1950s, so relations are those normally established between two nations with limited common interests.

To date, India's bilateral relations have achieved one major purpose—that of regional hegemony. In the future, the need is to turn those relations to the tasks of economic modernization and political stability—tasks that may ultimately require some foreign policy reorientation.

Indonesia's bilateral relations have recently been directed to precisely these latter objectives, but with a sustained interest in regional developments. Ties with Japan, although confined to the economic sphere and marked by serious problems, continue to be extensive, and no basic changes here are to be expected. With the United States also, special ties exist, both for economic and political-security reasons. Both of these relationships, however, fall considerably short of alliance, preserving Indonesia's right to call itself nonaligned and reflective of the new international era. The movement away from identification with the United States, moreover, may be accelerated as a result of doubts about American credibility.

Relations with China are currently more hostile than nonaligned, with a deep fear in Jakarta—warranted or unwarranted—of the future Chinese role in Southeast Asia. With the Soviet Union, relations are "normal," but scarcely warm or intimate. And India is not a nation of great consequence to Indonesia at this point in time. Thus, Indonesia represents a "nonaligned" nation with a decided tilt to its foreign policies, a tilt closely related to its earlier experiences and present needs.

The Soviet Union's bilateral relations stem in very considerable measure from its continuing concerns with China. The Sino-Soviet relation, as we have stressed, remains a hostile one, with Moscow hoping that in the post-Mao era, its stick-and-carrot policy will produce better results. The commitment to détente with the United States continues, as do tests on both sides of its meaning and extent. In Asia, Soviet-American differences and points of potential conflict remain, but they have been reduced in the last decade. The more intractable problems lie elsewhere. In this sense, developments out of Asia may well play a major role in determining the character of Soviet-American relations in Asia. Like China, the Soviet Union would undoubtedly benefit in the long run if it could establish a relatively equidistant relationship with the U.S. and the PRC, but that prospect does not seem an immediate one.

Soviet relations with Japan and India are reflections of the current status of the Soviet-Chinese-American triangle, with some additional considerations. In the case of Japan, Russia combats a long history of hostility and cultural distance. The lack of Soviet generosity continues, moreover. Consequently, relations are more minimal and less cordial than Russia's own interests would appear to dictate, both from economic and political perspectives. Here, the initiatives lie with Moscow.

In the case of India, on the other hand, the relationship may have become too intimate—product of India's needs and the USSR's commitment to containing China. The problems of an alliance between unequals have revealed themselves increasingly in this setting. In its relations with Indonesia, Russia has shown a willingness to overlook differences in an effort to establish a larger presence in the general region, but as long as the Indonesian government remains deeply anti-Communist, Soviet-Indonesian relations will be marked by ambiguity and reservation on both sides.

It can thus be seen that in its bilateral relations with countries other than China in the Pacific-Asian area, the Soviet Union has found it extremely difficult to strike the precise relationship it wishes—one that serves Soviet economic and political-strategic interests without extending Soviet commitments too far. Only a basic change in the Soviet-Chinese relationship itself would make possible a total reassessment of all other bilateral relations.

Finally, in the case of the United States, a position has been achieved—however precariously—of relative equidistance between China and the Soviet Union. The stress must be on the qualifying adjective "relative," because the nature of the two relations is and must continue to be different in many respects. Nevertheless, the United States can conduct a dialogue with both nations, can seek to resolve outstanding issues through negotiations, and in a host of other ways represents a centrist as well as central force in the American-Soviet-Chinese triangle. And as we have remarked, the U.S. currently stands in precisely the position that both of the other parties would ultimately like to achieve.

American-Japanese relations reflect the special ties that are natural between two nations so intimately involved, economically and in political-security terms. These relations also reflect the type of problems that comes under these circumstances, and between two nations greatly unequal in many respects. Nevertheless, those ties seem likely to continue, at least to the extent American initiatives are involved.

With India, the relation is closer to that of nonalignment, symbolic of the politics of the two nations, but also of the fact that South Asia as a region cannot have the same priority as East Asia for the United States. With Indonesia, relations are considerably more than "normal," but not as far-reaching as with Japan.

The bilateral relations of the United States in the Pacific-Asian region underline the fact that America remains a universal power, critical in its actions and inactions to peace or war, and to any meaningful international order, formal or informal. With the major societies, its relations currently range from nonalignment to modified alliance, with equidistance, special ties, low posture, and high posture all involved. This is a tribute to the complexity of the area, and the need for differentiated approaches. The overarching question, however, is whether the United States will have the stamina to retain its presence and power in Asia in the transitional era that lies ahead.

Multipower Relationships in the Major Regions

From these bilateral relations, certain broader patterns or configurations can be derived. Let us look at the power relationships as they pertain to the major regions. In the Pacific Ocean, the prospect is for the continued predominance of the United States, but with a growing Japanese economic presence and the strong possibility of an increase in Soviet and, possibly in the longer run, Chinese military presence. In this region, the Taiwan issue is likely to be the most thorny problem—although Taiwan can also be considered a part of the Northeast Asian region, as we have stressed.

In Northeast Asia, the power relationships are especially important and complex. If the status quo is disrupted, especially if the disruption comes through force, it could have the most serious repercussions. For this reason, the Korean problem (along with that of Taiwan) represents vital issues for each of the major societies. The equilibrium currently established is based on a Japan committed against major military power, aligned strategically with the United States, and a rough balance having been achieved between Soviet and Chinese power in the region. In this setting, the existence of the two Koreas and of an independent Taiwan provide further elements of the balance. A peaceful, evolutionary transition relating to these states would not necessarily upset the situation, but military conflict of any type would be very serious. Additional complications are conceivable: a rapid increase of Soviet military power in the region, based in Siberia; political changes in Japan resulting in major shifts of policy, whether toward pacificism or Gaullism; and a precipitous American withdrawal.

This is a region where experimentation in multipower guarantees and in regional disarmament may have meaning, as we suggested earlier. It is also a region closely interrelated with the Continental Center because of the Sino-Soviet issue. In the latter region, most projections would indicate a continuing preponderance of Soviet military power, with the gap not being closed by the Chinese, possibly even growing wider in the immediate future. Nevertheless, Peking intends to seek a credible nuclear deterrent, and there is no indication that it will cease its investments in several strategic systems along with selective modernization of its conventional forces. Thus, Central Asia will represent one of the most heavily militarized regions of the world, comparable with the Korean peninsula but on a much larger scale. All of the small Asian nations on the peripheries of Sino-Soviet boundaries will continue to be affected, having to choose between alignment and a precarious neutralism.

Southeast Asia, as we have noted, will continue to be the most unstable region in Asia, politically, economically, and in strategic terms. Although Indonesia will be a power of significance, it is doubtful as to whether it can play a dominant role in the entire region, even if it chose to make the effort. Given the nature of the region itself, and the probabilities of a weak regional configuration, the major societies external to Southeast Asia will continue to play an important role here, and one that will test the principles of peaceful coexistence, as well as those of détente. If the United States elects to opt out of the region, a certain contest between the Soviet Union and China for influence will ensue, with the odds strongly favoring China in the long run.

In contrast, in South Asia, regional relations seem relatively fixed, with the Soviet-Indian alliance underwriting a strong Indian influence throughout the subcontinent. There has been a substantial increase of interest on the part of the major powers in the Indian Ocean as a result of the energy crisis, and also of a neighboring state that is en route to medium power, Iran. But the interests of the United States will continue to be sufficiently modest, and those of China sufficiently dispersed, to make this region reasonably stable in power relations. Only serious upheavals within India affecting its capacities as a state could alter this picture.

In all of these analyses and projections, it is assumed, of course, that no nation's decision-making processes are simple, no set of policies reached without compromise and debate. One should be well aware of the fact that a wide range of factors enter into the determination of policies—and a range of models has recently been introduced to explain that process. Nothing here should be read to mean that a given nation's policies are the product of a monolithic consensus. Nonetheless, certain policies *are* enunciated and maintained. In their continuities and discontinuities, in their consistencies and paradoxes, they mirror the best consensus available, and reflect the range of changing and continuing perceptions of the policy-making elite on balance.

Transregional Power Configurations

Finally, let us suggest some of the transregional power configurations and possibilities for the future. First, the obvious should be reemphasized. Neither power nor major power relations can be conceived solely or, in many instances, primarily through military-strategic relations. The economic, social, and political factors so crucial to the concept of power itself are of equal importance in all relations undertaken by major societies. Thus, the possibilities of a Pacific Community will recur in the years ahead, and this idea deserves serious, detailed consideration. Similarly, ongoing operations such as the Asian Development Bank could easily be expanded—both in coverage and scope. On a broader scale, as we have noted, programs relating to food, population, and resources are points at which genuine international cooperation cutting across ideological and political lines seem most urgent. Indeed, it is in this area that the true tests of mankind's will to survive will come in the decades immediately ahead. These fields cannot be removed from politics, nor can ideological differences be fully overcome, as we have already discovered, but unless means of cooperation can be found, military power unfortunately is likely to become more, not less important.

In the strategic realm, bilateral American-Soviet negotiations continue to be critical, for it is here that the truly massive nuclear concentrations lie. But if SALT II is vital, so is the need to prevent nuclear proliferation. The possibility of such proliferation in Asia, as we have seen, is real—and events of the recent past make it a more dangerous prospect. Even small nations driven to desperation by an absence of trust in others are contemplating this course. Only if the international environment encasing them improves and meaningful controls on nuclear weapons are established can this threat be reduced.

The question of broader agreements on arms limitations thus directly concerns Asia. Can agreements pertaining to such regions as Korea or Northeast Asia be achieved? Would the "neutralization" of Southeast Asia also include agreements among the major powers with respect to military aid? When thoroughly probed, the issue of peaceful coexistence is found to be inextricably connected with this type of question.

The Pacific-Asian area, as was noted at the beginning of this work, represents approximately one-half of the world, whether measured in area, population, or resources. The relations of the major states within it thus encompass all of the critical issues confronting mankind: economic betterment, social development, political stability, and peace or war.

Looking at the recent past, and seeking to probe the alternatives that lie ahead, one can hold either a pessimistic or an optimistic view, depending on where one wishes to place the emphasis. On the pessimistic side, there remains the fact that none of the major problems suggested in the critical issues just outlined has been solved in Asia, nor are solutions clearly en route. Further, the attitudes as well as the institutions necessary for solution remain illusive. Consequently, there is no international order except that which springs out of balance-of-power politics. Now there is the possibility that one of the major powers, the United States, will withdraw in such a fashion as to contribute to a progressive destabilization with far-reaching repercussions. In any case, the foreign relations of each of the major societies (and the minor ones as well) are fragmented, lacking in a broad conceptual framework, and subject to erratic changes.

On the optimistic side, one accomplishment is clear. Nuclear war has been avoided, and indeed the major powers seem more than ever determined to prevent such a holocaust. At other levels as well, a sense of urgency is accumulating, and with it a growing willingness to discuss, possibly to experiment with new ideas and institutions at the supranational level. These trends must compete with a still vigorous, even militant nationalism—and there are no indications that this competition will cease, or that nationalism will fare badly on many occasions.

It is not empty rhetoric to assert that for each of the major Asian-Pacific nations, and particularly for the United States, this is a time of momentous decision. What stake does each nation have in the course of events in Asia? How can various national interests best be reconciled, and a viable order permitting diversity yet conducive to peace and development be constructed? For Americans, is it to be massive withdrawal, enclaves, or selective internationalism at this point?

Irrespective of the decisions of the moment, in the long run, no major state can withdraw from a vital region of the world completely, nor can it elect to interact intensively with only one type of society. We will continue to live in a highly complex international environment in which a wide range of relations remains indispensable. Bilateralism, regionalism, and internationalism on a broader scale, each have an important role to play. Foreign policy resources will continue to include economic, political, and military components, with the mix varying according to the given situation and time. Thus, to stress any single relationship or instrument is to misunderstand the nature of our times. To establish priorities, however, and to constantly reexamine them is essential. Similarly, to keep the instruments of foreign policy flexible and varied is of critical importance.

For the United States, the past has represented phases of intensive involvement, followed by equally massive disengagement. To move away from these extremes will require not merely policy revisions but sizable adjustments in our political culture.

Bibliographic Essay

In recent years, a vast array of studies pertaining to the issues raised in this volume has been published. Here it is possible to signal only a select number of these studies, and because of the constantly changing international panorama, I am placing the emphasis on recently published works.

International Politics

Turning first to the studies dealing in the broadest terms with the international order and basic political issues, the following are stimulating: Raymond Aron, *Peace and War* (Doubleday, New York, 1966); Seyom Brown, *New Forces in World Politics* (Brookings, Washington, D.C., 1974); Alastair Buchan, *The End of the Postwar Era: A New Balance of World Power* (Saturday Review Press, New York, 1974); Miriam Camps, *The Management of Interdependence* (Council on Foreign Relations, New York, 1974); James E. Dougherty, *National Security through World Law and Government: Myth or Reality?* (Foreign Policy Research Institute, Philadelphia, 1974); S.N. Eisenstadt, *Tradition, Change, and Modernity* (Wiley, New York, 1973); Ann Hollick and Robert Osgood, *The New Era of Ocean Politics* (Johns Hopkins Univ. Press, Baltimore, 1974); Ole R. Hosti, P. Terrence Hopmann, and John D. Sullivan, *Unity and Disintegration in International Alliances: Comparative Studies* (Wiley, New York, 1973); Alan James (ed.), *The Bases of International Order: Essays in Honour of C.A.W. Manning* (Oxford Univ. Press, New York, 1973); Catherine McArdle Kelleher (ed.), *Political-Military Systems: Comparative Perspectives* (Sage, Beverly Hills, Calif., 1974); Klaus Knorr, *Power and Wealth: The Political Economy of International Power* (Basic Books, New York, 1973); George Liska, *States in Evolution* (Johns Hopkins Univ. Press, Baltimore, 1973); Oskar Morgenstern, Klaus Knorr, and Klaus P. Heiss, *Long-Term Projections of Power: Political, Economic, and Military Forecasting* (Ballinger, Cambridge, Mass., 1973); Edwin O. Reischauer, *Toward the 21st Century: Education for a Changing World* (Knopf, New York, 1973); Marshall R. Singer, *Weak States in a World of Powers: The Dynamics of International Relationships* (Free Press, New York, 1972); Richard W. Sterling, *Macropolitics: International Relations in a Global Society* (Knopf, New York, 1974); and John G. Stoessinger, *Why Nations Go to War* (St. Martin's, New York, 1974).

303

Dealing with international security and military questions, many of them central to an understanding of American-Soviet relations, are these works: Walter C. Clemens, Jr., *The Superpowers and Arms Control: From Cold War to Interdependence* (Lexington Books, Lexington, Mass., 1973); Brian Crozier, *A Theory of Conflict* (Scribners, New York, 1975); Michael Haas, *International Conflict* (Bobbs-Merrill, New York, 1974); Robert E. Harkavy, *The Arms Trade and International Systems* (Ballinger, Cambridge, Mass., 1975); Morton Kaplan and others, *Strategic Thinking and Its Moral Implications* (Univ. of Chicago Press, Chicago, 1973); Geoffrey Kemp, Robert L. Pfaltzgraff, Jr., and Uri Ra'anan, *The Superpowers in a Multinuclear World* (Lexington Books, Lexington, Mass., 1974); Albert Legault and George Lindsey, *The Dynamics of the Nuclear Balance* (Cornell Univ. Press, Ithaca, 1974); Edward N. Luttwak, *The Political Uses of Sea Power* (Johns Hopkins Univ. Press, Baltimore, 1974); Laurence Martin, *Arms and Strategy: The World Power Structure Today* (McKay, New York, 1973); F.S. Northedge (ed.), *The Use of Force in International Relations* (Free Press, New York, 1974); George Quester, *Politics of Nuclear Proliferation* (Johns Hopkins Univ. Press, Baltimore, 1973); Charles V. Reynolds, *Theory and Explanation in International Politics* (Barnes and Noble, New York, 1974); and Stockholm International Peace Research Institute, *Nuclear Proliferation Problems* (MIT Press, Cambridge, Mass., 1974).

On economic themes in international politics pertinent to this study, see P.T. Bauer, *Dissent on Development* (Harvard Univ. Press, Cambridge, Mass., 1972); C. Fred Bergsten and others, *The Future of the International Economic Order: An Agenda for Research* (Lexington Books, Lexington, Mass., 1973); Lester R. Brown with Erik P. Eckholm, *By Bread Alone* (Praeger, New York, 1974); William P. Bundy (ed.), *The World Economic Crisis* (Council on Foreign Relations, New York, 1975); Edward W. Erickson and Leonard Waverman, *The Energy Question: An International Failure of Policy*, vol. 1: *The World*, vol. 2: *North America* (Univ. of Toronto Press, Toronto, 1974); S. David Freeman, *Energy: The New Era* (Walker, New York, 1974); Helen Hughes, *Prospects for Partnership: Industrialization and Trade Policies in the 1970s* (Johns Hopkins Univ. Press, Baltimore, 1973); Alexander King, *Science and Policy: The International Stimulus* (Oxford Univ. Press, New York, 1974); Mihaljlo Mesarovic and Eduard Pestel, *Mankind at the Turning Point: The Second Report to the Club of Rome* (Dutton, New York, 1974); Wilbur F. Monroe, *International Monetary Reconstruction: Problems and Issues* (Lexington Books, Lexington, Mass., 1974); Paul Streeten, *The Frontiers of Development Studies* (Halsted-Wiley, New York, 1972); and Mason Willrich (ed.), *International Safeguards and Nuclear Industry* (Johns Hopkins Univ. Press, Baltimore, 1973).

Asia

With respect to books providing a general coverage of Asia, I would suggest for historical background, John K. Fairbank,

Edwin O. Reischauer, and Albert M. Craig, *East Asia: The Modern Transformation* (Houghton-Mifflin, New York, 1965). Policy studies covering much of the area with which this work is concerned would include Coral Bell, *The Asian Balance of Power* (Adelphi Paper no. 44, Institute for Strategic Studies, London, 1968); Ralph N. Clough, *East Asia and U.S. Security (Brookings, Washington, D.C., 1975);* Fred Greene, *U.S. Policy and the Security of Asia* (McGraw-Hill, New York, 1968); Harold Isaacs, *Images of Asia* Harper and Row, New York, 1972); John W. Lewis (ed.), *Peasant Rebellion and Communist Revolution in Asia* (Stanford Univ. Press, Stanford, 1974); Ernest R. May and James C. Thompson, Jr., *American-East Asian Relations: A Survey* (Harvard Univ. Press, Cambridge, Mass., 1972); Edwin O. Reischauer, *Beyond Vietnam: The United States and Asia* (Alfred Knopf, New York, 1972); Robert A. Scalapino, *Asia and the Major Powers—Implications for the International Order* (American Enterprise Institute, Washington, D.C., 1972); Robert A. Scalapino (ed.), *The Communist Revolution in Asia,* 2nd ed. (Prentice-Hall, New York, 1969); Richard L. Walker (ed.), *Prospects in the Pacific* (Heldref, Washington, D.C., 1972); and Wayne Wilcox, Leo E. Rose, and Gavin Boyd, *Asia and the International System* (Winthrop, Cambridge, Mass., 1972).

Japan

Turning to Japan, an excellent general introduction is provided by Edwin O. Reischauer, *Japan—The Story of a Nation,* rev. ed. (Knopf, New York, 1974). The following works set forth the basic structure of Japanese politics: Nobutaka Ike, *Japanese Politics: Patron-Client Democracy* 2nd ed. (Knopf, New York, 1972); Hiroshi Itoh (trans. and ed.), *Japanese Politics—An Inside View* (Cornell Univ. Press, Ithaca, 1973); Frank C. Langdon, *Politics in Japan* (Little, Brown, Boston, 1967); Masao Maruyama, *Thought and Behavior in Japanese Politics* (Oxford Univ. Press, London, 1963); Theodore McNelly, *Politics and Government in Japan* (Little, Brown, Boston, 1967); and J.A.A. Stockwin, *Japan: Divided Politics in a Growth Economy* (Norton, New York, 1975).

Among the stimulating and differing works recently written by nonspecialists, I would select Zbigniew Brzezinski, *The Fragile Blossom* (Harper and Row, New York, 1972); and Herman Kahn, *The Emerging Japanese Superstate* (Prentice-Hall, Englewood Cliffs, N.J., 1970). Two interesting accounts by journalists are current: Frank Gibney, *Japan: The Fragile Superpower* (Norton, New York, 1975); and Robert Guillain, *The Japanese Challenge* (Hamish Hamilton, London, 1970). Also current is a perspective offered by a Japanese scholar, Masataka Kosaka, *100 Million Japanese: The Postwar Experience* (Kodansha, Tokyo, 1972).

Special mention should be made of a series of books dealing with Japan as a prime example of a successfully modernizing society, all published by the Princeton University Press, Princeton, N.J.: Marius B.

Jansen (ed.), *Changing Japanese Attitudes toward Modernization* (1965); William W. Lockwood (ed.), *The State and Economic Enterprise in Japan* (1965); Donald H. Shively (ed.), *Tradition and Modernization in Japanese Culture* (1971); Robert E. Ward (ed.), *Political Development in Modern Japan* (1968); and Robert E. Ward and Dankwart A. Rustow (eds.), *Political Modernization in Japan and Turkey* (1964).

A few more specialized works on Japanese politics should be mentioned, given the significance of that subject to potentialities in the foreign policy field: Hans Baerwald, *Japan's Parliament: An Introduction* (Cambridge Univ. Press, New York, 1974); Allan B. Cole, George O. Totten, and Cecil H. Uyehara, *Socialist Parties in Postwar Japan* (Yale Univ. Press, New Haven, 1966); Gerald Curtis, *Election Campaigning, Japanese Style* (Columbia Univ. Press, New York, 1971); Haruhiro Fukui, *Party in Power: The Japanese Liberal Democrats and Policy Making* (Univ. of California Press, Berkeley and Los Angeles, 1970); Chalmers Johnson, *Conspiracy at Matsukawa* (Univ. of California Press, Berkeley and Los Angeles, 1972); George R. Packard, *Protest in Tokyo: The Security Treaty Crisis of 1960* (Princeton Univ. Press, Princeton, N.J., 1966); Bradley M. Richardson, *The Political Culture of Japan* (Univ. of California Press, Berkeley and Los Angeles, 1974); Robert A. Scalapino, *The Japanese Communist Movement—1920-1966* (Univ. of California Press, Berkeley and Los Angeles, 1967); and Robert A. Scalapino and Junnosuke Masumi, *Parties and Politics in Contemporary Japan* (Univ. of California Press, Berkeley and Los Angeles, 1962).

On Japanese society in the late twentieth century, consult Ronald P. Dore, *City Life in Japan* (Univ. of California Press, Berkeley and Los Angeles, 1958); Chie Nakane, *Japanese Society* (Univ. of California Press, Berkeley and Los Angeles, 1972); and Ezra F. Vogel, *Japan's New Middle Class* (Univ. of California Press, Berkeley and Los Angeles, 1963)'.

Among the new books providing insights into Japan's economic structure, I would recommend James C. Abegglen, *Management and Worker: The Japanese Solution* (Tokyo, 1960); Robert E. Cole, *Japanese Blue Collar—The Changing Tradition* (Univ. of California Press, Berkeley and Los Angeles, 1971); Ronald P. Dore, Allen C. Kelly, and Jeffrey G. Williamson, *Lessons from Japanese Development: An Analytical Economic History* (Univ. of Chicago Press, Chicago, 1974); Kazushi Ohkawa and Henry Rosovsky, *Japanese Economic Growth: Trend Acceleration in the Twentieth Century* (Stanford Univ. Press, Stanford, 1973); Terutomo Ozawa, *Japan's Technological Challenge to the West, 1950-1974: Motivation and Accomplishment* (MIT Press, Cambridge, Mass., 1974); and Kozo Yamamura, *Economic Policy in Postwar Japan: Growth vs Economic Democracy* (Univ. of California Press, Berkeley and Los Angeles, 1967).

Recent general studies on Japanese foreign policy would include Donald C. Hellmann, *Japan and East Asia—The New International Order* (Praeger, New York, 1972); Douglas H. Mendel, Jr., *The Japanese People and Foreign Policy* (Univ. of California Press, Berkeley and Los Angeles,

1961); Robert E. Osgood, George R. Packard III, and John H. Badgley, *Japan and the United States in Asia* (Johns Hopkins Press, Baltimore, 1969); Henry Rosovsky (ed.), *Discord in the Pacific,* (American Assembly, Columbia Books, Washington, D.C., 1972); and Robert A. Scalapino (ed.), *The Foreign Policy of Modern Japan* (Univ. of California Press, Berkeley and Los Angeles, forthcoming).

The following works deal specifically with Japanese-American relations: Asahi Staff, *The Pacific Rivals—A Japanese View of Japanese-American Relations* (Weatherhill-Asahi, New York and Tokyo, 1972); Priscilla Clapp and Morton H. Halperin (eds.), *United States-Japanese Relations: The 1970s* (Harvard Univ. Press, Cambridge, Mass., 1974); Gerald Curtis (ed.), *Japanese-American Relations in the 1970s* (American Assembly, Columbia Books, Washington, D.C., 1970); Robert E. Osgood, *The Weary and Wary—U.S. and Japanese Security Policies in Transition* (Johns Hopkins Univ. Press, Baltimore, 1972); Robert A. Scalapino, *American-Japanese Relations in a Changing Era* (Library Press, New York, 1972); and Akio Watanabe, *The Okinawa Problem—A Chapter in Japan-U.S. Relations* (Melbourne Univ. Press, Melbourne, 1970).

On the decision-making process, see Donald C. Hellmann, *Japanese Domestic Politics and Foreign Policy* (Univ. of California Press, Berkeley and Los Angeles, 1969).

Five important works dealing with defense policies and security issues are John K. Emmerson, *Arms, Yen, and Power: The Japanese Dilemma* (Dunellen, New York, 1971); John K. Emmerson and Leonard Humphreys, *Will Japan Rearm?* (American Enterprise Institute, Washington, D.C., 1973); James William Morley (ed.), *Forecast for Japan: Security in the 1970s* (Princeton Univ. Press, Princeton, N.J., 1971); Hisahiko Okazaki, *A Japanese View of Détente* (Heath, Lexington, Mass., 1974); and Martin E. Weinstein, *Japan's Postwar Defense Policy, 1947–1968* (Columbia Univ. Press, New York, 1971).

China

In the past decade, a great number of studies have been published on the People's Republic of China. Once again, the emphasis here is on recent works. A perceptive general introduction is John K. Fairbank's *The United States and China,* 3rd ed. (Harvard Univ. Press, Cambridge, Mass., 1971). A balanced, comprehensive history of the Chinese Communist Party is provided by James P. Harrison, *The Long March to Power: A History of the Chinese Communist Party, 1921–1971* (Praeger, New York, 1972).

Works generally regarded as texts on Chinese politics for mature students, each worthy of attention and employing different perspectives, are Harold C. Hinton, *An Introduction to Chinese Politics* (Praeger, New York, 1973); Jan Prybyla, *The Political Economy of Communist China* (International Textbook, Scranton, Pa., 1970); Lucian W. Pye, *China—An Introduction* (Little, Brown, Boston, 1972); John Bryan Starr, *Ideology and Culture: An Introduction to the Dialectic of Contemporary Chinese Politics* (Harper and Row, New York, 1973); James R. Townsend, *Politics in China* (Little, Brown, Boston, 1974); and D.J. Waller, *The Government and Politics of Communist China* (Hilary House, New York, 1970).

General studies of Chinese politics somewhat different in character and also providing a valuable range of approaches are A. Doak Barnett, *Uncertain Passage—China's Transition to the Post-Mao Era* (Brookings, Washington, D.C., 1974); Jurgen Domes, *The Internal Politics of China—1949–1972* (Praeger, New York, 1973); Ping-ti Ho and Tang Tsou (eds.), *China in Crisis*, vol. 1: *China's Heritage and the Communist Political System* (Univ. of Chicago Press, Chicago, 1968); Lucian W. Pye, *The Spirit of Chinese Politics: A Psychocultural Study of the Authority Crisis in Political Development* (MIT Press, Cambridge, Mass., 1968); Stuart R. Schram (ed.), *Authority, Participation, and Cultural Change in China* (Cambridge Univ. Press, Cambridge, 1973); Franz Schurmann, *Ideology and Organization in Communist China*, rev. ed. (Univ. of California Press, Berkeley and Los Angeles, 1968); and Richard H. Solomon, *Mao's Revolution and the Chinese Political Culture* (Univ. of California Press, Berkeley and Los Angeles, 1971).

Among the general works written by nonacademics, I would signal two as of special worth: Stanley Karnow, *Mao and China: From Revolution to Revolution* (Viking, New York, 1972), and Edward E. Rice, *Mao's Way* (Univ. of California Press, Berkeley and Los Angeles, 1972). Two scholars who have written perceptively of journeys to China are Klaus Mehnert, *China Returns* (Dutton, New York, 1972), and Ross Terrill, *800,000,000: The Real China* (Little, Brown, Boston, 1972). If one makes the necessary corrections for his strong Sinophilic biases, Edgar Snow's *The Other Side of the River*, rev. ed. (Random House, New York, 1970), is useful, especially for his insights into the thinking of China's leaders during the 1960s.

Among the more specialized works on contemporary Chinese politics, the following should be consulted: A. Doak Barnett with a contribution by Ezra Vogel, *Cadres, Bureaucracy, and Political Power in Communist China* (Columbia Univ. Press, New York, 1967); A. Doak Barnett (ed.), *Chinese Communist Politics in Action* (Univ. of Washington Press, Seattle, 1969); Richard Baum, *Prelude to Revolution—Mao, the Party, and the Peasant Question, 1962–1966* (Columbia Univ. Press, New York, 1975); John Wilson Lewis (ed.), *The City in Communist China* (Stanford Univ. Press, Stanford, 1971); John Wilson Lewis, *Leadership in Communist China* (Cornell Univ. Press, Ithaca, 1963); John M.H. Lindbeck (ed.), *China: Management of a Revolutionary Society* (Univ. of Washington Press, Seattle, 1971); Roderick MacFarquhar, *The Origins of the Cultural Revolution—Contradictions among the People, 1956–1957* (Columbia Univ. Press, New York, 1974); Robert A. Scalapino (ed.), *Elites in the People's Republic of China*

(Univ. of Washington Press, Seattle, 1972); Frederick C. Teiwes, *Provincial Party Personnel in Mainland China* (Columbia University, East Asian Institute, New York, 1967); James R. Townsend, *Political Participation in Communist China* (Univ. of California Press, Berkeley and Los Angeles, 1967); Ezra F. Vogel, *Canton under Communism—Programs and Politics in a Provincial Capital, 1949–1968* (Harvard Univ. Press, Cambridge, Mass., 1969).

Studies focusing strongly on ideology and of special importance are Jerome Ch'en, *Mao and the Chinese Revolution* (Oxford Univ. Press, London, 1965); Arthur A. Cohen, *The Communism of Mao Tse-tung* (Univ. of Chicago Press, Chicago, 1964); Harry Harding, *Maoist Theories of Policy Making and Organization* (Rand Corp., Santa Monica, September 1969); James C. Hsiung, *Ideology and Practice: The Evolution of Chinese Communism* (Praeger, New York, 1970); Chalmers Johnson (ed.), *Ideology and Politics in Contemporary China* (Univ. of Washington Press, Seattle, 1973); Mao Tse-tung, *Selected Works of Mao Tse-tung,* 4 vols. (Peking Foreign Languages Press, Peking, 1961–1965); Stuart Schram, *The Political Thought of Mao Tse-tung* (Praeger, New York, 1963); *Mao Tse-tung* (Penguin, Baltimore, 1967); Benjamin I. Schwartz, *Communism and China: Ideology in Flux* (Harvard Univ. Press, Cambridge, Mass., 1968); and Frederic Wakeman, Jr., *History and Will: Philosophical Perspectives of Mao Tse-tung's Thought* (Univ. of California Press, Berkeley and Los Angeles, 1973).

For other special fields, on education see Theodore Hsi-en Chen, *The Maoist Educational Revolution* (Praeger, New York, 1974); Stewart Fraser, *Chinese Communist Education* (Wiley, New York, 1965); and R.F. Price, *Education in Communist China* (Praeger, New York, 1970). On the judicial system, see Jerome A. Cohen, *The Criminal Process in the People's Republic of China, 1949–1963: An Introduction* (Harvard Univ. Press, Cambridge, Mass., 1968); and Shao-chuan Leng, *Justice in Communist China: A Survey of the Judicial System of the Chinese People's Republic* (Oceana, Dobbs Ferry, N.Y., 1967).

Of the works dealing with sociological aspects of the PRC, in addition to those already mentioned, I would signal the earlier work of Marian J. Levy, Jr., *The Family Revolution in Modern China* (Octagon, New York, 1963); the recent study of Martin K. Whyte, *Small Groups and Political Rituals in China* (Univ. of California Press, Berkeley and Los Angeles, 1974); and C.K. Yang, *Chinese Communist Society: The Family and the Village* (MIT Press, Cambridge, Mass., 1965).

Also important from the perspective of those strongly favorable to the Communists are William Hinton, *Fanshen: A Documentary of Revolution in a Chinese Village* (Monthly Review Press, New York, 1966), and Jan Myrdal, *Report from a Chinese Village* (Heinemann, London, 1965).

Book-length studies of the Chinese military that warrant attention include Chester J. Cheng (ed.), *The Politics of the Chinese Red Army* (Hoover Institution, Stanford, 1966); Alexander George, *The Chinese Communist*

Army in Action (Columbia Univ. Press, New York, 1967); John Gittings, *The Role of the Chinese Army* (Oxford Univ. Press, London, 1967); Samuel B. Griffith II, *The Chinese People's Liberation Army* (McGraw-Hill, New York, 1967); Harry Harding and Melvin Gurtov, *The Purge of Lo Jui-ching: The Politics of Chinese Strategic Planning* (Rand Corp., Santa Monica, 1970); Ellis Joffe, *Party and Army: Professionalism and Political Control in the Chinese Officer Corps, 1949–1964* (Harvard Univ. Press, Cambridge, Mass., 1965); William W. Whitson (ed.), *The Military and Political Power in China in the 1970s* (Praeger, New York, 1972); and William W. Whitson, with Chen-hsia Huang, *The Chinese High Command: A History of Communist Military Politics, 1927–1971* (Praeger, New York, 1973.

Works not yet noted focusing on the Cultural Revolution, that major event unfolding between 1965 and 1968, are Richard Baum (ed.), *China in Ferment: Perspectives on the Cultural Revolution* (Prentice-Hall, Englewood Cliffs, N.J., 1971); Gordon A. Bennett and Ronald N. Montaperto, *Red Guard* (Doubleday, New York, 1971); Parris H. Chang, *Radicals and Radical Ideology in China's Cultural Revolution* (Columbia Univ. Press, New York, 1973); C.L. Chiou, *Maoism in Action: The Cultural Revolution* (Univ. of Queensland Press, St. Lucia, 1974); Lowell Dittmer, *Liu Shao-ch'i and the Chinese Cultural Revolution—The Politics of Mass Criticism* (Univ. of California Press, Berkeley and Los Angeles, 1974); William F. Dorrill, *Power, Policy, and Ideology in the Making of China's Cultural Revolution* (Rand Corp., Santa Monica, August 1968); Neale Hunter, *Shanghai Journal* (Praeger, New York, 1969); and Union Research Institute, *Chinese Communist Party Documents of the Great Proletarian Cultural Revolution, 1966–1967* (Hong Kong, 1968).

On the Chinese intellectuals in the post-1949 period, see Dennis J. Doolin, *Communist China: The Politics of Student Opposition* (Hoover Institution, Stanford, 1964); Merle Goldman, *Literary Dissent in Communist China* (Harvard Univ. Press, Cambridge, Mass., 1967); and Robert Jay Lifton, *Thought Reform and the Psychology of Totalism* (Norton, New York, 1963).

The noteworthy studies dealing with the Chinese economy include Nai-Ruenn Chen and Walter Galenson, *The Chinese Economy under Communism* (Aldine, Chicago, 1968); Audrey Donnithorne, *China's Economic System* (Allen and Unwin, London, 1967); Alexander Eckstein, *Communist China's Economic Growth and Foreign Trade* (McGraw-Hill, New York, 1966); Alexander Eckstein, Walter Galenson, and Ta-chung Liu (eds.) *Economic Trends in Communist China* (Aldine, Chicago, 1968); Victor D. Lippit, *Land Reform and Economic Development in China: A Study of Institutional Change and Development Finance* (International Arts and Sciences Press, White Plains, N.Y., 1974); *People's Republic of China: An Economic Assessment,* A Compendium of Papers Submitted to the Joint Economic Committee, 92nd Cong., 2 sess., 1972; W.E. Wilmott (ed.), *Economic Organization in Chinese Society* (Stanford Univ. Press, Stanford, 1972); and K.C. Yeh, *Communist China's Strategy Options and Priorities in Resource Allocation* (Rand Corp., Santa Monica, August 1973).

Turning finally to China's foreign policy, recent general works would include Winberg Chai (ed.), *The Foreign Relations of the People's Republic of China* (Putnam, New York, 1972); John Gittings, *The World and China, 1922–1972* (Harper and Row, New York, 1974); Harold C. Hinton, *China's Turbulent Quest* (Macmillan, New York, 1970); James C. Hsiung, *Law and Policy in China's Foreign Relations: A Study of Attitudes and Practices* (Columbia Univ. Press, New York, 1970); Douglas M. Johnston and Hungdah Chiu (eds.), *Agreements of the People's Republic of China, 1949–1967: A Calendar* (Harvard Univ. Press, Cambridge, Mass., 1972); Ishwer C. Ojha, *Chinese Foreign Policy in an Age of Transition: The Diplomacy of Cultural Despair* (Beacon, Boston, 1969); J.D. Simmonds, *China's World: The Foreign Policy of a Developing State* (Columbia Univ. Press, New York, 1970); Tang Tsou (ed.), *China in Crisis*, vol. 2: *China, the United States, and Asia* (Univ. of Chicago Press, Chicago, 1967); Francis O. Wilcox (ed.), *China and the Great Powers* (Praeger, New York, 1974).

Additional works focusing on the Sino-Soviet dispute are Tai Sung An, *The Sino-Soviet Territorial Dispute* (Westminster, Philadelphia, 1973); O. Edmund Clubb, *China and Russia: The "Great Game"* (Columbia Univ. Press, New York, 1971); William E. Griffith, *Sino-Soviet Relations— 1967–1965* (MIT Press, Cambridge, Mass., 1967); Morton H. Halperin (ed.), *Sino-Soviet Relations and Arms Control* (MIT Press, Cambridge, Mass., 1967); and Harold C. Hinton, *The Bear at the Gate: Chinese Policymaking under Soviet Pressure* (American Enterprise Institute, Washington, D.C., 1971). The classic study by Donald S. Zagoria, *The Sino-Soviet Conflict, 1956–1961* (Princeton Univ. Press, Princeton, N.J., 1962), is still very useful.

Studies concentrating on Sino-American relations not previously mentioned include A. Doak Barnett, *A New U.S. Policy toward China* (Brookings, Washington, D.C., 1971); Foster Rhea Dulles, *American Policy toward Communist China—The Historical Record: 1949–1969* (Crowell, New York, 1972); J.H. Kalicki, *The Pattern of Sino-American Crises* (Cambridge Univ. Press, New York, 1974); Roderick MacFarquhar and others, *Sino-American Relations, 1949–1971* (Praeger, New York, 1971); Richard Moorsteen and Morton Abramowitz, *Remaking China Policy: U.S.-China Relations and Governmental Decision Making* (Harvard Univ. Press, Cambridge, Mass., 1971); *U.S. Relations with the People's Republic of China*, Hearings before the Senate Committee on Foreign Relations, 92 Cong., 1 sess., 1971; *United States-China Relations: A Strategy for the Future*, Hearings before the Subcommittee on Asian and Pacific Affairs of the House Committee on Foreign Affairs, 91 Cong., 2 sess., 1970; and *U.S. Policy with Respect to Mainland China*, Hearings before the Senate Foreign Relations Committee, 80 Cong., 2 sess., 1966; and Kenneth T. Young, *Negotiating with the Chinese Communists: The United States' Experience, 1953–1967* (McGraw-Hill, New York, 1968).

Additional works relating to China's policies toward the Third World are King C. Chen, *Vietnam and China, 1938–1954* (Princeton Univ.

Press, Princeton, N.J., 1969); Melvin Gurtov, *China and Southeast Asia: The Politics of Survival* (Johns Hopkins Univ. Press, Baltimore, 1975); Cecil Johnson, *Communist China and Latin America, 1959–1967* (Columbia Univ. Press, New York, 1970); Joseph E. Khalili, *Communist China's Interaction with the Arab Nationalists since the Bandung Conference* (Exposition Press, New York, 1970); Bruce Larkin, *China and Africa, 1949–1970* (Univ. of California Press, Berkeley and Los Angeles, 1971); Neville Maxwell, *India's China War* (Pantheon, New York, 1970); Jay Taylor, *China and Southeast Asia: Peking's Relations with Revolutionary Movements* (Praeger, New York, 1974); Peter Van Ness, *Revolution and Chinese Foreign Policy* (Univ. of California Press, Berkeley and Los Angeles, 1971); and Donald S. Zagoria, *Viet-Nam Triangle* (Pegasus, New York, 1967). An earlier work by Allan S. Whiting, *China Crosses the Yalu* (Macmillan, New York, 1960), remains a most important study of China's intervention in the Korean War.

All individuals interested in China's domestic or foreign policies should consult the periodicals and translation services specializing in this field, including those put out by the People's Republic of China. The more important are *China Quarterly, Current Background*, 1960–, U.S. Consulate General, Hong Kong; *Current Scene*, 1961–, U.S. Information Service, Hong Kong; *Foreign Broadcast Information Service*, U.S. Government, Washington, D.C., *Peking Review* (weekly), Peking; *New China News Agency* (daily), Peking; *China Reconstructs* (monthly), Peking; *News from China's Provincial Radio Stations*, British Information Service, Hong Kong; *Selections from People's Republic of China Magazines*, U.S. Consulate General, Hong Kong; and *Survey of People's Republic of China Press*, U.S. Consulate General, Hong Kong.

India

Among the most recent general studies dealing with South Asian political systems or India specifically, the following can be recommended: William Norman Brown, *The United States and India, Pakistan, and Bangladesh*, 3rd ed. (Harvard Univ. Press, Cambridge, Mass., 1972); Ainslee T. Embree, *India's Search for National Identity* (Knopf, New York, 1972); Robert Kearney (ed.), *Politics and Modernization in South and Southeast Asia* (Halsted, New York, 1975); Richard Park (ed.), *Change and the Persistence of Tradition in India* (University of Michigan, Center for South and Southeast Asian Studies, Ann Arbor, 1971); and W. Howard Wriggins and James F. Guyot (eds.), *Population, Politics, and the Future of Southern Asia* (Columbia Univ. Press, New York, 1973).

Less recent political studies still of substantial value include Robert L. Hardgrave, *India: Government and Politics in a Developing Country* (Harcourt, Brace and World, New York, 1970); Rajni Kothari, *Politics in India*

(Little Brown, Boston, 1970); Beatrice P. Lamb, *India: A World in Transition*, 3rd. ed. rev. (Praeger, New York, 1968); W.H. Morris-Jones, *The Government and Politics of India* (Hutchinson University Library, London, 1964); Norman Palmer, *The Indian Political System*, 2nd ed. (Houghton Mifflin, Boston, 1971); C.H. Philips (ed.), *Politics and Society in India* (Praeger, New York, 1962); K.V. Rao, *Parliamentary Democracy in India* (Calcutta, 1961); Lloyd and Susanne Rudolph, *The Modernity of Tradition* (Univ. of Chicago Press, Chicago, 1967); Hugh Tinker, *India and Pakistan—A Political Analysis* (Praeger, New York, 1962); and Myron Weiner (ed.), *State Politics in India* (Princeton Univ. Press, Princeton, N.J. 1968).

A host of excellent specialized studies on Indian politics has recently been produced. Those having the greatest relevance to an overview would include Krishan Bhatia, *Indira: A Biography of Prime Minister Gandhi* (Praeger, New York, 1974); Paul R. Brass, *Language, Religion, and Politics in North India* (Cambridge Univ. Press, New York, 1974); Paul R. Brass and Marcus F. Franda (eds.), *Radical Politics in South Asia* (MIT Press, Cambridge, Mass., 1973); Stephen P. Cohen, *The Indian Army: Its Contribution to the Development of a Nation* (Univ. of California Press, Berkeley and Los Angeles, 1971); Jyotirindra Das Gupta, *Language Conflict and National Development: Group Politics and National Language Policy in India* (Univ. of California Press, Berkeley and Los Angeles, 1970); Rodney W. Jones, *Urban Politics in India: Area, Power, and Policy in a Penetrated System* (Univ. of California Press, Berkeley and Los Angeles, 1974); Rajni Kothari and others, *Context of Electoral Change in India—General Elections, 1967* (Academic Books, Bombay, 1969); George Rosen, *Democracy and Economic Change in India* (Univ. of California Press, Berkeley and Los Angeles, 1967); Rameshray Roy, *The Uncertain Verdict: A Study of the 1969 Elections in Four Indian States* (Univ. of California Press, Berkeley and Los Angeles, 1974); and Myron Weiner, *Party Politics in India: The Development of a Multi-Party System* (Kennikat Press, Port Washington, N.Y., 1972).

Three works presenting a broad social treatment of India, each highly relevant to India's political culture are David G. Mandelbaum, *Society in India*, 2 vols. (Univ. of California Press, Berkeley and Los Angeles, 1970); Adrian C. Mayer, *Caste and Kinship in Central India* (Univ. of California Press, Berkeley and Los Angeles, 1960); and M.N. Srinivas, *Social Change in Modern India* (Univ. of California Press, Berkeley and Los Angeles, 1966).

In the economic realm, contemporary works of importance would include Kuan-I Chen and J.S. Uppal (eds.), *India and China: Studies in Comparative Development* (Free Press, New York, 1971); Douglas Ensminger, *Rural India in Transition* (All India Panchayat Parishad, New Delhi, 1972); Howard L. Erdman, *Political Attitudes of Indian Industry* (Oxford Univ. Press, London, 1971); Francine R. Frankel, *India's Green Revolution: Economic Gains and Political Costs* (Princeton Univ. Press, Princeton, N.J., 1971); S.P. Gupta, *Planning Models in India, with Projections to 1975*

(Praeger, New York, 1971); A.H. Hanson, *The Process of Planning, A Study of India's Five-Year Plans, 1950–1964* (Oxford Univ. Press, New York, 1966); Stanley A. Kochanek, *Business and Politics in India* (Univ. of California Press, Berkeley and Los Angeles, 1974); Wilfred Malenbaum, *Modern India's Economy: Two Decades of Planned Growth* (Merrill, Columbus, Ohio, 1971); India Planning Commission (Republic); *Draft, Fifth Five-Year Plan, 1974–1979* (New Delhi, 1973); Gustav Ranis (ed.), *The Gap between Rich and Poor Nations* (Macmillan, London, and St. Martin's, New York, 1972); E.A.G. Robinson and Michael Kidron (eds.), *Economic Development in South Asia* (Macmillan, London, 1970); R.T. Shand (ed.), *Agricultural Development in Asia* (Univ. of California Press, Berkeley and Los Angeles, 1969); and Subramanian Swamy, *Economic Growth in China and India, 1952–1970: A Comparative Appraisal* (Univ. of Chicago Press, Chicago, 1973).

Older works of continuing importance would include P.T. Bauer, *Indian Economic Policy and Development* (Allen and Unwin, London, 1961); D.R. Gadgil, *Planning and Economic Policy in India* (Gokhale Institute of Politics and Economics, Poona, 1961); John P. Lewis, *Quiet Crisis in India* (Brookings, Washington, D.C., 1962); and Gunnar Myrdal, *Asian Drama*, 3 vols. (Twentieth Century Fund, New York, 1968).

For general works on Indian foreign policy of note, see A. Appadorai, *Essays in Indian Politics and Foreign Policy* (Vikas, Delhi, 1971); J. Bandyopadhyaya, *The Making of India's Foreign Policy* (Allied, Bombay, 1970); William J. Barnds, *India, Pakistan, and the Great Powers* (Praeger, New York, 1972); Balwant Bhaneja, *The Politics of Triangles: The Alignment Patterns in South Asia, 1961–1971,* Research, Delhi, 1973; S.M. Burke, *Mainsprings of Indian and Pakistani Foreign Policies* (Univ. of Minnesota Press, Minneapolis, 1975); Bhabani Sen Gupta, *The Fulcrum of Asia: Relations among China, India, Pakistan, and the U.S.S.R.* (Pegasus, New York, 1970); K.P. Misra (ed.), *Studies in Indian Foreign Policy* (Vikas, Delhi, 1969); H.G. Pant, *India's Foreign Policy* (Panchseel, Jaipur, 1971); Parliament of India, House of the People Secretariat, *Parliament and Foreign Policy—A Study* (Government Printing House, New Delhi, 1971); and Paul F. Power, *India's Nonalignment Policy: Strengths and Weaknesses* (Heath, Boston, 1967).

More specialized studies of worth include V.S. Budhray, *Soviet Russia and the Hindustan Subcontinent* (Somaiya, Bombay, 1973); Michael Brecher, *India and World Politics—Krishna Menon's View of the World* (Oxford Univ. Press, London, 1968); P.J. Eldridge, *The Politics of Foreign Aid in India* (Vikas, Delhi, 1969); Margaret Fisher, Leo E. Rose, and Robert Hüttenback, *Himalayan Battleground* (Praeger, New York, 1962), S. Gupta, *Kashmir: A Study in India-Pakistan Relations* (Asia Publishing House, Bombay, 1966); H.V. Hodson, *The Great Divide* (Hutchinson, London, 1969): Lorne J. Kavis, *India's Quest for Security: Defense Policies, 1947–1965* (Univ. of California Press, Berkeley and Los Angeles, 1967); Neville Maxwell, *India's China War* (Cape, London, 1970); K.P. Misra, *The Role of the United Nations in the Indo-Pakistani Conflict, 1971* (Vikas, Delhi, 1973); Norman D. Palmer, *South Asia and United States Policy* (Houghton Mifflin, Boston, 1966); Bimal Prasad, *Indo-Soviet Relations, 1947–1962* (Paragon Cook Reprint, New York, 1973); Mohan Ram, *Politics of Sino-Indian Confrontation* (Vikas, Delhi, 1973); Arthur Stein, *India and the Soviet Union* (Univ. of Chicago Press, Chicago, 1969); K. Subrahmanyam, *Perspectives in Defence Planning* (Abhinar, New Delhi, 1972); and Howard Wriggins, with the assistance of Stanley J. Heginbotham and James W. Morley, *India and Japan: The Emerging Balance of Power in Asia and Opportunities for Arms Control* (Columbia Univ. Press, New York, 1971).

Indonesia

Much of the current writing on Indonesia is included in more general studies on Southeast Asia or comparative studies. Among the recent works on culture and politics not yet mentioned, these are worthy of attention: Richard Allen, *A Short Introduction to the History and Politics of Southeast Asia* (Oxford Univ. Press, New York, 1970); Richard Butwell, *Southeast Asia: A Political Introduction* (Praeger, New York, 1975); Sudershan Chawla, Melvin Gurtov, and Alain-Gerard Marsot (eds.), *Southeast Asia under the New Balance of Power* (Praeger, New York, 1974); Bernhard Grossmann, *Southeast Asia in the Modern World* (O. Harrassowitz, Wiesbaden, Germany, 1972); Michael Leifer, *Dilemmas of Statehood in Southeast Asia* (Univ. of British Columbia Press, Vancouver, 1972); Joel S. Migdal, *Peasants, Politics, and Revolution: Pressure toward Political and Social Change in the Third World* (Princeton Univ. Press., Princeton, N.J., 1975); Jan M. Pluvier, *South-East Asia from Colonialism to Independence* (Oxford Univ. Press, New York, 1974); Lucian W. Pye, *Southeast Asia's Political Systems,* 2nd ed. (Prentice-Hall, Englewood Cliffs, N.J., 1974); Roger M. Smith (ed.), *Southeast Asia: Documents of Political Development and Change* (Cornell Univ. Press, Ithaca, 1974); and J. Robert E. Waddell, *An Introduction to Southeast Asian Politics* (Wiley, Sydney and New York, 1972).

On economics, see Asian Development Bank, *Southeast Asia's Economy in the 1970s* (Manila, Nov. 1, 1970); and U Hla Myint, *Southeast Asia's Economy: Development Policies in the 1970s* (Praeger, New York, 1972). Certain educational issues are raised in Yip Yat Hoong (ed.), *Development of Higher Education in Southeast Asia: Problems and Issues* (Regional Institute of Higher Education and Development, Singapore, 1973); and Muhammad Shambul Huq, *Education and Development Strategy in South and Southeast Asia* (East-West Center Press, Honolulu, 1965).

Among the recent works on Indonesian culture and politics, these studies should be consulted: Herbert Feith and Lance Castles, *Indonesian Political Thinking, 1945–1965* (Cornell Univ. Press, Ithaca, 1970); Claire Holt (ed.), with the assistance of Benedict R. Anderson and James Siegel, *Culture and Politics in Indonesia* (Cornell Univ. Press, Ithaca, 1972);

Oly Hong Lee (ed.), *Indonesia after the 1971 Elections,* Hull Monographs on Southeast Asia, no. 5 (Oxford Univ. Press, London, 1974); J.D. Legge, *Sukarno: A Political Biography* (Praeger, New York, 1972); R. William Liddle, *Political Participation in Modern Indonesia,* Cultural Report Series Monograph no. 19 (Yale University, Southeast Asian Studies, New Haven, 1973); Leslie Palmer, *Communists in Indonesia: Power Pursued in Vain* (Doubleday Anchor, Garden City, N.Y., 1973); Peter Polomka, *Indonesia since Sukarno* (Penguin, Baltimore, 1971); and Allan M. Sievers, *The Mystical World of Indonesia: Culture and Economic Development in Conflict* (Johns Hopkins Univ. Press, Baltimore, 1974).

Among the older works of continuing value, see Herbert Feith, *The Decline of Constitutional Democracy in Indonesia* (Cornell Univ. Press, Ithaca, 1962); Clifford Geertz, *The Religion of Java* (Free Press, New York, 1960); *Peddlers and Princes* (Univ. of Chicago Press, Chicago, 1963); *The Social History of an Indonesian Town* (MIT Press, Cambridge, Mass., 1965); Hildred Geertz, *The Javanese Family* (Free Press, New York, 1961); *Indonesian Cultures and Communities* (HRAF Press, New Haven, 1963); Donald Hindley, *The Communist Party of Indonesia, 1951–1963* (Univ. of California Press, Berkeley and Los Angeles, 1964); G. McTurnan Kahin, *Nationalism and Revolution in Indonesia* (Cornell Univ. Press., Ithaca, 1952); J.D. Legge, *Indonesia* (Prentice-Hall, Englewood Cliffs, N.J., 1964); Ruth T. McVey, *Indonesia* (Yale Univ. Press, New Haven, 1963); Selosoemardjan, *Social Change in Jogjakarta* (Cornell Univ. Press, Ithaca, 1962); Robert Van Niel, *The Emergence of the Modern Indonesian Elite* (Van Hoeve, The Hague, 1960); W.F. Wertheim, *Indonesian Society in Transition: A Study of Social Change* (Van Hoeve, The Hague, 1959); and Ann Willner, *The Neo-Traditional Accommodation to Political Independence: The Case of Indonesia* (Center of International Studies, Woodrow Wilson School, Princeton, N.J., 1966).

For more specialized political studies of recent vintage, see Antonie C.A. Dake, *In the Spirit of the Red Banteng: Indonesian Communists between Moscow and Peking, 1959–1965* (Mouton, The Hague, 1973); Daniel S. Lev, *Islamic Courts in Indonesia: A Study in the Political Bases of Legal Institutions* (Univ. of California Press, Berkeley and Los Angeles, 1972); Ali Moertopo, *Some Basic Thoughts on the Acceleration and Modernization of 25 Years' Development* (Paragon Press, Malang, 1972); Nugroho Notosusanto and Ismail Saleh, *The Coup Attempt of the "September 30 Movement" in Indonesia* (Pemmas, Jakarta, 1967). Four recent works are devoted to Indonesian foreign relations. Two are general studies: Ide Anak Agang Gde Agung, *Twenty Years of Indonesian Foreign Policy, 1945–1965* (Mouton, The Hague, 1973); and Centre for Strategic and International Studies, *The World of Strategy and the Foreign Policy of Nations* (Paragon Press, Malang, 1973). One focuses on the Peking-Jakarta ties of earlier years, Sheldon W. Simon, *Indonesia—The Broken Triangle—Peking, Jakarta, and the PKI* (Johns Hopkins Press, Baltimore, 1969), and one on economic relations with Japan, Yusuf Panglaykim, *Business Relations between In-*

donesia and Japan (Paragon Press, Malang, 1974).

On Indonesian economics specifically, see Clifford Geertz, *Agriculture Involution: The Process of Ecological Change in Indonesia* (Univ. of California Press, Berkeley and Los Angeles, 1966); Bruce Glassburner (ed.), *The Economy of Indonesia—Selected Readings* (Cornell Univ. Press, Ithaca, 1971); and Gary E. Hansen, *Rural Local Government and Agricultural Development in Java* (Cornell University, Center for International Studies, Ithaca, 1974).

In the realm of periodicals, *The Indonesian Quarterly*, first published in 1972 by the Centre for Strategic and International Studies, Jakarta; *Indonesia*, Cornell Modern Indonesia Project; and the *Bulletin of Indonesian Economic Studies*, Monash University, Melbourne, Australia, are especially useful.

The Soviet Union

General studies of Soviet society and politics published in recent years would include L.G. Churchward, *Contemporary Soviet Government* (Routledge and Kegan Paul, London, 1975); Richard Cornell, *The Soviet Political System: A Book of Readings* (Prentice-Hall, New York, 1970); Darrell P. Hammer, *USSR: The Politics of Oligarchy* (Dryden Press, Hinsdale, Ill., 1974); John N. Hazard, *The Soviet System of Government*, 4th ed. (Univ. of Chicago Press, Chicago, 1968); Samuel Hendel (ed.), *The Soviet Crucible*, 4th ed. (Duxbury, North Scituate, Mass., 1973); Paul Hollander, *Soviet and American Society* (Oxford Univ. Press, New York, 1973); Zev Katz, Rosemarie Rogers, and Frederic Harned, *Handbook of Major Soviet Nationalities* (Free Press, New York, 1975); David Lane, *Politics and Society in the USSR* (Random House-Knopf, New York, 1971); Mervyn Matthews, *Class and Society in Soviet Russia* (Walker, New York, 1972); Ellen Mickiewicz, *Handbook of Soviet Social Science Data* (Free Press, New York, 1973); Henry W. Morton and Rudolf L. Tokes, *Soviet Politics and Society in the 1970s* (Free Press, New York, 1974); Joseph L. Nogee (ed.), *Man, State, and Society in the Soviet Union* (Praeger, New York, 1972); Robert J. Osborn, *The Evolution of Soviet Politics* (Dorsey, Homewood, Ill., 1974); Sidney I. Ploss, *The Soviet Political Process—Aims, Techniques, and Examples of Analysis* (Ginn, Waltham, Mass., 1971); John S. Reshetar, *The Soviet Polity: Government and Politics in the USSR* (Dodd, Mead, New York, 1971); Michael Tatu, *Power in the Kremlin from Khruschev to Kosygin* (Viking, New York, 1969); and Robert C. Tucker, *The Soviet Political Mind*, rev. ed. (Norton, New York, 1971).

Many earlier books are of continuing value, among them John Armstrong, *The Soviet Bureaucratic Elite* (Praeger, New York, 1959); Harold J. Berman, *Justice in the USSR*, rev. ed. (Random House Vintage, New York, 1963); Zbigniew Brzezinski and Samuel Huntington, *Political Power—U.S.A./U.S.S.R.* (Viking, New York, 1964); Robert Conquest, *Power and Policy in the USSR: The Struggle for Stalin's Succession, 1945–1960*

(Macmillan, London, 1962); Alexander Erlich, *The Soviet Industrialization Debate, 1924–1928* (Harvard Univ. Press, Cambridge, Mass., 1960); Merle Fainsod, *How Russia Is Ruled* (Harvard Univ. Press, Cambridge, Mass., 1953); *Smolensk under Soviet Rule* (Random House Vintage, New York, 1963); Carl J. Friedrich (ed.), *Totalitarianism* (Grosset and Dunlap, New York, 1964); Alex Inkeles and Raymond Bauer, *The Soviet Citizen* (Harvard Univ. Press, Cambridge, Mass., 1961); and Barrington Moore, Jr., *Soviet Politics—The Dilemma of Power: The Role of Ideas in Social Change* (Harper and Row, New York, 1965).

A larger number of more specialized works on the Soviet social or political system have recently been available. Studies of the Stalin and immediate post-Stalin period worthy of attention include Seweryn Bialer (ed.), *Stalin and His Generals* (Pegasus, New York, 1969); E.H. Carr and R.W. Davies, *Foundations of a Planned Economy*, vol. 1, parts 1 and 2 (Macmillan, New York, 1969); Robert Conquest, *The Great Terror* (Macmillan, London, 1968); Sheila Fitzpatrick, *The Commissariat of Enlightenment* (Cambridge Univ. Press, London, 1970); Zvi Gitelman, *Jewish Nationality and Soviet Politics: The Jewish Sections of the CPSU, 1917–1930.* (Princeton Univ. Press, Princeton, N.J., 1972); Moshe Lewin, *Russian Peasants and Soviet Power* (Northwestern Univ. Press, Evanston, Ill., 1968); Gregory J. Massell, *The Surrogate Proletariat* (Princeton Univ. Press, Princeton, N.J., 1974); Roy Medvedev, *Let History Judge: The Origins and Consequences of Stalinism* (Knopf, New York, 1971); Olga Narkiewicz, *The Making of the Soviet State Apparatus* (Manchester Univ. Press, Manchester, 1970); Roger Pethybridge, *The Social Prelude to Stalinism* (St. Martin's, New York, 1974); Robert C. Tucker, *Stalin as Revolutionary 1879–1929* (Norton, New York, 1973); Adam B. Ulam, *Stalin: The Man and His Era* (Viking, New York, 1973).

For contemporary works dealing with such special topics as nationalities, leadership, ideology, and the party, see Edward Allworth and others, *Soviet Nationality Problems* (Columbia Univ. Press, New York, 1971); Carl Beck and others, *Comparative Communist Political Leadership* (McKay, New York, 1973); Jerome M. Gilison, *British and Soviet Politics* Johns Hopkins Univ. Press, Baltimore, 1972); Erich Goldhagen (ed.), *Ethnic Minorities in the Soviet Union* (Praeger, New York, 1968); Loren R. Graham, *Science and Philosophy in the Soviet Union* (Vintage, New York, 1974); Werner G. Hahn, *The Politics of Soviet Agriculture 1960–1970* (Johns Hopkins Univ. Press, Baltimore, 1972); John Hazard, *Communists and Their Law* (Univ. of Chicago Press, Chicago, 1969); Grey Hodnett and Val Ogareff, *Leaders of the Soviet Republics, 1955–1972* (Australian National Univ., Canberra, 1973); Grey Hodnett and Peter J. Potichnyj, *The Ukraine and the Czechoslovak Crisis* (Australian National Univ., Canberra, 1970); Gayle D. Hollander, *Soviet Political Indoctrination* (Praeger, New York, 1972); David Joravsky, *The Lysenko Affair* (Harvard Univ. Press, Cambridge, Mass., 1970); Wolfgang Leonhard, *Three Faces of Marxism* (Holt, Rinehart, and Winston, New York, 1974); Borys Levytsky, *The*

Soviet Political Elite (Hoover Institution, Stanford, 1970); *The Uses of Terror: The Soviet Secret Police, 1917–1970* (Coward, McCann, and Geoghegan, New York, 1972); Robert Miller, *One Hundred Thousand Tractors: The MTS and the Development of Controls in Soviet Agriculture* (Harvard Univ. Press, Cambridge, Mass., 1970); Joel C. Moses, *Regional Party Leadership and Policy-Making in the USSR* (Praeger, New York, 1974); Alec Nove and J.A. Newth, *The Soviet Middle East* (Allen and Unwin, London, 1967); Peter Reddaway (ed.), *Uncensored Russia* (American Heritage Press, New York, 1972); George Saunders (ed.), *Samizdat* (Monad, New York, 1974); Aryeh L. Unger, *The Totalitarian Party* (Cambridge Univ. Press, New York, 1974).

Works of special interest with respect to Soviet military policies include Leon Goure, Foy D. Kohler, and Mose L. Harvey, *The Role of Nuclear Forces in Current Soviet Strategy* (Center for Advanced International Studies, Univ. of Miami, 1974); Roman Kolkowicz, *The Soviet Military and the Communist Party* (Princeton Univ. Press, Princeton, N.J., 1967); *The Soviet Union and Arms Control* (Johns Hopkins Press, Baltimore, 1970).

Among recent sociological and educational studies, these are of importance: Walter D. Connor, *Deviance in Soviet Society* (Columbia Univ. Press, New York, 1972); H. Kent Geiger, *The Family in Soviet Russia* (Harvard Univ. Press, Cambridge, Mass., 1968); Mark W. Hopkins, *Mass Media in the Soviet Union* (Pegasus, New York, 1970); Alex Inkeles, *Social Change in Soviet Russia* (Simon and Schuster, New York, 1971); David Lane, *End of Inequality?* (Penguin, Baltimore, 1971); Bernice Q. Madison, *Social Welfare in the Soviet Union* (Stanford Univ. Press, Stanford, 1968); James R. Millar (ed.), *The Soviet Rural Community: A Symposium* (Univ. of Illinois Press, Urbana, 1971); Robert J. Osborn, *Soviet Social Policies: Welfare, Equality, and Community* (Dorsey, Homewood, Ill., 1970); G.V. Osipov (ed.), *Industry and Labour in the USSR* (Tavisoock, London, 1969); Jean Pennar, Ivan I. Bakalo, and George Z.F. Bereday, *Modernization and Diversity in Soviet Education: With Special Reference to Nationality Groups* (Praeger, New York, 1971); Seymour M. Rosen, *Education and Modernization in the USSR* (Addison-Wesley, Reading, Mass., 1971); Alex Simirenko (ed.), *Social Thought in the Soviet Union* (Quadrangle, Chicago, 1969); and Murray Yanowitch and Wesley A. Fisher, *Social Stratification and Mobility in the USSR* (International Arts and Sciences Press, New York, 1973).

Among the works on Soviet economics of the past few years, the following are very useful: William L. Blackwell, *The Industrialization of Russia: An Historical Perspective* (Crowell, New York, 1970); Morris Bornstein and Daniel R. Fusfeld (eds.), *The Soviet Economy: A Book of Readings,* 4th ed. (Dorsey, Homewood, Ill., 1974); Emily Clark Brown, *Soviet Trade Unions and Labor Relations* (Harvard Univ. Press, Cambridge, Mass., 1966); Robert W. Campbell, *Soviet-Type Economics* (Macmillan, New York, 1974); Michael Ellman, *Planning Problems in the USSR: The Contribution of Mathematical Economics to their Solution, 1960–1971* (Cambridge Univ.

Press, New York, 1973); Iain F. Elliot, *The Soviet Energy Balance* (Praeger, New York, 1974); John G. Eriksen and Robert Farrell (eds.), *The Development of Soviet Society: Plan and Performance* (Institute for the Study of the USSR, Munich, 1970); George R. Feiwel, *The Soviet Quest for Economic Efficiency: Issues, Controversies, and Reforms* (Praeger, New York, 1972); Mose L. Harvey, Leon Goure, and Vladimir Prokofieff, *Science and Technology as an Instrument of Soviet Policy* (Center for Advanced International Studies, Univ. of Miami, Coral Gables, Fl., 1972); Michael Kaser, *Soviet Economics* (McGraw-Hill, New York, 1970); Abraham Katz, *The Politics of Economic Reform in the Soviet Union* (Praeger, New York, 1972); Leonard Kirsch, *Soviet Wages* (MIT Press, Cambridge, Mass., 1972); Moshe Lewin, *Political Undercurrents in Soviet Economic Debate: From Bukharin to the Modern Reformers* (Princeton Univ. Press, Princeton, N.J., 1974); E.G. Liberman, *Economic Methods and the Effectiveness of Production: A Study of Soviet Economic Reforms* (Doubleday, New York, 1973); Jan Marczewski, *Crisis in Socialist Planning: Eastern Europe and the USSR* (Praeger, New York, 1974); Alec Nove, *The Soviet Economy*, 2nd rev. ed. (Praeger, New York, 1969), and *An Economic History of the USSR* (Lane, London, 1969); Gur Ofer, *The Service Sector in Soviet Economic Growth* (Harvard Univ. Press, Cambridge, Mass., 1973); John Quigley, *The Soviet Foreign Trade Monopoly: Institutions and Laws* (Ohio State Univ. Press, Columbus, Ohio, 1974); Anthony C. Sutton, *Western Technology and Soviet Economic Development, 1945–1965* (Hoover Institution, Stanford, 1973); U.S. Congress, Joint Economic Committee, *Soviet Economic Prospects for the Seventies* (Washington, D.C., 1973); Karl-Eugen Waedekin, *The Private Sector in Soviet Agriculture* (Univ. of California Press, Berkeley and Los Angeles, 1973); and Charles Wilber, *The Soviet Model and Underdeveloped Countries* (Univ. of North Carolina Press, Chapel Hill, 1969).

Recent general studies of Soviet foreign policy include Vernon V. Aspaturian, *Process and Power in Soviet Foreign Policy* (Little, Brown, Boston, 1971); L.I. Brezhnev, *On the Policy of the Soviet Union and the International Situation* (Doubleday, Garden City, N.Y., 1973); Michael P. Gehlen, *The Politics of Coexistence* (Indiana Univ. Press, Bloomington, 1967); Leon Goure and others, *Convergence of Communism and Capitalism, The Soviet View* (Univ. of Miami, Coral Gables, Fl., 1973); Sir William Hayter, *Russia and the World: A Study in Soviet Foreign Policy* (Taplinger, New York, 1970); Erik P. Hoffman and Frederick J. Fleron, *The Conduct of Soviet Foreign Policy* (Aldine-Atherton, Chicago, 1971); C. G. Jacobsen, *Soviet Strategy—Soviet Foreign Policy: Military Considerations Affecting Soviet Policy-Making* (MacLehose-The Univ. Press, Glasgow, 1972); Barbara Jelavich, *St. Petersburg and Moscow: Tsarist and Soviet Foreign Policy, 1814–1974* (Indiana Univ. Press, Bloomington, 1974); Foy D. Kohler, Mose L. Harvey, Leon Goure, and Richard Soll, *Soviet Strategy for the Seventies: From Cold War to Peaceful Coexistence* (Univ. of Miami, Center for Advanced International Studies, Coral Gables, Fl., 1973); W.W. Kulski, *The Soviet Union in World Affairs: A Documented Analysis, 1964–1972*

(Syracuse Univ. Press, Syracuse, N.Y., 1973); Ivo J. Lederer, *Russian Foreign Policy—Essays in Historical Perspective* (Yale Univ. Press, New Haven, 1964); Kurt London (ed.), *The Soviet Impact on World Politics* (Hawthorn, New York, 1974); Anatol Rappaport, *The Big Two* (Pegasus, New York, 1971); Richard F. Rosser, *An Introduction to Soviet Foreign Policy* (Prentice-Hall, Englewood Cliffs, N.J., 1969); Alvin Rubenstein (ed.), *Foreign Policy of the Soviet Union* (Random House, New York, 1972); Marshall D. Shulman, *Stalin's Foreign Policy Reappraised* (Harvard Univ. Press, Cambridge, Mass., 1963); Adam B. Ulam, *Expansion and Coexistence: Soviet Foreign Policy, 1917–1973*, 2nd ed. (Praeger, New York, 1974); Robert G. Wesson, *Soviet Foreign Policy in Perspective* (Dorsey, Homewood, Ill., 1971); *The Russian Dilemma: A Political and Geopolitical View* (Rutgers Univ. Press, New Brunswick, N.J., 1974); and William Zimmerman, *Soviet Perspectives on International Relations, 1956–1967* (Princeton Univ. Press, Princeton, N.J., 1969).

For several studies on special aspects of foreign policy, see William C. Fletcher, *Religion and Soviet Foreign Policy, 1945–1970,* (Oxford Univ. Press, New York, 1973); Franklyn D. Holzman, *Foreign Trade under Central Planning* (Harvard Univ. Press, Cambridge, Mass., 1974); Paul Marer, *Soviet and East European Foreign Trade, 1946–1969* (Indiana Univ. Press, Bloomington, 1972); and Glen Alden Smith, *Soviet Foreign Trade: Organization, Operations, and Policy, 1918–1971* (Praeger, New York, 1973).

Works dealing with Soviet policy toward specific countries and regions include Zbigniew K. Brzezinski, *The Soviet Bloc—Unity and Conflict*, rev. ed. (Harvard Univ. Press, Cambridge, Mass., 1967); Walter C. Clemens, Jr., *The Superpowers and Arms Control: From Cold War to Interdependence* (Heath, Lexington, Mass., 1973); Helen D. Cohn, *Soviet Policy toward Black Africa* (Praeger, New York, 1972); Michael Confino and Shimon Shamir, *The USSR and the Middle East* (Wiley, New York, 1973); Robert H. Donaldson, *Soviet Policy toward India: Ideology and Strategy* (Harvard Univ. Press, Cambridge, Mass., 1974); W. Raymond Duncan (ed.), *Soviet Policy in Developing Countries* (Ginn-Blaisdell, Waltham, Mass., 1970); Robert O. Freedman, *Soviet Policy toward the Middle East since 1970* (Praeger, New York, 1975); Charles Gati (ed.), *Caging the Bear—Containment and the Cold War* (Bobbs-Merrill, Indianapolis and New York, 1974); J.P. Jain, *Soviet Policy towards Pakistan and Bangladesh* (Radiant, New Delhi, 1974); Geoffrey Jukes, *The Soviet Union in Asia* (Univ. of California Press, Berkeley and Los Angeles, 1973); Roger E. Kanet (ed.), *The Soviet Union and the Developing Nations* (Johns Hopkins Univ. Press, Baltimore, 1974); Ivo J. Lederer and Wayne S. Vucinich (eds.), *The Soviet Union and the Middle East: The Post-World War II Era* (Hoover Institution, Stanford, 1974); Jaan Pennar, *The U.S.S.R. and the Arabs—The Ideological Dimension* (Crane Russak, New York, 1973); Robert Slusser, *The Berlin Crisis of 1961*, (Johns Hopkins Univ. Press, Baltimore, 1973); Oles M. Smolansky, *The Soviet Union and the Arab Middle East under Khrushchev* (Bucknell Univ. Press, Lewisburg, Pa., 1974);

Adam B. Ulam, *The Rivals—America and Russia since World War II* (Viking, New York, 1971); Wayne S. Vucinich (ed.), *Russia and Asia: Essays on the Influence of Russia on the Asian Peoples* (Hoover Institution, Stanford, 1972); Robert S. Walters, *American and Soviet Aid: A Comparative Analysis* (Univ. of Pittsburg Press, Pittsburgh, 1970); William Welch, *American Images of Soviet Foreign Policy: An Inquiry into Recent Appraisals from the Academic Community* (Yale Univ. Press, New Haven, 1970); and Thomas W. Wolfe, *Soviet Power and Europe, 1945–1970* (Johns Hopkins Univ. Press, Baltimore, 1970).

The United States

The literature on American domestic politics is so extensive that I shall limit myself here to mention of recent works on the presidency, Congress, and other aspects of the contemporary American scene that have a direct bearing on either the process or the substance of American foreign policy.

Starting with the presidency, in addition to the classical works by Corwin, Rossiter, and Neustadt, we have had a recent torrent of books, some of which express quite different views, but most of which advocate curbs on presidential powers, reflecting current tides. Raoul Berger, *Executive Privilege: A Constitutional Myth* (Harvard Univ. Press, Cambridge, Mass., 1974); Robert A. Divine, *Foreign Policy and U.S. Presidential Elections, 1952–1960* (New Viewpoints, New York, 1974); Alonzo L. Hamby, *Beyond the New Deal: Harry S. Truman and American Liberalism* (Columbia Univ. Press, New York, 1973); Erwin C. Hargrove, *The Power of the Modern Presidency* (Temple Univ. Press, Philadelphia, 1974); Charles Roberts (ed.), *Has the President Too Much Power?* (Harper's, New York, 1974); Arthur M. Schlesinger, Jr., *The Imperial Presidency* (Houghton-Mifflin, Boston, 1973); and Rexford G. Tugwell and Thomas E. Cronin, *The Presidency Reappraised* (Praeger, New York, 1974).

To Congress, the parties, and foreign policy, much less attention has been paid. Among the studies worthy of attention, however, the following should be noted: Holbert N. Carroll, *The House of Representatives and Foreign Affairs* (Pittsburgh Univ. Press, Pittsburgh, 1958); Nelson W. Polsby, *Congress and the Presidency* (Prentice-Hall, Englewood Cliffs, N.J., 1971); Nelson W. Polsby (ed.), *Congressional Behavior* (Random House, New York, 1971); H. Bradford Westerfield, *Foreign Policy and Party Politics* (Yale Univ. Press, New Haven, 1955).

On other aspects of American government and society as they relate to foreign policy, see Raymond Bauer, Ithiel de Sola Pool, and Lewis Anthony Dexter, *American Business and Public Policy* (Atherton, New York, 1963); Bernard C. Cohen, *The Press and Foreign Policy* (Princeton Univ. Press, Princeton, N.J., 1963); *The Public's Impact on Foreign Policy* (Little, Brown, Boston, 1973); Thomas M. Franck and Edward Weisband, *Secrecy and Foreign Policy* (Oxford Univ. Press, New York, 1974); Robert S. Frank, *Message Dimensions of Television News* (Lexington Books, Lexington, Mass., 1973); Morton H. Halperin, with the assistance of Priscilla Clapp and Arnold Kanter, *Bureaucratic Politics and Foreign Policy* (Brookings, Washington, D.C., 1974); Lyman B. Kirkpatrick, Jr., *The U.S. Intelligence Community: Foreign Policy and Domestic Activities* (Hill and Wang, New York, 1973); Robert Presthus, *Elites in the Policy Process* (Cambridge Univ. Press, New York, 1974); Leon V. Sigal, *Reporters and Officials: The Organization and Politics of Newsmaking* (Lexington Books, Lexington, Mass., 1973); and William Watts and Lloyd Free, *State of the Nation—1974* (Potomac Associates, Washington, D.C., 1974).

For five recent studies of the American military that are relevant to foreign policy considerations, see Charles Walton Ackley, *The Modern Military in American Society* (Westminster Press, Philadelphia, 1972); James Clotfelder, *The Military in American Politics* (Harper and Row, New York, 1973); Zeb Bradford, Jr., and Frederic J. Brown, *The United States Army in Transition* (Sage, Beverly Hills, Calif., 1973); William L. Hauser, *America's Army in Crisis* (Johns Hopkins Univ. Press, Baltimore, 1973); and Col. George Walton, *The Tarnished Shield: A Report on Today's Army* (Dodd, Mead, New York, 1973).

Among the many general studies on American foreign policy, the following are worthy of attention, bearing in mind the diversity of views that reflect the American scene today—both with respect to interpretations of the past and ideas for the future: Raymond Aron, *The Imperial Republic—The United States and the World—1945–1973* (Prentice-Hall, Englewood Cliffs, N.J. 1974; Lincoln P. Bloomfield, *In Search of American Foreign Policy: The Humane Use of Power* (Oxford Univ. Press, New York, 1974); Henry Brandon, *The Retreat of American Power* (Doubleday, Garden City, N.Y. 1973); James Chace, *A World Elsewhere: The New American Foreign Policy* (Scribner, New York, 1973); John H. Gilbert (ed.), *The New Era in American Foreign Policy* (St. Martin's Press, New York, 1973); Stanley Hoffmann, *Gulliver's Troubles* (McGraw-Hill, New York, 1968); Alan M. Jones, Jr., *U.S. Foreign Policy in a Changing World: The Nixon Administration, 1969–1973* (McKay, New York, 1973); Harold B. Malmgren (ed.), *Pacific Basin Development: The American Interests* (Heath, Boston, 1972); Donald R. Lesh (ed.), *A Nation Observed—Perspectives on America's World Role* (Potomac Associates, Basic Books, New York, 1974); Drew Middleton, *Retreat from Victory: A Critical Appraisal of American Foreign and Military Policy from 1920 to the 1970s* (Hawthorn, New York, 1973); Lynn H. Miller and Ronald W. Pruessen (eds.), *Reflections on the Cold War: A Quarter Century of American Foreign Policy* (Temple Univ. Press, Philadelphia, 1974); Donald E. Nuechterlein, *United States National Interests in a Changing World* (Univ. Press of Kentucky, Lexington, 1973); Robert E. Osgood and others, *America and the World*, vol. 2: *Retreat From Empire?—The First Nixon Administration* (Johns Hopkins Univ. Press, Baltimore, 1974); Henry Owen (ed.), *The Next Phase in Foreign Policy* (Brookings, Washington, D.C., 1973); Guy Pauker, Steven Canby, A. Ross Johnson, and William B. Quandt, *In Search of Self-Reliance: U.S. Security Assistance to the Third World under the Nixon Doctrine* (Rand Corp.,

Santa Monica, June 1973); Eugene V. Rostow, *Peace in the Balance—The Future of American Foreign Policy* (Simon and Schuster, New York, 1972); and Robert W. Tucker, *A New Isolationism: Threat or Promise?* (Potomac Associates, Basic Books, New York, 1972).

Works focusing primarily on conflict and security issues in American foreign policy include Bernard Brodie, *War and Politics* (Macmillan, New York, 1973); Alexander L. George and Richard Smoke, *Deterrence in American Foreign Policy: Theory and Practice* (Columbia Univ. Press, New York, 1974); Richard G. Head and Ervin J. Rokke, *American Defense Policy*, 3rd rev. ed. (Johns Hopkins Univ. Press, Baltimore, 1973); William R. Kintner and Richard B. Foster, *National Strategy in a Decade of Change: An Emerging U.S. Policy* (Lexington Books, Lexington, Mass., 1973); Harland B. Moulton, *From Superiority to Parity: The United States and the Strategic Arms Race, 1961–1971* (Greenwood Press, Westport, Conn. 1973); Alton H. Quanbeck and Barry M. Blechman, *Strategic Forces: Issues for the Mid-Seventies* (Brookings, Washington, D.C., 1973); and Robert L. Pfaltzgraff, Jr. (ed.), *Contrasting Approaches to Strategic Arms Control* (Lexington Books, Lexington, Mass., 1974).

For works dealing specifically with SALT or American-Soviet relations, see Morton A. Kaplan (ed.), *Salt: Problems and Prospects* (General Learning Press, Morristown, N.J., 1973); William R. Kintner and Robert L. Pfaltzgraff, Jr., *Salt: Implications for Arms Control in the 1970s* (Univ. of Pittsburgh Press, Pittsburgh, 1973); Thomas G. Paterson, *Soviet-American Confrontation: Postwar Reconstruction and the Origins of the Cold War* (Johns Hopkins Univ. Press, Baltimore, 1973); Carl Solberg, *Riding High: America in the Cold War* (Mason and Lipscomb, New York, 1973); and Mason Willrich and John B. Rhinelander, *Salt: The Moscow Agreements and Beyond* (Free Press, New York, 1974).

On the strategic significance of Micronesia, see James H. Webb, Jr., *Micronesia and U.S. Pacific Strategy: A Blueprint for the 1980s* (Praeger, New York, 1974).

For recent studies relating to economic aspects of American foreign policy, including relations with the developing world, see James W. Howe and others, *The U.S. and the Developing World: Agenda for Action* (Praeger, New York, 1974); John P. Lewis and Ishan Kapur, *The World Bank Group, Multilateral Aid, and the 1970s* (Lexington Books, Lexington, Mass., 1973); Robert A. Packenham, *Liberal America and the Third World: Political Development Ideas in Foreign Aid and Social Science* (Princeton Univ. Press, Princeton, N.J., 1973); Rutherford M. Poats, *Technology for Developing Nations: New Directions for U.S. Technical Assistance* (Brookings, Washington, D.C., 1972); Ernest H. Preeg, *Economic Blocs and U.S. Foreign Policy*, (National Planning Association, Washington, D.C., 1974); Mira Wilkins, *The Maturing of Multinational Enterprise: American Business Abroad from 1914 to 1970* (Harvard Univ. Press, Cambridge, Mass., 1974); and Joseph A. Yager and Eleanor B. Steinberg, *Energy and U.S. Foreign Policy* (Ballinger, Cambridge, Mass., 1975).

Index

Abdul Razak bin Hussein, Tun, 18
Afghanistan: Soviet pressure on India through, 115; as buffer state, 117; relations with U.S., 187–188; relations with USSR, 187–188
Africa: relations with China, 86. *See also* Third World Aid: questioned, 23, 213, 262–263, 273, 274–275; to South Asia, 23, 102, 114–115, 120, 126, 127, 128, 129, 273, 274, 275–276; to Southeast Asia, 135, 145, 183, 251–252, 262–263; military, limits on, 159, 300; to Siberia, 172–173; to South Korea, 226; quid pro quo policies, 226–228; responsibilities of, 257, 258, 259, 277; problems of corruption, 258–259
Aidit, D. N.: Indonesian Communist leader, 148
Alliances: role of military bases in, 6; Sino-Soviet, 11, 55, 81, 92, 93, 96, 172, 247, 286, 287; Soviet-Japanese, 43; Sino-Japanese, 43, 83, 174; Communist/Kuomintang, 66, 76; Congress-Communist Parties (India), 101–102; Soviet-Indian, 125–126, 271; Sino-Indonesian, 133, 142; changing character of, 154, 288, 292; Japanese-American, 218, 219; Sino-American, 244
Anti-Americanism: in Japan, 28; in India, 102, 128, 273, 274, 275
Arab states. *See* Middle East
ASEAN (Association of Southeast Asian Nations) 141, 143
Asian Development Bank, 211, 300

Australia: interest in Pacific Ocean region, 4, 212; regional setting, 5; establishing Asian ties, 8; relations with Indonesia, 153. *See also* Southeast Asia
Austria: as buffer state, 14, 225
Authority relationships: among Communist states, 11

Balance-of-power politics: by small states, 14, 289; minimal in a leftist Japan, 28–29; by China, 76, 87, 92; effect of U.S. Asian withdrawal on, 94, 245, 261; behind détente, 204; international order through, 301
Bandung, Conference of 1954, 112
Bandung, Indonesia: anti-Chinese riots in, 149
Bangladesh: regional setting, 5; relations with India, 21, 22, 119–121, 122, 125; domestic politics, 120; U.S. aid to, 128; relations with USSR, 189. *See also* South Asia
Bangladesh War: Indian role in, 105, 107, 113, 115, 119, 125
Bhutan: regional setting, 5; relations with India, 118. *See also* South Asia
Bickel, Professor Alexander, 198
Blockade: as possible tactic, 122, 123, 179; Japan vulnerable to, 38, 179
Border problems: Sino-Soviet, 13–15, 70, 71, 74, 87, 92, 156–157, 168, 286, 298; Sino-Indian, 115, 116, 117, 276; Indian-Bangladeshi, 119, 120
Brezhnev, Leonid, 67, 70, 73, 74, 150, 159, 169
Brezhnev Doctrine, 75